PRAISE FOR *FROM SOURCE TO SEA*

"An enjoyable refuge from everyday life."

Clive Aslet, *The Times*

"Chesshyre cuts an engaging figure… He has a true journalist's instinct for conversational encounters – Kurdistani picnickers in the river meadows upstream of London, pub thugs in the badlands of the lower Thames, other Thames Path pilgrims he rubs up against along the way… rich in history and thick with characters, fables and happenstance – a highly readable and entertaining saunter along England's iconic river."

Christopher Somerville, author of *Britain's Best Walks*

"I found myself quickly falling into step beside Tom Chesshyre, charmed by his amiable meanderings, pointed observations and meetings with strangers along the way… but most of all Chesshyre champions the joys of a good walk through fascinating surroundings – with beer and blisters at the end of the day."

Fergus Collins, BBC *Countryfile Magazine*

"Readers should perhaps prepare themselves for a whole new wave of Whither England? *type books in the months and years ahead, and Chesshyre's is a not unwelcome early attempt to answer that seemingly urgent question."*

Ian Sansom, *The Times Literary Supplement*

PRAISE FOR *PARK LIFE*

"Recurring lockdowns have reminded us all of the importance of parks in our lives – as places of refuge, respite, relaxation and reconnection. In Park Life, *Tom Chesshyre guides his readers around the world in 50 parks, opening up all sorts of intriguing historical, cultural and environmental vistas along the way."*

Jonathon Porritt, Forum for the Future

"Chesshyre's inspired selection from around the world amplifies how parks are so much more than green spaces."

Richard Hammond, author of *The Green Traveller*

"*This timely guide to urban escapes will not only add dozens more to your to-do list, but also help you appreciate your own local little wonder a little more, too.*"

Wanderlust

PRAISE FOR *SLOW TRAINS AROUND SPAIN*

"*A lovely book.*"

Michael Portillo

"*In the spirit of Laurie Lee in* As I Walked Out One Midsummer Morning *and in the manner of Philip Larkin chronicling his slow southward journey in* The Whitsun Weddings, *Chesshyre takes us on a wondrously hypnotic meander across Spain. His attention to detail and unwillingness to be rushed, either as passenger or author, make this a highly relaxing and subtly addictive read.*"

Glen Mutel, National Geographic Traveller

"*If you ever need convincing that it's better to take the train than to fly, this is the book that makes a persuasive case… a fine read.*"

Nicky Gardner, hidden europe

"*Tom Chesshyre's* Slow Trains Around Spain *trundles gently through Spain much like the trains he so loves. By turns humorous and sharply insightful, he affectionately paints a vivid portrait of a deeply divided and contrasting country, bringing to life its characters and landscapes like few other travel writers can. Always curious, witty and intelligent, his writing style and subject matter are deeply rewarding.*"

Francisca Kellett

PRAISE FOR *SLOW TRAINS TO VENICE*

"*He casually, and beautifully, bats away the earnestness of travel literature.*"

Caroline Eden, The Times Literary Supplement

"There is something nostalgic about the clatter of wheels and sleeper trains… by the end, the reader will struggle to resist the urge to follow his lead."

The Economist

"Bristling with vitality, Chesshyre's new tome is a joyfully rudderless romp through Europe's railway system… It's a work of brilliant geekery, but for the most part it's a love letter to the continent, a Eurocentric work for our Brexit-beleaguered times."

National Geographic, Top Ten Travel Books for Summer 2019

"Beethoven with attitude, masochism in Lviv, the smell of cigarettes in the corridor, adventurous great aunts who travelled on the roofs of crowded trains, Carniolan pork-garlic sausage, Jimi Hendrix in the Slovene Ethnographic Museum and, of course, the 13:49 from Wrocław. Tom Chesshyre pays homage to a Europe that we are leaving behind and perhaps never understood. Che bella corsa! He is the master of slow locomotion."

Roger Boyes, *The Times*

"We love reading about train travel… Pick up Slow Trains to Venice *by Tom Chesshyre.*"

Sunday Times Travel Magazine

PRAISE FOR *TICKET TO RIDE*

"Trains, dry wit, evocative descriptions, fascinating people and more trains – what's not to like?"

Christian Wolmar, author of *Blood, Iron & Gold: How the Railways Transformed the World*

"This is an engaging, enjoyable and warm-hearted book that will appeal as much to general readers as to lovers of trains."

Simon Bradley, author of *The Railways: Nation, Network and People*

"Like mini-odysseys, Chesshyre's railway journeys are by turns gentle and awesome, and full of surprises."

John Gimlette, author of *Elephant Complex: Travels in Sri Lanka*

"Funny and illuminating from Crewe to Korea, Ticket to Ride *is a hugely entertaining account of the author's travels on the rails the world over – chance encounters fly like sparks."*

Sara Wheeler, author of *The Magnetic North*

PRAISE FOR *TALES FROM THE FAST TRAINS*

"Compulsory reading."

Mark Smith, *The Man in Seat 61*

"If you've 'done' Paris and Bruges and are wondering, 'Where next?', then this may be a quiet revolution."

Andrew Marr

"Splendid 21st-century railway adventure. At last this IS the age of train."

Simon Calder, *The Independent*

PRAISE FOR *TO HULL AND BACK*

"Tom Chesshyre celebrates the UK... discovering pleasure in the unregarded wonders of the 'unfashionable underbelly' of Britain. The moral, of course, is that heaven is where you find it."

Frank Barrett, *The Mail on Sunday*

"You warm to Chesshyre, whose cultural references intelligently inform his postcards from locations less travelled."

Iain Finlayson, *The Times*

PRAISE FOR *HOW LOW CAN YOU GO?*

"Highly readable Bill Bryson-esque travel writing."
Clover Stroud, *The Sunday Telegraph*

"A hilarious record of a low-cost odyssey around the least salubrious corners of Europe."
Celia Brayfield, *The Times*

PRAISE FOR *A TOURIST IN THE ARAB SPRING*

"This witty, perceptive book provides a fascinating read for lovers of thoughtful, imaginative and well-written travel literature."
Frank Barrett, *The Mail on Sunday*

"A charming travel companion, entertaining and engaging."
The Times Literary Supplement

PRAISE FOR *GATECRASHING PARADISE*

"Chesshyre, one of the most dependably interesting modern travel writers, explores the offbeat atolls of this sinking archipelago."
Wanderlust

"It should be mandatory reading for all visitors [to the Maldives]."
Francisca Kellett, *Tatler*

"Tom Chesshyre gives a behind the scenes look at the islands [which] are among the most sought-after holiday destinations."
The Mail on Sunday

LOST IN THE LAKES

An Hachette UK Company
www.hachette.co.uk

Summersdale Publishers Ltd
Part of Octopus Publishing Group Limited
Carmelite House
50 Victoria Embankment
LONDON
EC4Y 0DZ
UK

www.summersdale.com

Printed and bound by CPI Group (UK) Ltd, Croydon, CR0 4YY

ISBN: 978-1-80007-519-1

Substantial discounts on bulk quantities of Summersdale books are available to corporations, professional associations and other organizations. For details contact general enquiries: telephone: +44 (0) 1243 771107 or email: enquiries@summersdale.com.

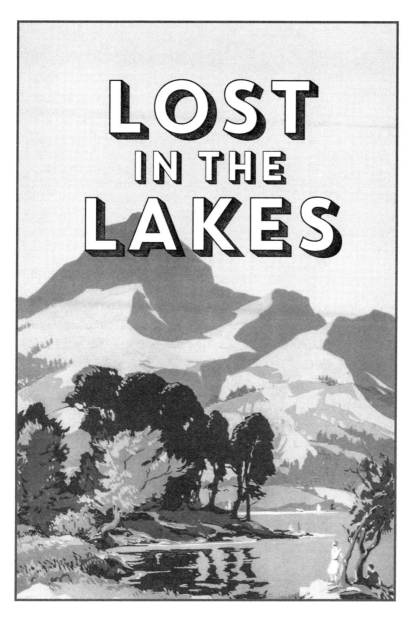

LOST
IN THE
LAKES

NOTES FROM A 379-MILE HIKE
AROUND THE LAKE DISTRICT

TOM CHESSHYRE

summersdale

ABOUT THE AUTHOR

Tom Chesshyre is the author of 11 travel books. He worked on the travel desk of *The Times* for 21 years and is now a freelance writer. His books are *How Low Can You Go?: Round Europe for 1p Each Way (Plus Tax)*, *To Hull and Back: On Holiday in Unsung Britain*, *Tales from the Fast Trains: Europe at 186 MPH*, *A Tourist in the Arab Spring*, *Gatecrashing Paradise: Misadventures in the Real Maldives*, *Ticket to Ride: Around the World on 49 Unusual Train Journeys*, *From Source to Sea: Notes from a 215-Mile Walk Along the River Thames*, *Slow Trains to Venice: A 4,000-Mile Adventure Across Europe*, *Slow Trains Around Spain: A 3,000-Mile Adventure on 52 Rides* and *Park Life: Around the World in 50 Parks*. He lives in Mortlake in London.

For Robert and Christine

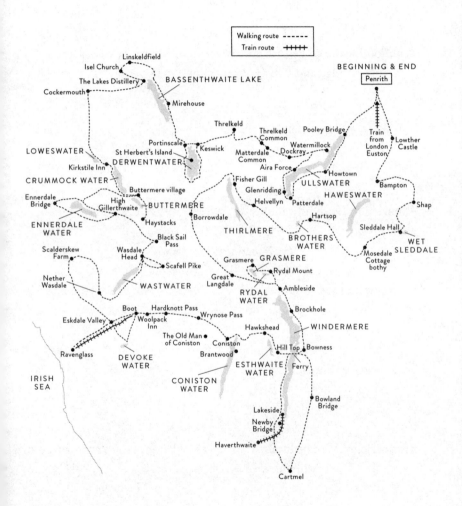

CONTENTS

The fleeting hour of life of those who love the hills is quickly spent, but the hills are eternal.
Alfred Wainwright

PREFACE

Falling in love with the Lakes can happen in a flash – and most Lakeland lovers remember that eureka moment.

For me it happened in my late teens when visiting a friend in the village of Threlkeld beneath the jagged ridge of Blencathra. With little idea how to reach the summit other than proceeding vaguely in its direction, my friend being no mountaineer, we had plodded across the scree. Up, up, up we went into a misty Cumbrian mid-afternoon, pausing to puff on Benson & Hedges cigarettes or glug Paddy Irish Whiskey from a hip flask. Shocking now, looking back: 1) How unprepared we were (no compass, no map), 2) Quite how established in bad ways we had become at an early age (no thoughts of water or snacks).

Slowly, we stumbled along rocky paths, puffing and occasionally slugging. Not exactly lost, but winging it, for sure. Then the breakthrough came. The skies cleared, as they can so suddenly in the Lakes, and the sun blazed down in dazzling, heavenly shafts. Great sweeps of fells emerged all around in delicious shades of emerald and mauve marked with splashes of copper and mustard and streaks of silver-grey.

It was simply magnificent. There amid the dreamy patchwork was the sliver of Derwentwater beside the market town of Keswick (home to a famous pencil museum we never visited). There, we imagined, was the ghostly outline of Scafell Pike, England's highest mountain, at 978 metres. Mysterious smaller waters – tarns – glittered near peaks. Serpentine valleys slid between soaring slopes. Somewhere beyond the undulating horizon lay the Irish Sea.

It was not just the setting that tugged at the heart strings, though. It was the way of life, too. The camaraderie over pints and darts by the fireside at The Sally (or Salutation Inn) in the village. Nights out "on the town" in Keswick in the company of new pals, ending up almost inevitably at Starlights, a nightclub playfully and perhaps not so subtly nicknamed "Starshites" (but much-loved, nevertheless).

You could, if you were sociable, get to know all sorts in a few days. Threlkeld's population was, and is, little more than 400, while Keswick's is around 5,200 – the Lake District's second largest town after the "metropolis" of Windermere/Bowness (8,359 inhabitants). Take away all the tourists with their windbreakers and laminated maps and the Lakes is a small world. The entire population? A mere 41,600.

Night skies were haunting; so dark it seemed the universe might engulf us. Constellations glittered above eerie silent slopes. This was a long way from the North and South Circulars, Piccadilly Circus and journeys on the Tube back home. The Lake District had "caught" me hook, line and sinker. I had fallen for the fells.

* * *

Much has been written about the Lakes – more than 50,000 books by the estimation of Hunter Davies, not only the Beatles' official biographer but also author of a series of his very own insightful tomes about the region. Staggering when you think about the sheer volume, and an awful lot to read. Yet it begs a question: why are so many people so fascinated by this watery corner of north-west England?

This is a matter with which many have grappled over the years, one of the most famous being William Wordsworth (1770–1850), the unofficial Lakeland Bard. For as well as being a groundbreaking poet, Wordsworth is perhaps less known for having penned an illuminating book entitled *Guide to the Lakes* in 1810, although the story goes that, back in his day, a parson once congratulated Wordsworth on his *Guide* and asked him if he had written anything else (a bit cheeky, if actually true).

This *Guide* was hugely influential. Wordsworth had been born in Cockermouth in the north-west of the Lake District and was, in his twenties, the leader of the pack of Lake Poets, who formed in the late eighteenth century and were known for their romantic streak of appreciation for nature at a time when industrialization was beginning to boom. This sea change to the British economy (and the world's) introduced a new threat to England's lovely Lakeland region: many a wealthy Lancastrian factory owner had taken to building big "statement" houses on the shores of Wordsworth's beloved lakes.

These were opulent, ostentatious retreats for the bigwigs who were as pleased as punch to have posh new pads away from the grind and grime of the hard streets of Manchester and Liverpool, where their fortunes were being made. Wordsworth, who like so many others adored the local scenery, looked on in horror.

"I do not know any tract of country in which, in so narrow a compass, may be found an equal variety in the influences of light and shadow upon the sublime and beautiful features of the landscape", he gushed in his *Guide*, before attacking all the gaudy country homes, "gross transgressions", popping up on the profits of mills. Humankind was encroaching on nature and doing no good, a theme not lost on modern readers of his *Guide* considering what humankind is up to in the twenty-first century. One section in his book is entitled simply *Changes, and Rules of Taste for Preventing their Bad Effects*. In other words: stay away you vulgarians! Leave us alone!

So intent was Wordsworth to block the invasion of the countryside by city folk of all ilk – wealthy factory owners with their fancy architects as well as mass crowds of ordinary people working in factories who might feel like a change of scene during their time off – he campaigned in his later years to prevent railways encroaching into his beloved Lakeland. And he succeeded. Were it not for his sermonizing on the subject, trains would undoubtedly have rolled on further than the eastern edge of Windermere, where tracks terminate to this day.

Yet the effect of Wordsworth's guidebook, in which he (rather high-handedly perhaps) hoped to educate the unenlightened on how to understand and enjoy the landscape of the Lakes, was, ironically, to begin the type of mass influx he had hoped to discourage, unsettling the peace of villages that had previously seen few holidaymakers. "Tourism" had begun, many of the first arrivals clutching Wordsworth's *Guide* or other similar publications that were soon on the market.

This was a time when Napoleon's nefarious affairs on the Continent meant that holidays abroad, the almost exclusive preserve of the grand-touring well-to-do back then, were tricky; the first vogue for "staycations" had nothing to do with pandemics or watching pennies during cost-of-living crises. And Wordsworth, who was in later years almost besieged by curious travellers hoping to catch a glimpse of the, by then, Poet Laureate at his house, Rydal Mount, was to make a tidy profit from the book. It proved to be a stroke of luck: more lucrative than much of his "higher" poetry (as his sister, Dorothy, had cannily predicted).

All of this was quite a turnaround. Just 50 years before Wordsworth's birth, the novelist Daniel Defoe had reached the Lake District in the 1720s, during a journey for his entertaining travel book *A Tour Thro' the Whole Island of Great Britain*, and had found the way blocked by what he regarded as "unpassable hills". It was all too much, even for the man who had dreamed up Robinson Crusoe. Defoe decided there and then that "all the pleasant part of England was at an end", the mountains were "horrid" and he would have nothing to do with them. This, at the time, was the conventional wisdom; the region was deemed rough and, frankly, dangerous. That it was sparsely populated was quite understandable: who on earth would want to live there?

Fast-forward to now, however, and things are slightly different. As many as 20 million visitors annually are attracted to the Lakes, as of 2017 a UNESCO World Heritage Site, and thousands swarm to see Wordsworth's childhood home in Cockermouth as well as his later dwellings in Grasmere and Rydal. Horrifying, you might think. Impossibly overrun. Wordsworth must be spinning in his grave – et cetera. On the other hand, this continuing massive influx just goes to show that the poet's concerns about outsiders destroying the beauty of the Lakes have yet to come to pass. Sure, the extraordinary tourist figures might make us think otherwise, but it seems Wordsworth's "sublime" landscape somehow must have retained its glorious sublimity: why else would so many people still want to come?

This said, for me, there has always been a quandary about visiting the Lakes. Yes, there may have been many, many guides explaining where to go and what to see, dating back many years. So many, as Hunter Davies pointed out, it is almost overwhelming. And sure, they are all usually extremely helpful, even those penned before Wordsworth's try.

The first proper book – after a short journal by another Poet Laureate, Thomas Gray, in 1769 in which he falls for the "peace, rusticity and happy poverty" of Grasmere – dates from as early as 1778 and is written by Thomas West: *A Guide to the Lakes: Dedicated to the Lovers of Landscape Studies and to All Who Have Visited, or Intend to Visit the Lakes in Cumberland, Westmorland and Lancashire*. A "clickbait" title well ahead of its time, with a rousing opening passage encouraging readers to visit the region's:

> Alpine finery, finished in nature's highest tints... the pastoral and rural landscape, varied in all the stiles: the soft, the rude [as in rough and craggy], the romantic, the sublime. [That word cropping up again.] Such as spend their lives in cities, and their time in crowds, will here meet with contrasts that enlarge the mind by contemplation... whoever takes a walk into these scenes, will return penetrated with a sense of the creator's power and unlearnable wisdom in heaping mountains upon mountains, and enthroning rocks upon rocks... [bringing] at once rapture and reverence.

Enticing stuff. Yet the Lakes, despite so much helpful literature of this sort going back so far, from the days of quills and inkpots to the slick and informative Rough Guides and Lonely Planets of today, have always seemed such a tricky place to visit and see *in one go*.

Looking at a map of the Lake District National Park with its fells (mountains) and peaks, dales (valleys) and forests, screes and passes – ancient glacial ribbon lakes twisting every which way – a question had long lodged in my mind: *so where exactly do you start?* Unlike with a river, the rambler has neither a "source" nor banks to follow. Unlike with a coastline, there is no obvious way. Unlike with Hadrian's Wall, not so far away to the north, you have no marked beginning or end on one official "trail".

* * *

Since around the mid-twentieth century, the approach to the Lakes common among walkers has been to bite off one section of the wild terrain at a time, normally covering an ascent, often in a loop beginning and ending in the same place. This way of "conquering" the landscape was famously advocated by Alfred Wainwright (1907–1991), the Lakeland rambling guru who described the routes to no fewer than 214 summits in his fabulously precise and elaborately named *A Pictorial Guide to the Lakeland Fells: Being an Illustrated Account of a Study and Exploration of the Mountains in the English Lake District*, published in seven smart volumes between 1955 and 1966.

This first-rate series of guides was to take on almost legendary status, the 214 ascents quickly becoming known in mountain-climbing circles as "the Wainwrights". Soon, many folk set off to Britain's Lakeland, intent on ticking off – or "bagging" – as many summits as possible. Nothing wrong with that.

Alternatively, requiring less strain on the knees and fewer worries about weather in the mountains, the casual rambler could simply take a leisurely circuit of one or more of the lakes. With well-signed lakeside tracks and little chance of getting lost, these walks make perfect day trips: the pleasant 10 miles round Derwentwater, perhaps, or a joyful stroll by the shores of beautiful Buttermere (4½ miles) or beside lovely little Grasmere (3 miles). Nothing wrong with that approach, either. Highly recommend it.

But how about a long cross-country walk around the whole of the Lakes, exploring hidden corners while covering the main sights, getting a real feel for the region, scampering up the odd peak yet not feeling any pressure to bag the mountaintops?

Having visited many times as a reporter, it has been my great fortune to dip into the Lakes over the years for work, ever since that first memorable trip to Threlkeld. Each time, whether exploring the fells in Langdale Valley for a day, investigating a tarn above Grasmere or visiting waterfalls in the foothills of Helvellyn (writing stories for newspaper columns with names like *The Great British Weekend* or *Britain at its Best*), hiking and the Lakes have always seemed to go hand in hand. Notebook, pen and guidebook are, of course, always packed – and walking boots, too.

On each visit, my curiosity about this hallowed landscape so eulogized by the poets – "the loveliest spot that man hath ever found", said Wordsworth – has been piqued. How, though, to see it all, not as a serious climber, but as an "average Joe" walker interested in Wordsworth's "sublime" scenery, the villages and towns, as well as the people, along the way?

I consulted a series of Ordnance Survey maps. There were 1,342 miles of public footpaths and 544 miles of bridleways to explore across 912 square miles of land (the national park is 32 miles across and 40 miles from north to south). I read a large number of books, Wordsworth's included. I plotted a vague route: a big wobbly circle taking in all 16 main lakes, which would form the focus of the hike, and some of the principal mountains. I bought a train ticket to Penrith.

With a month free, a backpack and a spring in my step, off I went. This is the story of what happened next.

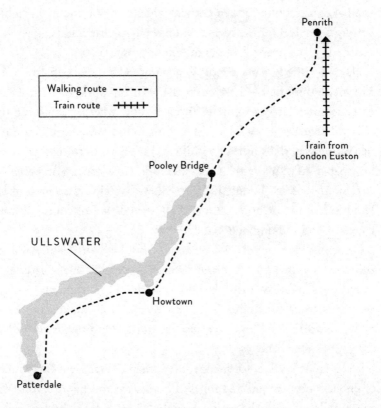

CHAPTER ONE

LONDON EUSTON TO PENRITH AND ONWARD TO PATTERDALE, VIA POOLEY BRIDGE AND ULLSWATER

INTO THE ENGLISH ALPS

On the train to Penrith, a trio of businessmen – colleagues – sat at my table (mostly) in silence. Perhaps there was hidden tension between them, maybe they had had an unsuccessful outing to London, or it could simply have been they knew each other so well no chatter was required. It seemed the latter was most likely. Every now and then, one would say: "Sandwiches?" The other two would nod and sandwiches would be produced. "Tea?" Nods. One of them would fetch tea. "Biscuits?" Nods. Biscuits were offered round. My Lake District map, half unfurled on the table, scattering of Lakes books and backpack, had clearly caught their attention, but not one of them commented: "Off for a hike then?" or "What route are you planning?" It was, it struck me, extremely English behaviour, lasting the entire 2 hours to Preston, whereupon they quietly disembarked.

Behind me, a pair of businesswomen who had only just met were discussing relationships. The older woman, whose work involved the "integration of smart meters", said that the problem with her ex-husband was he had not been "career-focused or driven, we split seven years ago". She was raising a daughter alone. The younger woman, involved in "import/export", sighed. "Men," she said. "At first my partner was very laid-back." He had since become quite the opposite. The older woman said that was a pity and told the younger woman about a disastrous date with a man in Bristol who had turned up late, drunk. They both had a good laugh about this, whereupon they too had disembarked at Preston.

The newspapers were full of gloom. "WE'LL FIGHT FOR EVERY METRE VOWS ZELENSKY AS HE FEARS NEW ASSAULT", ran a headline referring to the war in Ukraine and the determination of Volodymyr Zelensky, the Ukrainian president, to keep Russian troops out of the eastern Donbas region. "NOW THE COST OF LIVING CRISIS REALLY BITES", declared another story, pointing out that VAT on eating and drinking was due to increase and highlighting that cucumbers were about to triple in price while 30 pence would soon be added to the cost of a dozen eggs. In other news, the number of Covid cases in London hospitals was at its highest for two months. Meanwhile, in a prominent article, "ROCK BREAKS SILENCE OVER OSCARS SLAP", the comedian and actor Chris Rock said he was "still kind of processing what happened" after being slapped by fellow actor Will Smith at the weekend's Oscars ceremony. Pictures of this shocking event had gone viral on social media during the past couple of days, with just about everyone seeming to have an opinion. The world may have been slowly falling apart, but it was this Hollywood slap that seemed to be grabbing most attention, news-wise, that day – with a photograph of Chris Rock looking distressed glaring out on the front page of the *Evening Standard*.

Our Avanti West Coast train spun onward, tilting into turns and devouring distance.

Then something wonderful happened on the left-hand side of the track.

Gentle rolling hills began to rise; gentle, heart-leaping rolling hills with coppery contours of old bracken and snow-dusted tops. Drystone walls spread out in a spider's web across the landscape, punctuated by sheep beside a glinting winding river. Great beams of early-April sunlight lit up the frost-tipped hills, filtering between clusters of clouds. The landscape (my destination) was bathed in orange light and the horizon had turned apricot and indigo. The train slowly pulled in to Penrith Station at 7.30 p.m., a 3-hour ride from Euston (though geographically it felt much longer than that).

"Have you got far to go?" asked the conductor, watching me lug the backpack on to platform two. I explained where I was staying. "That's just round the corner, close to all the pubs," he said. "Have a good one!"

With that, the strange silence of the businessmen, the relationship woes on the seats behind, the downbeat news headlines and all thoughts of Big City life seemed to float away. I had begun my hike in the Lakes – the first few steps at least, with a very long way to go. I left the station, passing the jagged silhouette of the medieval ruins of Penrith Castle before crossing the street by a shiny National Farmers'

Union building and a McDonald's with a Drive Thru. I was ready. Ready to walk for mile upon mile in "Britain's number-one tourist destination", as so many refer to this small north-west corner of the country. Ready to lose myself in the foothills and fells. Ready, happily ready, for whatever might come my way.

"You can always take the bus"
Penrith

Station Hotel was indeed just round the corner, a looming red-brick building beside the castle. Inside was a lounge with a long wooden bar, a pool table and darts, plus a divided-off restaurant. The pool table, busy on a Thursday night, was surrounded by signed pictures and shirts of sports stars, mainly England footballers: Harry Kane, Wayne Rooney and Stuart Pearce.

"Tony, the owner, is a sports fan," said Kathleen, the manageress.

She gave me my key and asked me about my trip.

"My husband, if he were here, he'd know the way, he's a postie," she said, on hearing about tomorrow's target: Patterdale at the southern tip of Ullswater, the second largest of the lakes after Windermere in the south. "He pretty much knows everywhere. I don't have a Scooby-Doo. I'd quite happily walk with the dog round here, but it's busy roads and heavy car-parking fees."

Kathleen and her husband, it turned out, lived in a village to the east of Penrith, a town of around 15,000 people just outside the boundaries of the Lake District National Park on its north-east edge, and by far the biggest place on my route.

My main concern for the next day was picking the best way out of town: by "best", I meant the quietest. Having perused the Ordnance Survey map on the train up, I had an idea that this was via a street behind a large leisure centre, across the A66 and over Eamont Bridge, before turning sharply right across fields.

Merv, the chef, was consulted. Merv was sitting by the bar drinking a pint as the evening's food service was over. He seemed to think the route was OK. "Just walk from there to Pooley Bridge, get the steamer to Glenridding and have a couple of beers along the way," was his advice. He had ruffled grey hair and wore a wrinkled old blue jumper, looking extremely content to be drinking a beer after his shift.

I explained I was on a hiking trip and that catching long boat rides would defeat the purpose. "You can always take the bus," he replied, as though this made even more sense.

Kathleen nodded: "Take a bus!"

Merv and Kathleen seemed to be ganging up on me (in a nice way). I asked if many walkers came by the Station Hotel.

"Oh yeah, we get loads," Kathleen replied. "They come here first before heading into the middle of the Lakes, coming off Junction 40 [of the M6]. We get loads of elderly hikers. They're absolute diamonds. A lot of them come on their own and they're very knowledgeable."

The Station Hotel also attracted cyclists. "Last week we were absolutely chocka with coast-to-coast cyclists," she added; this route covers about 140 miles between the west-Cumbrian coast and the sea at the mouth of the river Tyne, beyond Newcastle.

Kathleen, who was dressed in a shimmering silver dress as though about to attend a cocktail party, brought me a pint of lager.

Apropos of nothing, Merv told me he used to play cricket for Glenridding, the village next to Patterdale. "It's regularly voted the most scenic ground in the country," he said.

Then he talked walking for a while. "Striding Edge," he said, referring to a notorious rocky ridge leading to the top of Helvellyn, the third highest Lake District peak, at 950 metres. "It can be dangerous. Very. I've done it a few times. First, you get a weather report from the information centre in the car park at Glenridding. It may be a gorgeous morning, but then the wind and the clouds could come in. So you need to know."

He paused and sipped his pint. "When the wind comes you just lie flat and wait. You could quite easily get blown off the edge. It's a sheer drop. You shouldn't even attempt to stand up in a storm. The wind. It's atrocious. If you see it coming, you should lie down."

He paused once again and said more brightly: "On a clear day, mind you, it's fantastic scenery."

Merv's real name was David, he went on to say: "But everyone just calls me Merv." He did not elaborate. He was aged 55 and had worked at the Station Hotel for 18 years as chef.

He gestured for me to come close so he could impart what appeared to be top-secret information. "When Kathleen calls time [which could happen early on a quiet night], you can sit here in the gentleman's club." He pointed to a couple of seats beside the entrance to the restaurant.

"Aye," said Kathleen, overhearing Merv. "There's a guest who stays here every week on business and I serve him there, three pints he has each night. You can have what you want there."

For food, Kathleen recommended crossing the street to the Agricultural Hotel, known to locals as The Aggie. Then she talked pubs. There were a lot of pubs in Penrith. "There used to be fifty-seven in my dad's day, now there are about twenty," she said. "The Aggie, The Cross Keys, The George, The Woolpack, The Royal, The Druids Arms, The Dog Beck, The Board and Elbow…" She reeled off almost all of them.

I asked her what she thought of William Wordsworth and what the poet meant to the Lake District. Wordsworth's grandparents had lived in Penrith, close to Market Square, and William and Dorothy had often come to visit. Their mother died in the family house there in 1778 (when William was eight).

"I think that if you mention him to anyone young, they wouldn't have heard of him," she replied. "I did a bit at school, so I know."

Then Kathleen talked housing. "The house opposite mine [in her village] was just bought by an incomer and he's rented it out," she said. The practice of buying as an investment for holiday lets was getting her down. "It's making it more difficult for the younger generation to get on the property ladder. A lot of houses are being bought by outsiders now."

This, I already knew, was a hot topic across the Lake District and the county of Cumbria within which the Lakes falls, recently raised in the House of Commons by the local MP, Tim Farron of the constituency of Westmorland and Lonsdale. He had called on new laws to allow local councils to introduce tough limits on second homes across Britain as well as to ensure that council tax is paid to cover local services. Many second-homers were dodging the latter by setting up ownership as a "small business", a technical loophole allowing them to avoid the tax. The net result was a "catastrophe", Farron said, with a "collapse of affordable housing" and "communities at risk of dying".

Kathleen agreed: "Before [all the outsiders], everyone knew everyone. A lot of us would drink and socialize together. It's not like that now."

* * *

Up a staircase covered in a tartan carpet and surrounded by purple walls with grainy pictures of locomotives, I dumped my backpack in a small room with a fine view of the castle. The mattress sagged. The TV was the size of a cereal box. The bathroom fan made a sound like ice being crushed in a kitchen mixer. But I had not come to the Lakes to hang about in hotel rooms. Anyway, I was hungry. I went out to eat.

Across the street, The Aggie had stopped serving, too. Down a hill of tightly terraced houses on a road that alternated between being dead quiet and akin to a Formula One racing track (the people of Penrith, that evening at least, seemed to drive like demons), I passed a Mexican restaurant (too late for orders) and the Little Chippy fish-and-chip shop (closed). The Romanian World Ltd grocery shop was also shut. So was the Polish grocery shop. Aside from the many open pubs, none serving food that I could find, there was also an open Bargain Booze shop. Alcoholic beverages were plentiful in Penrith. Solid substances for consumption at 9 p.m. were not.

Close by, however, I came to Deniz Food, a kebab shop, just beyond the house where Wordsworth's grandparents lived. This building is now home to an old-fashioned clothing business named N Arnison & Sons and faces the market square beside the old George Hotel, where Bonnie Prince Charlie is said to have stayed in 1745 on his ill-fated expedition down south. Plenty of history in Penrith: it was the capital of the independent kingdom of Cumbria up to 1070 and Penrith Castle, by my hotel, was once the northern headquarters of Richard III.

By some small miracle, Deniz Food was open. I ventured inside to find walls decorated with pictures of Istanbul and rock formations in Cappadocia. I had not expected to eat a kebab on my first night in Cumbria. I ordered and got chatting to Ken, originally from Kent, who was in charge.

"We moved up here three years ago," he said, as my chicken shish kebab sizzled. "Kent was getting me down. Too crowded and the schools were going downhill." He had three children aged thirteen, eight and three. He was 34 and his family roots were from near Ankara, although he was born in Britain. "The kids love it, the nature, and it's calmer and safer in Penrith. We were a bit worried about moving." But he had had a taste of living in the north of England when his parents moved from Lewisham in London to Chester when he was a boy. "So I knew the North and I thought: *just go a bit more up to the Lakes*. We'd never been before. We like it. There's more community. Down south you don't get hellos. It's better round here. The world down south is too fast."

Were there downsides? Ken thought about this for a while: "There's not so much big-brand shopping." He paused and thought a bit more. "And it's difficult to get Krispy Kreme doughnuts. In Penrith you can't find them. I have to go down the M6 to get them from a service station." His children loved Krispy Kreme doughnuts.

Ken returned to his earlier topic. "Down south, you can't even ask people for directions. Down south, they'll just ignore you, or they'll get suspicious and worried," he said, thinking of the difference between Kent and Cumbria. Ken looked extremely relieved to have made it to Cumbria.

I said goodbye. I ate Ken's top-notch chicken shish kebab beneath an awning on a little square known as Great Dockray. I returned to the Station Hotel, where Merv, sitting in the "gentleman's club", advised me again to take a bus to Patterdale. I declined once more, saying I wanted to walk. Merv's drinking companion said: "But every other bugger takes the bus!" And with that I returned to the little room facing the old castle, reflecting on just how open and sociable Penrith seemed to be. The world down south did feel "too quick and fast" – and withdrawn – by comparison. Tomorrow, things would be even slower still.

First glittery glimpse
Penrith to Pooley Bridge

Before setting forth, a little explanation of my intended route and my (very limited) credentials as a mountain walker.

Regarding the way ahead, the plan was to drop briefly south to Ullswater, cross north-westward to Keswick and then Cockermouth via the shores of Derwentwater and Bassenthwaite Lake, the only "lake" in the Lake District officially known as a lake, i.e. having the word "lake" in its name. The rest were referred to as "waters" or "meres", although the word *mere* comes from Old English and means "lake". So, not confusing at all.

From Cockermouth, Wordsworth's hometown up in the far north-west, my feet would lead south via lonely Loweswater and tucked-away Crummock Water to Buttermere, said to be an especially charming mere. It was on a mountain overlooking Buttermere (named Haystacks) that Alfred Wainwright chose to have his ashes scattered – he said he enjoyed the scenery there so much. Lake District endorsements do not come higher than that.

After Buttermere, the aim was to pop westward to remote Ennerdale Water, where I had pencilled in a rest day at a hostel by a forest. Afterward, it would be southward to Wastwater, beside England's highest mountain, Scafell Pike, which I had half a mind to climb. Next, the route would weave further south still to Devoke Water, officially a "tarn" rather than a lake, and the largest such tarn in the Lake District. The difference between a tarn, which derives from the ancient Scandinavian word *tjörn* (pond), and a lake is a grey area, the deciding factor seemingly being that tarns are generally smaller and higher than ordinary lakes. That said, some meres and waters may be smaller than the largest tarns. So, not confusing at all, again.

From Devoke Water, it was to be east to Coniston Water, passing Esthwaite Water and Hill Top, Beatrix Potter's old house. From there the route would lead further east into the heart of Lakeland tourism – Windermere, the biggie of the Lake District at 11 miles long and 1 mile wide, and the town of Bowness-on-Windermere. Then I would duck south to the pretty town of Cartmel, with its famous Michelin-starred restaurants, and return up Windermere to Ambleside, the walkers' HQ on the lake's northern tip.

Grasmere and Rydal Water could be explored from Ambleside, before I slipped across into Langdale Valley, traversing north into Borrowdale Valley and visiting Thirlmere, Brothers Water and Haweswater, moving steadily eastward between the three. All that would be left would be a dozen miles north back up to Penrith, thus completing the loop. I would have touched upon the 16 main lakes/waters/meres and given the region a thorough investigation one way or another. It would take about 30 days and I had booked accommodation in advance, putting pressure on myself not to slip up. I had a schedule to keep to, or the chain of bookings would fall apart.

So far as my walking ability was concerned, this was where worries crept in.

Hiking in steep and rugged terrain with a heavy backpack was something I had never tried. Yes, I had ambled along the Thames for a previous walking book, *From Source to Sea: Notes from a 215-Mile Walk along the River Thames*, but that was on the nice flat Thames Path. My backpack for the Lakes weighed 11 kilogrammes when I set off to Penrith, containing guides, maps and notebooks, as well as an emergency storm shelter, a first-aid kit, waterproof overtrousers, a compass, whistle, torch, laptop, sleeping bag (for a night planned in a bothy), various chargers and some spare clothing.

I was wary of gaining altitude, getting stuck and having to turn back, especially early on. So, I would not be cutting across 800-metre fells, at least not at the start. If the weather came in, as Merv mentioned, anything might happen. I was heading off as a very cautious casual rambler, who might – who knew? – gain confidence along the way. I hoped so, anyway. It was also cold in early April; 1°C overnight in Penrith with snow on the mountaintops ahead looking dreamy at a distance, but perhaps not so great close up.

Those were the basics. I was aiming to amble in a big, long lazy loop. Let the Wainwright summits be the Wainwright summits. All those peaks poking into the clouds would be a (delightful) sideshow. I was heading into the hills and letting the lakes of the Lake District lead the way… doing my own thing.

* * *

Penrith to Patterdale is 15 miles, according to Google Maps. A decent distance with a bulging backpack stuffed largely with books, but that was the whole point: I wanted to push myself early on to see what I could do.

Leaving Station Hotel at 6.30 a.m., I cut across the castle grounds and continued beyond the leisure centre and the A66 roundabout.

The sky was luminous grey. The temperature was chilly. Beyond the stone arches of Eamont Bridge, the Ordnance Survey map's trusted green dotted line – designating a public right of way – soon slipped beneath the M6, a symbolic moment of sorts as this felt like a boundary. Behind lay the Big Bad World, while ahead awaited remote dales, mighty fells and trickling becks (streams), to use the Lake District lingo. It did not take long after leaving Penrith to disappear into countryside.

In this state of reverie, I almost immediately, true to the title of this hiking book, became quite thoroughly lost.

How, I am not sure, but I soon found myself in a cattle field, following what I believed to be the dotted green line into a muddy passage leading to another pasture. Large brown cows defended this passage at both ends, every which one regarding me with whatever thoughts they may then have been thinking.

On my long Thames walk, such cattle occasionally barred the way, so I reasoned: *this is quite normal,* and I ambled onward, discovering that several of the creatures appeared to have taken against being disturbed that April morning. They moved toward me with what looked like narrowed, angry eyes. I moved away from them, not quite running for fear of triggering a stampede, but going fast. It was then I discovered a railway line, the one from Euston, blocking the way. Within 2 hours of departing, and after weeks of planning, I had already messed up. Not wanting to retrace my steps past the cattle, I followed the fence along the railway and found a track going under it that led to a farm. There, I hopped over a gate and slipped back to the official footpath, whispering *apologies, apologies, apologies* (to the farmer) and vowing to pay more attention from then on.

Not the best start. Proceeding with caution beyond the village of Sockbridge and a church with a sturdy stone tower, I tramped onward beside a tea-coloured river. Dogs barked. Woodpeckers pecked. Startled grouse flapped away. A chestnut horse and two Shetland ponies observed me. I strode across a field on wispy grass and the first glittery glimpse of "lake" appeared ahead: Ullswater, all 7½ glorious miles of it stretching beyond the hills and eventually leading to Patterdale in the south.

I stood for a while, transfixed, staring at this little slate-grey corner of water: 1 down, 15 more of the "big ones" to go. There was something enticing about Ullswater. It had a secretive, intangible allure.

After this field, the path turned abruptly into the grounds of a holiday camp called Hole House Farm Caravan Park. This consisted of a cluster of pistachio-coloured holiday homes shaped like cargo containers. There were 65 of them, each had a name (*Rio Sierra, Knightsbridge, Bordeaux*), and they cost from £50,000 to £80,000. I know this because I met Dave Coulston, who runs the farm and who was fixing boards on one of the patios.

"My grandad began this sixty years ago," said Dave, wearing a lumberjack shirt, hammer in hand. He explained that prices depended on views and whether the holiday homes, known as "static holiday homes", had views of Ullswater with patios. "You get them with a fifteen-year lease," he said.

"So buyers do not actually own their static holiday homes," I asked.

"That's right," Dave said. "Most caravan parks work like that."

For this deal, static-holiday-temporary-homeowners got use of a kids' play area, a football pitch and an on-site laundry. Wi-Fi was also available.

I asked if Hole House was a working farm as well as a caravan park.

"Oh yes, it's a proper farm too: beef and sheep," said Dave, and just as he was about to go into this, Tony arrived.

Tony was shuffling down the lane in a duffle jacket and a cap. He was on assignment for *The Durham Drinker* magazine, produced by the Durham branch of the Campaign for Real Ale, and was about to catch a bus from Pooley Bridge, a village just down the hill by Ullswater, to Penrith, where he was reviewing pubs. He was of retirement age and had a twinkle in his eye. He asked me where I had stayed in Penrith.

"That's the farmer's pub, that is," he said. "No ales there. All the young farmers, all they drink is champagne. Ain't that right, Dave?" Tony seemed to know Dave.

Dave just laughed and began hammering the deck.

Tony said he was visiting The Royal, The Aggie and "a few others" for *The Durham Drinker*. Penrith, he said, was good value for beer drinkers. A pint could be had for £2.80, half of "down south in London". He especially praised Penrith's Fell Bar: "It's famous throughout Cumbria for its ales." He had been a pub reviewer for 12 years, and also contributed to the *Good Beer Guide*. He recommended the White Lion in Patterdale. Then he tipped his cap and tootled off down a lane, looking quite content with his lot in life, as well he might.

After a pleasant stroll down a path along the river Eamont, I reached Pooley Bridge, the head of Ullswater.

Pooley Bridge was a tiny village set around a high street, and it had a recent sad story.

In December 2015 the old stone bridge – which had crossed the usually peaceful river Eamont since 1764 and had given the village its name – collapsed during flooding caused by Storm Desmond. Pooley Bridge for a while had no bridge, causing great traffic trouble in the north-eastern Lakes. A temporary bridge was, however, soon erected and then, finally, a strong new single-span stainless-steel bridge was completed in October 2020. Across the Lake District, more than 450 bridges had been damaged by Storm Desmond, presenting Cumbria County Council with an enormous headache, but steadily all repairs had been completed. To celebrate the official opening, a local farmer had driven his flock of Swaledale sheep across the elegant new structure.

The village was home to three pubs, a tea room, a gift shop selling unusual bamboo socks, an award-winning restaurant-with-rooms named 1863 and the jetty for the steamer ferry south to Glenridding that Merv had recommended. This was not really powered by steam but used an old boat that once was.

There was also a brand-new bookshop named Verey Books. Being so new, this was spotless and shiny, with everything just so. A bright café on one side offered pastries, brownies, lattes and cappuccinos, and a board advertised "Words on Wednesday" evenings with readings. An assistant, noticing me poking around, quizzed me and said: "Let me get you Al! Al is the owner! Al is a poet!"

Shortly afterward, she returned with a tall, skinny man wearing a stripy jumper: Al. His full name was Al Verey and he invited me for a coffee, telling me he had previously been an English teacher as well as a guide at Dove Cottage, Wordsworth's Grasmere home, before changing career and realizing his long-held ambition to open a bookshop. Al was modest about his poetry: "I'm not published." So, switching tack, I asked him what he thought of another poet: Wordsworth. Ullswater was, after all, prime Wordsworth territory. "The happiest combination of beauty and grandeur which any of the lakes affords" was how he had described Ullswater in his *Guide*, and it was by a south-western stretch of the lake that the poet had found inspiration for his famous verse about daffodils, "I Wandered Lonely as a Cloud".

Al chose his words carefully as he considered what he liked most about the Lakeland Bard: "I think it's that sense of putting grand words to grand scenery. That's what Wordsworth did."

Al paused and seemed to look inside himself for a moment, as all good poets, no doubt, must. Then Al said: "The still, sad music of humanity, that rolls through all things."

And after a second of letting that sink in, Al admitted: "I nicked that."

It was from Wordsworth's "Lines Composed a Few Miles above Tintern Abbey".

We drank coffees and discussed books about the Lake District for a while, Al saying that his shop had been having a "good start, everyone is very positive, we're just gearing up". I wished him well and went across the lane to dip my hand in my first lake.

"Dehydration is the mother of all disaster"
Pooley Bridge to Patterdale

Ullswater was captivating from Pooley Bridge, with boulders and driftwood scattered by the shore while a vast luminous pool of gently swelling water reflected the soft-blue sky and tiny cotton-bud clouds. On the horizon, russet-green fells capped with snow tumbled into the distance like hidden Himalayas. I was quite blown away by the "beauty and grandeur", too.

A tourist noticeboard said the shape of Ullswater was "like a crooked finger". Looking at the Ordnance Survey map this description seemed just right. Further on, down the eastern shore, another sign soon warned: "DANGER TO SWIMMERS: YOU ARE STANDING ON PART OF A WATER INTAKE STRUCTURE." This operation was run by United Utilities, it said, which was pumping water from Ullswater to Haweswater, a reservoir 3 miles to the south-east. Muffled commentary from one of the steamers drifted across the lake, the red funnel of the sleek vessel drawing the eye. I entered a campsite by the waterfront and stopped for a break at The Gathering café.

Cath, who ran this café/kiosk, brought over a mango smoothie, and paused to talk. There were no other customers. As it was still cold, people were staying away, she said, but it was not as nippy as yesterday: "It was perishing yesterday. Big fluffy snowflakes. Then we had hail stones. But then it's beautiful when it all stops, and you can see the snow on the hills when it's sunny and clear."

Cath told me her business had thrived during the Covid-pandemic lockdowns as "outdoor catering was top of the tree". As she was saying this, Steve approached. Steve worked at Waterside House Campsite. One by one, I seemed to be meeting a large proportion of the folk who ran Ullswater's tourism industry.

"Very popular pitches by the lake," he said. "Very. You have to book them months in advance. Every pitch there." He pointed to the best spots facing the water. "Each one is reserved every night this summer."

Cath and Steve began talking about rising business costs, which were putting pressure on them to increase prices. Steve thought this was to do with Brexit. Without the influx of European Union workers for low-paid jobs, there were staff shortages across the Lakes, he said, and this was pushing up wages.

"I voted Remain," he said, sounding stoic. "But now we've just got to get on with it."

Things did not sound great. We talked about this for a while, then another customer came to the kiosk so Cath departed, and Steve went off to get a coffee too.

I walked on along Ullswater.

Further on, beyond Ullswater Yacht Club, the way ahead followed a narrow lane with the occasional farmer driving by in a pickup truck pulling a sheep trailer. Along this lane was a sign for Sharrow Bay, a renowned Lakeland hotel. "OPEN TO NON-RESIDENTS", it said, but I already knew this was not true as when I tried to book, I found the hotel had just gone into administration.

This failure had shocked many in the hospitality industry, prompting one prominent hotel reviewer, Fiona Duncan of *The Daily Telegraph*, to pen an "Ode to Sharrow Bay", no less. The semi-legendary property had been opened originally in 1948 by two men, Francis Coulson and Brian Sack, and was considered Britain's first country house hotel, run "like a benign mini-fiefdom", said Duncan in her ode, with chintz galore, "garish flower arrangements", formal teas, and "pink swirly carpets". Sticky toffee pudding had allegedly been invented in its kitchen, which had gained two Michelin stars at its height.

During a visit in the 1970s, Hunter Davies had been blown away both by the cooking as well as by learning that a diner on the next-door table had come up that day from London just to have lunch, a return journey of 600 miles. "One thought Northerners would not encourage such nonsense", he commented dryly. Both Coulson, in 1998, and Sack, in 2002, had passed away, moving on "doubtless to velveteen armchairs in the sky", said Duncan, and the company that had taken over had failed to survive the pandemic.

Curious, I walked down a mossy driveway lined with azaleas. A Range Rover was parked outside and some of the windows of the hotel, originally a fishing lodge from 1814, were boarded up. A tattered Union Jack hung on a pole by a crumbling wall. The front door, flanked by flamboyant stone angels, was locked. I went round the side to see if I could find anyone to ask about the famous old hotel, but nobody was about.

From the terrace, looking south-west, the snow-capped ridge of Helvellyn arose. What a location for a hotel. What a sad, but perhaps inevitable, outcome. The owners who had taken over from Coulson and Sack had hoped to freeze time and maintain the hotel's original twee appeal, but as Duncan had pointed out, old-fashioned places in the Lakes merely offering a comfortable bed and good food were being outstripped by designer spa hotels with flashy cocktail bars, programmes of activities and "buzz and glamour". No chance for fusty old Sharrow Bay up against all that, Lakeland legend though it may have been.

I walked on along Ullswater once more.

A path soon led inland, linking to another, higher trail that was parallel to the lake and passed between pine trees and golden-yellow gorse before crossing the gently winding water of Swarthbeck Gill (a *gill* or *ghyll* is a narrow stream, also in local lingo, though the difference between what makes a gill and a beck is tricky to discern precisely, as often they are quite similar in size, though gills/ghylls tend to flow through ravines). It was a secretive, contemplative woodland. I was all alone – most hikers seemed to have taken a lower path closer to the lake – and on my way "proper" in the Lakeland wilds. I could already tell I was going to have plenty of thinking time in the weeks ahead and I had much on my mind: tricky work decisions (I had recently lost regular shifts at a newspaper making cutbacks), big life moves (maybe moving out of London), family matters (my father sadly had early-stage Parkinson's), the question of children (were my partner, Kasia, and I ever going to have any? I, for one, was knocking on).

Quite apart from these personal matters, the world seemed so uncertain on so many levels, as the headlines on the train up had captured: Britain's place in affairs having "left" Europe and the economic turmoil that may or may not be connected to that decision (depending on your take; Steve at the campsite's becoming increasingly prevalent); the many frankly depressing examples of incompetence at government level (and aloof responses to criticism); the sad goings-on in south-east Europe. What was Vladimir Putin capable of in Ukraine? Anything seemed possible. Without wishing to sound melodramatic, the potential for further – nuclear? – disaster put everything in perspective; all else was small fry, really. Along the trails ahead, it would not just be the scenery and the encounters that carried my thoughts.

Though perhaps that's not so unusual. Isn't one of the reasons for a very long walk to take time out, to tease out your thoughts and let the landscape bring you a sense of calm and consideration and even, if you are lucky, a few conclusions? Wasn't that what drew people to pilgrimages so many centuries ago (and indeed today, too)? That sense of inner peace that, maybe, waited down the footpaths, in my case, the footpaths of the Lakes ahead.

Or perhaps I was just overthinking it all a bit.

Into the cool woodland air I stepped, enjoying the solitude for a while. Across the glittering surface of Ullswater, a fell arose called Gowbarrow, looking handsome and immense with expanses of brooding, shadowy bracken, perilous crumbling cliffs and great cascades of inhospitable scree. Rough landscape. Despite the tourist hordes, the Lake District is home to tough, treacherous terrain aplenty (as well as Beatrix Potter and Peter Rabbit, of course).

* * *

The path led down a slope through more woodland, arriving at Howtown Hotel in Howtown, which seemed to comprise not much more than Howtown Hotel and a pier for steamers. I stopped for a sandwich at the old-fashioned-but-open hotel, beginning to feel quite tired from the long walk. Worn out and ready to take off my backpack, which really was heavier than anything I had lugged around any distance before, I was looking forward to slumping at a table and zoning out as you do after a long walk (and I still had 6 miles to go to Patterdale). At the café counter, however, before I could place my order, an assistant who reminded me of Agatha Christie's Miss Marple asked an unexpected question.

"Are you meeting a young lady here?" she said.

I said that I was unaware that I would be.

"There was a young lady in here who was wanting to meet someone and couldn't find them: it wasn't you?"

Not me, I answered, feeling put under (gentle) interrogation.

"She was doing the Ullswater Way," Miss Marple continued, eyeing my reaction.

I said that I was doing the same – the Ullswater Way is the official name of the 20-mile path that rings Ullswater – but I had no plans to meet a young lady.

Miss Marple examined me once again, seemed satisfied, and then said "oh fiddlesticks" when she could not get the till to work properly.

Quite what all that was about, I wasn't sure.

I enjoyed a half-hour of "nothing", other than eating a ham sandwich and glancing at the map. Then, after a nose around the ivy-clad hotel's front lounge with its blazing fire, gilt-framed landscape paintings and porcelain figurines, I was soon moving on along a rocky path above the lake again, falling in stride with three ex-rugby players from Wilmslow. They had caught the boat from Glenridding to Howtown and were walking back to Glenridding along Ullswater, having had a drink at the Howtown Hotel. Their names were Tari, Sammy and Keith. Tari was a property investor,

Sammy a project manager and Keith was "doing something in finance".

"Dehydration is the mother of all disasters when you're walking," said Tari, referring to their refreshments at the Howtown Hotel bar, which he said was "a right hidden gem".

They had come to the area both to walk and to watch Wilmslow play Penrith at rugby the next day.

When asked what they enjoyed about Ullswater, their answers were as follows.

Tari: "The walking."

Keith: "There is a sociability when you walk."

Sammy: "The beer."

With that they hiked onward and two new walkers emerged in the opposite direction, one wearing fluorescent orange shorts, a woolly hat, a fleece and walking boots, the other in an identical ensemble except his shorts were fluorescent yellow. How their legs were not cold I do not know.

"Aye up," said the man in orange shorts.

"Aye up," I replied, to match his greeting.

"Aye up," said the man in yellow shorts in reply to my "aye up".

"Aye up," I replied once again.

And we continued on our ways.

Another walker, a solitary man dressed head-to-toe in black with a long grey beard, a stick and a slight limp came along from the direction of Patterdale.

"All right," he said.

"All right," I replied.

"All right," he said as though to confirm my "all right".

We continued on our ways.

A pair of walkers, a man and a woman in matching olive-coloured North Face jackets were next to appear ahead.

"You OK?" the man asked, making me wonder whether I did not look OK.

"I'm OK," I replied. "You OK?"

"Yeah, OK," he said.

Hiker talk, I was noticing, could be limited at times. But at least we were acknowledging one another; more than could be said in some parts of Britain, as Ken had mentioned in the Penrith kebab shop.

I came to a row of cottages on the edge of Patterdale, soon after discovering that my hostel, just up a street from Ullswater, was shut. A sign said that there was a private booking, as though it was closed to everyone else that night. The door was locked, and no one was around. I took off the backpack, slumped on the front step and wondered what to do. I had no phone reception, so could not check the internet or call. Had I really somehow got the second night's booking wrong? I supposed this was possible. My feet, I noticed, ached quite badly. I imagined that I might have a blister on my left big toe but was too lazy to check. My shoulders felt raw from the backpack. I had run out of energy, water and snacks, and seemed to have nowhere to sleep for the night. In this state I sat for a while, I am not sure how long. After this indeterminate period, a man wearing a red jacket appeared.

"Do you know anything about this hostel?" I asked.

"Yes, I work here," he replied.

The hostel, I learned, would open for check-in at 5 p.m., the sign for a private booking was left over from the day before. It was 4 p.m., however, the man in the red jacket said I could wait in a lounge. This I did, in a space with a large atrium and chesterfield armchairs: Britain's most comfortable chesterfield armchairs if you have just completed an 18-mile walk, which was the length my phone estimated; Google Maps' 15 miles had been along a more direct route, following main roads.

At 5 p.m., a charming receptionist with purple hair apologized about the front door being locked when I arrived, apparently it was "policy" to let early arrivals wait in the lounge.

"After Covid everyone decided they didn't want to do it any more," she said, by way of explaining why there had not been enough staff around to allow the lounge to be open. By "it" she had been referring to working in the hostel. "It's been the same in all hospitality. We're very short-staffed."

I thanked her, took my key and checked in to a small room with a bunk bed, bare brick walls and a sink; a shared bathroom was down the hall. Leaving my bag, I walked stiffly – my body seemed to be seizing up – to the White Lion pub, where I was met, inside, by a large wooden carving of a lion that the barman said had once been at South Lakes Safari Zoo; the landlord of the White Lion had heard the zoo was getting rid of it and picked it up for a bargain. I ordered and quickly drank a pint of Wainwright ale. Then I ordered and quickly ate an enormous Cumberland sausage and mash with Yorkshire-pudding dinner. Both excellent.

The barman told me that Patterdale is "a very quaint little village, not like Windermere. If you don't know about it, you might not come" and said that a lot of coast-to-coast walkers, covering more or less the same route as the cyclists visiting Station Hotel in Penrith, stay at the White Lion.

He pointed to a group of four guys in the corner: "Coast-to-coasters." The pub, which was about "three hundred or four hundred years old", served Coast to Coast pale ale to such guests. I listened to some Oasis and R.E.M hits for a while quite contentedly (happy simply to be still). I inspected the eclectic interior: the coat of armour, a collection of old gin bottles and a sign by the bar that said: "SAVE WATER, DRINK BEER". Then I shuffled slowly back to the hostel and promptly fell into a deep slumber on my bunk. It was around 9.30 p.m. and I was whacked, but glad to be on the move. In little over 24 hours, I had moved from Britain's biggest city and now found myself surrounded by fells in the heart of Wordsworth's old stomping ground. Amazing the places you could get to by trains and green dotted trails (no need for all the security queues of an airport or squeezing into a pesky plane).

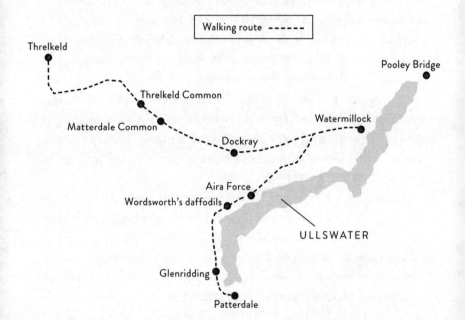

CHAPTER TWO

PATTERDALE TO THRELKELD, VIA GLENRIDDING, AIRA FORCE AND WATERMILLOCK

SLOWLY, SLOWLY UP THE FELLS

The Lake District did not seem short of job opportunities, even if a cost-of-living crisis was well under way.

"We're still trying to figure it out. We never had a problem with staffing before, but it's hospitality-wide. I'm sure Brexit has played a part. We're in quite a predicament. I think we'll be OK in the summer. We'll get in some university help," said Ellie, the hard-working manager of YHA Patterdale, as she served her guests full English breakfasts. She had helped to clean the hostel the previous afternoon, had been up late in reception and was also covering breakfast shifts.

The hostel, Ellie said, had 15 rooms, plus dorms and a campsite, and had opened in 1971 as part of the Youth Hostel Association (YHA), although there had been a hostel at the location since the 1930s. She had worked at YHA Patterdale since 2016 and she was rightly proud of her hostel, which was run efficiently and with friendliness, despite the shortages. Some guests came back year after year, Ellie said, many because they enjoyed the "1970s retro Scandinavian style". This was evident especially in the lounge with its high atrium, wide rectangular fireplace, long strip-windows facing woodland and a staircase that seemed to float upward from the reception. "Regulars love it," she said. You could see why.

Like Pooley Bridge, Patterdale was a tiny village and comprised the hostel, a handful of cottages, the White Lion pub, the well-regarded Patterdale Hotel and a former post office. This had sadly closed, the barman at the White Lion had said, which was particularly regretful as it was famous in fell-walking circles for being the first shop to stock Alfred Wainwright's hiking guides to the Lakes. A slate plaque on the facade of the building explained this, and the story went that in 1955 Wainwright had self-published 2,000 copies of his first Lake District book at the not-inconsiderable cost of £900, whereupon the post office at Patterdale had taken six. These had sold within a week and were "a cause for much inward rejoicing and relief", as Wainwright had been worried nobody would be interested. Since then, more than 2 million copies of his *Pictorial Guide to the*

Lakeland Fells had been shifted and he had become a cult figure in mountain-hiking circles.

Patterdale's other claim to fame, apart from Wordsworth having spent part of his youth nearby and having once reportedly purchased a property (Wordsworth, you quickly learn, crops up just about everywhere), is that in the fifth century St Patrick is said to have preached in the valley. Whether legend or not, Patterdale is believed to derive from "Patrick's Dale".

Steamers, murders and mines
Patterdale to Glenridding

After breakfast, I proceeded down the hill from the White Lion, which was flying the flag of Ukraine in solidarity with the country's war against Russia. It was a gloriously sunny, hopeful, but cold morning. My target for the day was Brackenrigg Inn in Watermillock, up the western side of Ullswater, where I had booked a room. It was to be a light day's hike compared to yesterday, or so I thought. Google Maps indicated a mere 7 miles, although I was already doubtful about the accuracy of Google Maps when it came to walking in the fells of the Lake District. My feet, legs and shoulders seemed fine after yesterday. Thankfully, no blister had appeared on my left big toe.

Ullswater lay ahead. Finches and robins were hopping in the hedgerows. I dropped by St Patrick's Church, admiring both its distinguished, pink-tinted facade, dating from the mid-nineteenth century, and the many daffodils swaying gently in the morning breeze, forming a yellow sea amid the gravestones. The church was locked at 8.45 a.m. and was otherwise remarkable for a large sign that said: "FREE WIFI INSIDE CHURCH". The Lord was evidently moving with the times in Patterdale.

Not far on was Merv's cricket ground, which was indeed exceedingly scenic, surrounded by fells. Beyond was a Mountain Rescue centre, and then a path between silver birches that led to the village of Glenridding and Ullswater Steamers' headquarters, based on a pier in a building doubling as a ticket office.

I was curious to see these steamers, especially one called *Lady of the Lake,* said to be the oldest working passenger vessel in the world. So I went over. This was how I met Wayne, working in the ticket office, who at first said it was against the rules to go down the pier to take a picture of *Lady of the Lake* without a ticket. Wayne had bleached blonde hair, earrings and nose-rings, and he was well on top of *Lady of the Lake* facts: "She was launched in 1871, on 26 June at 2.30 p.m. She's one hundred feet long and fifteen feet wide, with a four-foot draw. She weighs forty-three tonnes and has a capacity of two hundred and three."

Wayne said all this almost without drawing a breath. "It's just the elegance of the vessel that makes it special," he said, quickly into his stride. "The aspect ratio of the *Lady of the Lake.* If you look at it, the width compared to the length, it's fantastic."

By this, I gathered, that he meant it was particularly long and thin.

"There are now two Cummins diesel engines with a straight speed of ten miles an hour," he added.

Wayne seemed to know all the figures – how long had he worked for Ullswater Steamers? "Oh, only two months," he replied. "But I'm a stats man. I used to work in a factory: a polystyrene factory with sixty-two employees in Newcastle. It was under my command. I was the boss. It turned over twenty million pounds a year."

How had he ended up at Ullswater Steamers?

"Well, I retired to the Lakes, and then I got this job," he said. "I first came to the Lake District forty-five years ago, when I camped at the Waterside campsite. Then I'd come every weekend from Durham staying in a static [holiday home]. I bought a static fifteen years ago. Then I sold that and got a lodge. Then I sold that and bought a cottage dating from 1751 in Langwathby." This was just north-east of Penrith. "It's got one pub, one post office. Heaven."

It turned out that Wayne, 61, was a triathlete and ran 3 miles in the fells five times a week, often swimming across Ullswater and back for training. He looked around the ticket office. No customers were about. "Come on," he said and let me go down the pier to take a snap of *Lady of the Lake*. Very nice chap, Wayne.

I retraced my steps into Glenridding, passing a shop selling gingerbread vodka and brambleberry gin, and the Glenridding Hotel, which had a prominent sign outside: "HIRING NOW: WHY NOT JOIN INN?" Yet more Lakeland job opportunities. At Glenridding's tourist office, I waited as a man enquired about conditions on Striding Edge, the ridge that Merv had warned about when windy.

Tourist: "What's it like up there?"

Tourist assistant: "It's got snow and ice on it."

Tourist: "Ah ok. I went up there with my dad when I was younger but I'm leading others so had better not." He paused. "What about Kettle Crag?"

Tourist assistant: "It's full winter up there. You'd need an ice axe to do it."

Tourist, sounding a little despondent: "Ah, ok."

Spring had clearly not quite sprung on the mountaintops.

The tourist departed.

Like Pooley Bridge, Glenridding had been hit hard by the floods of 2015. I asked the tourist assistant what it had been like to live in the village then.

"People don't really want to talk about that," she said. But then she pulled out a board with pictures showing the 2015 damage. The tourist office had almost been swept away, the roads had turned into rivers and the ground floors of nearby properties inundated.

"We've had additional walls for flood protection since then," she said. "And they've dug down." This meant that Glenridding Beck could flow more easily when waters rose, without breaking its banks.

"I usually hide this," said the tourist assistant, referring to the picture board; the floods were a bad memory and unlikely to induce happy holiday feelings, which the tourist office was, of course, in the business of inducing.

Beryl, a local woman of retirement age wearing a large floppy hat had been listening to us. She joined in. "For three days we were cut off. It was like wartime," she said. "There was even a food bank. I didn't complain, I got smoked salmon from that. I also got toiletries from the hotel. Oh yes, the floods were horrendous. This shop was completely washed down to the lake." By that she meant all its objects for sale, not the building itself. Once the storm had passed, this had created opportunities. "I went down to the shore with my cousin and we said: 'What's the point, they don't want it. It's damaged goods.'" So, they had gathered up the items from the shop. "These earrings were from there," Beryl said, moving her hair to one side. "We'd open the boxes and find necklaces and earrings. There were pictures too. I have them up in my house, the water hadn't got to them yet as they had been wrapped in plastic. We had T-shirts that washed up too, cuddly toys as well." The tourist assistant running the tourist office, listening to Beryl, did not seem to mind one bit as everything had been damaged.

Beryl had a lovely, soft-grey whippet with her named Storm, named so as he was "born on a stormy night".

Then Beryl told me that a neighbour of hers had just moved in with a younger man: "He's aged seventy-two."

She and the tourist assistant had a laugh about that.

Then Beryl told me a tragic story. It was about the son of a local farmer, who had been drinking at the White Lion pub in Patterdale in 1835 when miners from the Greenside Lead Mine, just to the west of Glenridding, operating from the late eighteenth century up to 1962, had attacked him after getting drunk on payday.

"There was a fracas between miners and farmers in the pub," said Beryl. "Thomas Grisdale [the farmer's son] had gone to intervene when a brawl broke out. Two men, miners named Bainbridge and Greenwell had been involved. They got chucked out. But then later, when Grisdale was walking home, Greenwell and Bainbridge waylaid him. Greenwell stabbed him and three-quarters of an hour later, Grisdale was dead. Greenwell was sentenced to be hanged by the Appleby assizes, but the judge was merciful and, instead, he was sent to Botany Bay. He was meant to serve twelve years but only served six and then he was a free man to run around Australia. I always stand before the grave [of Grisdale] at St Patrick's Church. He died when he was only twenty-seven years old. It's terribly sad."

After this murder, which had greatly shocked the peaceful valley, the practice of paying miners twice a year was cancelled; wages had previously been collected from Penrith and then used to settle bills at shops as well as to hit the hostelries and "go mad and get drunk". It was becoming dangerously riotous, as poor Grisdale had discovered. "It had been a powder keg ready to blow," said Beryl, who was proving to be a source of all sorts of information.

She was not finished. Beryl told me that one man who used to work at Greenside Lead Mine still lived in Patterdale: "The last of the lot." Not knowing his address, she described where he lived and said he probably would not mind me popping round.

Which was how I found myself *going backward* to Patterdale, past the Ullswater Steamer pier and St Patrick's Church, and meeting Eddie Poole, aged 91.

Eddie lived in a bungalow overlooking St Patrick's Church with his wife, Anne. He too had a whippet, which was shivering outside his living-room window waiting to be let back in when I called. He was swarthy with a shock of grey hair and was wearing a brown jumper with a diamond pattern. Anne wore a purple fleece and held a stick. Both, like Beryl, had mischievous senses of humour and did not seem at all put out by an outsider coming by without an appointment. They invited me through their kitchen, decorated with ribbons awarded to prize foxhounds, to sit in their living room near a painting of a fox. A copy of the *Westmorland Herald* sat on a side table. The whippet stared quizzically at me through the window. Anne went to make tea.

I asked Eddie what it was like working in the lead mine.

"We'd never been used to anything else, it was just a job," he said. "It wasn't really hard. I was an engineer, a fitter. I went down every day. If something was wrong, I'd fix it. I think I must be about the last to have worked there. Most of the people in the village worked in the mine back then. It was far better, then. I don't think there's much community now. Not as it used to be. The community was much better back then."

"There are far too many holiday cottages and second homes," said Anne.

"Now if I go out, I just go out," said Eddie. "Back then I'd go out and there would always be someone to talk to."

"The place just isn't the same," said Anne.

Eddie and Anne, who were married in 1960 and had three children, used to live closer to the village centre. Eddie had left the mine in 1955 and "gone into haulage". He said: "I was brought up in Glenridding. When the mines were on, practically everyone was on the mine. It's just one of those things. They expected it. It had been going for years. I was there for ten years."

Working in the mine, however, had health drawbacks. "People definitely died younger, in their fifties and sixties back then," said Anne. "Take a walk around the churchyard and you can see."

I mentioned Thomas Grisdale. Were there tensions between farmers and miners, or did that belong to a different era?

"Well, there was a fight every bloody day," said Eddie. "If you were walking home from here at chucking-out time. It was easily done. They had had it bloody easy the farmers, compared to the miners. The farmers were much better off."

Eddie and Anne moved from the village centre in 1993. "It was getting noisy and dangerous down there," said Eddie. "The place was full of tourists. We used to have five or six terriers, and they couldn't run free with all the traffic."

Eddie looked across to his whippet in the window: "I better let the bloody bugger in!" Eddie got up and opened the window. The whippet jumped in and Eddie said: "When that dog catches a rabbit he never kills it, just lets it go again. The bugger!"

Eddie pronounced this word "boug-a".

"To be quite honest, tourists have been coming even before our time," said Eddie. "The buggers are good. People have work from them. As regards to the village though, once the mines closed, it wasn't a village any more."

Then Eddie clarified something: "I weren't a *miner*: lazy buggers! I was a *fitter*."

Anne chipped in, with a mocking voice: *"We can't do this. It's broken."*

Miners, as opposed to fitters such as himself, were quick to down tools, it seemed, if something was not right.

With that, we all shook hands and I walked up the west side of Ullswater.

Daffodils and diversions
Glenridding to Watermillock, via Glencoyne Bay and Aira Force

I had three missions for this stretch: 1) To find the spot where William Wordsworth was inspired by banks of daffodils to write "I Wandered Lonely as a Cloud", 2) To see a much-heralded waterfall at Aira Force and 3) To make it to Brackenrigg Inn at Watermillock reasonably early so I could put my feet up. This latter goal seemed both sensible and possible, despite having talked to a large percentage of the populations of Glenridding and Patterdale that morning.

Ashes, yews and cypress trees lined the secluded path below the main road as I plodded on up Ullswater, coming to a gravel beach. Here I asked a local for the location of Wordsworth's famous daffodils. "That's news to me," he said, when I mentioned that the tourist-office people had said it was close by. "But I wouldn't question the tourist-office people," he added.

I thanked him for his assistance. An information board in a car park pointed the way to a spot called Glencoyne Bay, also referred to as Wordsworth Point, where William and Dorothy came on 15 April 1802 and saw their daffodils. Dorothy recorded the moment in her journal, providing William with something to go on when he finally got round to penning his lines:

> When we were in the woods beyond Gowbarrow Park, we saw a few daffodils close to the water side. We fancied that the lake had floated the seed ashore and that the little colony had so sprung up. But as we went along there were more and yet more and at last under the boughs of the trees, we saw that there was a long belt of them along the shore, about the breadth of a county turnpike road. I never saw daffodils so beautiful they grew among the mossy stones about and about them, some rested their heads upon these stones as on a pillow for weariness and the rest tossed and reeled and danced and seemed as if they verily laughed with the wind that blew upon them over the lake, they looked so gay ever glancing ever changing. This wind blew directly over the lake to them. There was here and there a little knot and a few stragglers a few yards higher up but they were so few as not to disturb the simplicity and unity and life of that one busy highway. We rested again and again. The Bays were stormy, and we heard the waves at different distances and in the middle of the water like the sea.

William was to borrow Dorothy's descriptions – "gay", "dancing", "laughing" – in his best-known poem, written two years later. He also personified the flowers, just as Dorothy had in her journal.

The great thing was, if you visited Glencoyne Bay in the spring, they would probably be tossing and reeling as ever. They were when

I went. The "turnpike" of flowers still ran in a wide band along the shore, bathed in sunshine by the water's edge. I had them all to myself and it was a very strange sensation, as though I had stepped into the poem.

William and Dorothy had been walking together from Pooley Bridge to Patterdale on the day they saw all the flowers, so William had not really been "wander[ing] lonely as a cloud". Apart from this, the big difference between then and today was the presence of the cars tearing by on the road above. Wordsworth Point was slightly tricky to reach, squeezed as it was between the A592 and the water. No wonder no one else was there.

Daffodils done, it was not far up Ullswater to Aira Force.

This was another of Wordsworth's inspirations. In his poem "Airey-Force Valley", however, he ignored the waterfall itself and concentrated on the surrounding scenery:

> A soft eye-music of slow-waving boughs,
> Powerful almost as vocal harmony
> To stay the wanderer's steps and soothe his thoughts.

Up a path into the "soft eye-music" I went, observing the tumbling waterfall from an old stone bridge in a gully before returning down to the National Trust's tea room for lunch on the little veranda. Then I noticed something. Looking at the map, the Ullswater Way appeared to cut inland from Aira Force, moving through Gowbarrow Park and then into Swinburn's Park, requiring a long diversion to Brackenrigg Inn. Why the Ullswater Way did not follow the shores of Ullswater, as I had expected, I was unsure; perhaps there was not enough room with the road.

I asked a National Trust employee in a booth if I had it right.

"Yes," he said. "This is the difficult bit."

After looking at my map and showing me the way, we began talking about writing. It turned out that before becoming a National Trust employee, Richard had written rock-music biographies. "I wrote one on Robert Smith of The Cure, and Johnny Marr of The Cure – that did OK until he wrote his autobiography," he said. "Then a friend asked me to ghost the Robbie Williams section of a biography of Take That. For a short while, I was an expert on everything to do with Robbie Williams, until I forgot it all."

Richard had not written about music since that job; the life of Robbie Williams seemed to have undone him. Instead, he had settled into his work for the National Trust.

I was meeting all sorts by the shores of Ullswater.

Inland up a hill behind the car park at Aira Force, the path rose to about 350 metres on what turned out to be a great diversion along the Ullswater edge of Gowbarrow Fell, with sweeping lake views, buzzards wheeling above and rocky slopes leading to a forest with lichen-covered pines. Cones crunched underfoot. The air smelled of pine resin. Snow began to fall. I crossed fields near a holiday park and went down a hill to the Brackenrigg Inn. Somehow, I had covered 15 miles in the day: double what I had expected.

It was 6 p.m. I went to the little reception, where a woman said: "I'll just be a sec," as the phone had begun to ring as I arrived and she wanted to answer it. On completing the call, she looked up at me as though she had never seen me before in her life and asked: "Can I help you?" And then it dawned on her that she *had* seen me before and that I had already asked to check in. "Oh sorry," she said and gave the key.

I dropped my bag in my room and promptly went to the bar. I will not pretend otherwise: one of the great joys of walking around in the Lake District, as I was rapidly discovering, is the moment you stop walking around in the Lake District and begin to have something to drink after stopping to walk around; my preference being one of the many bitters and ales that seem to be produced by a proliferation of small local breweries. Perfect for quenching thirst and providing calories to replace all the ones you have just burned off by walking so far. I ordered a pint of The Rambling Bookkeeper, a fine, smooth ale named after Alfred Wainwright, who had an accountancy qualification and worked at the borough treasurer's office in Kendal, in the east of the Lakes, until he retired in 1967. His walking books were just a (very successful) sideline.

The Rambling Bookkeeper, it turned out, was produced by a microbrewery called Brack'N'Brew, based at the back of the Brackenrigg Inn. The pub had been brewing its own produce since 2015, with five different ales including The Steamers Stout, Boathouse Blonde, Aira Force and Alfred's. The barman, who had slicked-back hair and who was enjoying occasionally singing and dancing to a succession of soul-music tracks, said rhetorically as he passed over the pint of The Rambling Bookkeeper: "Why would you name two beers after one man?"

I answered that I did not know, but the barman had turned and was already at the other end of the bar, clicking his fingers, crooning about missing his "baby" (his sweetheart) and clicking his fingers some more. He seemed to be really into it.

After The Rambling Bookkeeper, I ordered a Steamboat Stout and a pizza from the soul-man barman and asked if I could take the table by the window. The pub was quite empty, a fire burning brightly in the fireplace on one side.

"It's reserved," he said. "You can go over there."

This was a table tucked behind other tables, facing a wall at the back. "Ah ok," I said, guessing a rush of people must be about to come.

In this corner I sat and ate my pizza and drank my stout, staring at the wall. The other tables remained empty. I asked a waitress when it was going to get busy, and she replied enigmatically: "In about a week's time."

Feeling a little nonplussed, I returned, after eating the pizza, to sit at the bar, whereupon I asked the barman whether he knew all the old soul songs, as he seemed something of an expert. I had hoped to break the ice a bit with this question and perhaps find out more about the Brack'N'Brew brewery.

"Not all of them, that would be impossible," he replied, and before I had a chance to respond, he had turned and was already at the other end of the bar, clicking his fingers and singing about his long-lost "baby" once more. Feeling a little nonplussed again, I returned to my room to read some of Wordsworth's *Guide* and check the map for the next day. A long day's walk appeared to lie ahead.

"You've gotta do what you've gotta do"
Watermillock to Threlkeld, via Dockray

To begin a hike in the Lake District on a crisp, bright morning with golden sunlight bathing the fells, curly-horned sheep baaing in the fields and crows flapping in the treetops was heartwarming and uplifting in equal measure. The countryside lay ahead in a state of perfection. A dog barked. A cockerel crowed. Birds trilled in hedgerows. A kestrel sailed forth from a tree. Way down below, Ullswater glimmered in a blaze of serpentine silver.

I was not without nerves about this section of the walk to Threlkeld, the village I had visited all that time ago as a teenager. It appeared to traverse great swathes of isolated mountains rising as high as 541 metres, at a place called Wolf Crags, and passing close to another peak named Clough Head, measuring 726 metres. I was hoping the paths would be easy to follow, no strolling on to screes or getting lost on hilltops, please. It was a measure of my lack of experience of mountain walking that I should have felt such unease. This was, after all, (absolutely) nothing compared to what was to come later during this story of a 379-mile Lakeland hike. Experienced fell walkers might well tut at such rookie lack of cool. And I would not blame them.

But I am aiming to tell it how it was on this long walk around the Lakes, and that was how it was: I was unsure about how the day would work out. No following the meandering shore of a gently lapping lake any more. I was heading up into the hills, at the mercy of winding little dotted green lines on the Ordnance Survey map, contours of mountains swirling and large patches of seemingly impassable land.

To reach this wild landscape required retracing my steps through yesterday's pine forest, ignoring signs for the villages of Dacre, Penruddock and Greystoke, before reaching Gowbarrow once more. A different path led around the far side of the mountain there, rising to a spot called Airy Crag – 481 metres at the top. I took this path, the fells alight with the early sunshine, which had turned the scenery a delicious caramel colour. Long morning shadows had formed across a tumbledown hilltop of gorse and grass, with the rocky summit at Airy Crag marked by a National Trust plaque.

The trail was easy to follow (I need not have worried). I descended a steep hill where sacks of granite boulders had been helicoptered in and left to be spread out to improve the path. "What a lovely day!" said a woman walking a chestnut dog, capturing exactly how I felt about it too. The track led to the side of the fast-moving Aira Beck, which fed Aira Force waterfall. I passed an old barn and arrived after 5 miles at the Royal Hotel in the tiny village of Dockray.

The Royal Hotel was a three-storey structure with a huge Scottish royal coat of arms on one side. A notice by the entrance explained that Mary, Queen of Scots, had stayed in 1568 "while being escorted from Scotland". The pub had then been named the Cross Keys but this was changed after her visit to the Royal Hotel.

Inside, I asked if breakfast was available, and the manager/waiter looked at his watch. It was 9.29 a.m. and service, he said, ended at 9.30 a.m. He considered this for a moment. "No problem!" he said and very soon heaps of Cumberland sausages, poached eggs, bacon, fried tomatoes and toast were delivered. Yoghurts, cereals, fruit and juices were also available on a sideboard. Cyndi Lauper and Madonna hits played. Bookshelves in the dining room teemed with interesting old travel books: Paul Theroux, Jan Morris, Eric Newby. The manager/waiter told me that he was from Warsaw in Poland. He had lived in the Lakes for ten years.

Did he like it, I asked.

"Oh yes!" he said, as if surprised that anyone might not. We chatted for a while about Warsaw (my other half is Polish and she had once worked in the city, so I knew it well). He introduced me to the chef, who was Polish too. An elderly local woman came in for a cup of tea and we all sat around chatting for a while.

What a top place, the Royal Hotel.

A road led on from this inn to High Row, which was where the wide-open expanse of Matterdale Common began.

Ahead, patches of snow lay beside stone walls and the path was deserted. The Ordnance Survey map showed I was following the Old Coach Road, which was a wide stony track and, I noticed, marked on the map with a green *and* orange dotted line signifying both an "other public access route" (the green dots) and a "traffic-free cycle route" (the orange dots). Quite what this meant, I was not sure, but it seemed to be a bigger deal than a mere "footpath" (small dotted green line) or bridleway (wider green dashes), which were what I had covered so far.

Snow had settled prettily on Clough Head fell and the trail up through Matterdale Common felt a world away from lakeside affairs and the bustle of Penrith. A forest of pine trees rose to the right before ceasing abruptly at a boundary fence. Skylarks flittered in the tall grass growing by the track, squeaking happily as the countryside opened out like a prairie in the American Wild West. As I soaked up the sheer enjoyment of such splendid solitude, a man on a bicycle wheeled up behind and I almost jumped out of my skin. "Sorry, mate, didn't mean to startle ya," he said, looking at me slightly oddly. I think I may have been muttering to myself about how much I liked

Matterdale Common when he passed.

Then, not long afterward, a man from Preston drove up, coming in the opposite direction in a shiny Land Rover Discovery: encounter number two on the Old Coach Road.

"You all right, mate?" he asked, rolling down a window and coming to a halt.

This was the middle of nowhere, not a building in sight. Scree and boulders marked the rugged slopes of Wolf Crag above the track. The wind had picked up, whipping fiercely across the hills. It was freezing cold, and I was feeling the weight of the backpack. Perhaps that had showed.

I said I was fine, thanks.

The driver, who was alone, was talkative. He told me he had driven over from Preston to try out his new vehicle in scenery fit for a four-wheel drive. There was little point in owning a Land Rover Discovery and just using it to go to Asda. He wanted to test it out. "Green lanes," he said. Apparently, this track was a "green lane" where vehicles were allowed, even though the Ordnance Survey map appeared to indicate otherwise. "I'm just following satnav, to be honest, mate. All legal roads. I'm off to some tracks south of Windermere after this."

The man from Preston was named Matt, bald with mirrored sunglasses resting on his head. He wore a gilet and looked warm in his tan leather seat. He warned me about boulders on the track ahead. "They only did a little bit of damage to the car," he said, advising me not to take a farmers' track at that point. "I was tempted but, to be honest, God knows where that goes. Watch out!"

With that, he tooted his horn and spun onward.

Not long after this conversation, the ridge of Blencathra, also known as Saddleback, rose to the north, with a thin white line of snow across the top as though it had been painted with whitewash. The peculiar effect, from a distance, was of a mountain with little white teeth pointing up.

It was a marvellous, if odd, sight. Streams ran down steep slopes in lemony streaks sliding between scree, bracken and burgundy-tinted heather. Threlkeld, my destination, lay at the foot of this fell: a scattering of dwellings beyond the great undulations of northern Lake District grassland in the foreground. Turning round at this point, looking back toward Dockray, empty landscape was all the eye could see. Silence reigned beneath a sky dotted with high clouds. It was still, elemental, isolated and quite awe-inspiring.

Another shiny Land Rover Discovery drove past, this one with a couple in the front who faintly (and a touch smugly) smiled at me as they purred by. Another cyclist passed. Then I crossed a field and bypassed a quarry where a sign said "DANGER, NO ACCESS" and met a woman who had just been in the quarry walking her dog. I had seen her leave from a gate.

"Are people allowed in there?" I asked, considering having a look.

"Well not really," she replied, but as she lived close by, she knew where it was safe.

The quarry, she said, was disused and was now full of old excavators (mechanical diggers) belonging to a group called the Vintage Excavator Trust. "My neighbour calls it the biggest pile of rust in the north-west," she said. "It's boys and their toys really."

Walking with me toward Threlkeld, she explained that the granite quarry, which had been used to supply ballast for the Cockermouth, Keswick and Penrith Railway (closed in 1972 due to falling passenger numbers), had itself shut up shop in the 1980s.

"The granite was also used to make sets for cobbled streets," she said. "Large parts of Manchester and Leeds are probably cobbled from here. To be a *set worker* making those cobbles was a prized skill. There is a campaign to reopen the railway that has been going for years but I don't think it'll get anywhere."

Her name was Moira, a retired lawyer from Manchester. "There are quite a lot of retired middle-class white liberal people here," she said. "White. Don't forget: *white*. It's the countryside, isn't it? You don't get much diversity."

On this somewhat disquieting (thought-provoking) note, we parted, and I crossed the old railway line, now a footpath, and the A66, passing down a lane to The Salutation Inn, aka The Sally, where I had played darts and hung out so many moons ago. This was where I believed I had booked a room for the night, although the barmaid said the room was across the street at the Horse & Farrier, a sister pub, as renovations were just being completed in the rooms of The Sally.

Restoration had just finished in the public areas by the bar as well, to such an extent it was difficult to recognize the place of my teenage visits. Carpets had been replaced with pared-down wooden floorboards and a conservatory-style room was at the back facing a sun terrace; none of which I could recall. A dartboard hung in a corner, pleasingly, just as before, and a fire was ablaze in the old fireplace. A message on a board on the mantelpiece read: "Everybody has to believe in something. I believe I'll have another BEER."

I was the only customer and it was 2 p.m. I had walked about 10 miles, according to my phone.

The barmaid seemed pleased to have someone to talk to. I ordered a pint of Wainwright and the barmaid apologized. "Last week we had to put up the prices of pints by about thirty to forty-five pence," she said. "The dearest one went up sixty pence, and I'm still making a loss on that. The breweries put the prices up. It's fuel costs and ingredient costs. Everything has gone up."

The barmaid, though, seemed down about things. "During Covid some people realized that hospitality was not the industry for them," she said. "With the hours it's not a social industry, and wages aren't high either. We also had a bit of abuse from members of the public." This was about the one-way systems to encourage social distancing during the pandemic. "'Why don't you do this or that?' people would say. I just got verbal abuse, but I know someone who got physical abuse. I was lucky. People have switched to other jobs with more pay and less difficult hours."

Another reason, aside from Brexit, for all the "hiring" signs I had seen.

The barmaid was on a roll. "The biggest problem is transport. If you haven't got transport, how do you get to work? There is a good bus here but it stops at 9 p.m." That was no good for pub workers. "I commute forty miles a day. It's getting to the point where I can't afford to work here. I love this industry. I love this job. I don't want to leave." But the price of petrol was beginning to make work unviable.

She discussed the make-up of the village of Threlkeld. "There are two sides to the village here," she said. "You've got the originals and the ones who've moved in. Those ones [those who have moved in] don't come into the pub as much."

She switched tack: "Holiday homes and second homes, that's the biggest problem. In the village where I live there are twenty-three houses. We didn't use to need cars, but then they [the local authorities] stopped the bus route about six years ago. So people had to move out if they didn't have cars and the elderly people couldn't go anywhere. So houses were sold and they became holiday homes. Ten of them were sold. That has a knock-on effect on schools. Attendance numbers go down. More and more schools are closing as not enough children are turning up. And they now say that no one wants the bus route anyway because there are fewer people needing it. But that's because so many moved out because there was no bus! I understand that people want to live up here, but people need to understand that there is a knock-on effect for locals. If you are born and bred round here, you should be able to afford to live here and be able to work here. My daughter lives with me. She just can't afford to get out. My other daughter and her boyfriend have got a place, but they're struggling. People are having to move to Workington, Whitehaven and Maryport on the coast because it's cheaper, but the standard of living is not as good."

The barmaid paused. She had become quite emotional. Then she said quietly: "But you've gotta do what you've gotta do." This was spoken as though she sounded utterly defeated by the situation: *what can I, or any of us, do?*

The issue of outsiders buying properties thus pricing out locals and ruining old ways of life was not going away. From Kathleen in Penrith to the barmaid at The Sally and the campaigning efforts of the Liberal Democrat MP Tim Farron, it kept cropping up. Many others saying the same were to come. Half of the barmaid's village, which she asked me not to name, had "gone". As with Kathleen, it was both clear she wanted it back and that it would never be quite the same again, either.

* * *

My room at the Horse & Farrier was the best yet, with a smart bathroom featuring olive-green tiles and shiny chrome fittings, a wide bed, a neat little writing desk and decor in shades of grey that somehow managed to be tasteful shades of grey, soothing even, rather than dull. It was above a busy, labyrinthine bar with many snugs and nooks and a low ceiling. All very cosy in the Horse & Farrier.

The receptionist had told me about the Threlkeld Quarry and Mining Museum, so, without further ado, I re-crossed the A66 and entered the quarry, going along a road without any "DANGER, NO ACCESS" signs, passing many rusty old excavators. The description given by the woman walking her dog earlier had been spot on.

As I arrived, feeling as though I was floating along without the backpack, I came to a little red locomotive attached to a series of carriages on a narrow-gauge track. In these carriages sat tourists waiting for the loco to go. I asked a gap-toothed man with a grey beard and a filthy fluorescent jacket whether I could join the train journey, which appeared to be about to travel in the direction of the quarry's centre. He replied: "Yes, if you get a ticket. We won't go without you." He indicated with his eyes that tickets were purchased from a little building across a car park. I returned with one, took a seat in a tiny wooden booth and the train duly departed with a hoot, rolling beyond a heap of coal. It clattered. It clanked. It bumped. We passed yet more rusty old excavators. The wheels squealed upward along the edge of a crater with silver-birch trees and boulders. It was a great sensation, moving without walking. The train clanked a great deal more and seemed to feel the strain of the hill, eventually coming to a halt 5 minutes later, beside an old yellow crane with "LOUGHSIDE QUARRIES" written on it.

Everyone disembarked and had a look at the old crater and the excavators. Some of us then went to the front of the train to peer at the locomotive.

The driver was a short, wiry man with a bushy moustache. He wore a flat cap and an old-fashioned train driver's jacket.

"We have one steam loco and a few diesel locos," he said. "We're getting the boiler tube fixed on the steam loco at the moment. This one [the loco that had been pulling our train, a diesel] spent its working life down a coal mine in Yorkshire." He explained a little about the quarry's original purpose supplying ballast for regional railways. Then he complained that the Cockermouth, Keswick and Penrith Railway should never have been closed in the 1970s. "We need it back now to put Keswick on a railway line. If they want folk to stop using motor cars, people need an alternative."

The rail enthusiast beside me asked the driver about the locomotive's engine. "The type of engine on this train is a Gardner four cylinder with fifty horsepower," the driver replied, quick as a shot. "It's a steady pull up all the way, a steep incline. We do six journeys a day, seven days a week – fewer in slack times."

I asked the driver his name and he told me it was Ian Hartland. "What's your official title?" I asked, expecting perhaps an answer of "head driver" or "chief engineer".

"Managing director," he said, pausing for effect. "Well, actually I own this quarry."

Ian had bought the quarry in 1990 and opened the museum 25

years ago. "When this quarry was shut in 1982, almost everybody in the area used to work here," he said. "Go back a hundred years and there were three hundred people round here working in this quarry. We felt the Lake District needed something to reflect its industrial heritage. People don't realize that before tourism it was industrial in these parts."

The museum was run by a group of volunteers and paid staff, with 9,000 visitors annually. "We could probably double that," said Ian. "But we want to make enough to make it pay, but not too many people to spoil it."

He tipped his cap. We returned to the carriages. The train ran down the hill. We all disembarked and had a look around the curious little museum, with its displays on the excavation of iron ore, lead, copper, silver, granite, slate and much else in the Lakes over the years. In one corner, I stumbled upon a display all about Greenside Lead Mine, Eddie's mine, which had once been a source of lead for bullets in the American Civil War as well as of silver, found in small traces amid the lead.

Greenside Lead Mine, I soon learned, had also been the site of a highly unusual final episode in its working life. In 1959, the Atomic Weapons Research Establishment (AWRE) had co-opted the almost depleted mine, having selected it for a test to simulate an underground nuclear explosion. As madcap as this may sound, taking place as it did in the middle of the lovely Lake District, the project went ahead. The AWRE was keen to establish whether a clever "de-coupling" system of explosions could be being used by the Soviet Union to conceal the seismic effect of underground nuclear tests. So, in the hills above Glenridding, with its tea rooms and the Ullswater Steamer pier, an almighty blast was conducted involving more than 4,000 pounds of high explosive. This top-secret project was code-named Operation Orpheus and was carried out alongside American scientists.

The operation was at first a failure and then a tragedy before the scientists completed their task on the second go. The double explosion did not work on the initial try as one of the sets of explosives had failed to blow. A pair of men who went to examine what had happened then died from heavy fumes while deep underground. Finally, the experiment was set up once again and, in April 1960, the double explosions were triggered. The results were as the scientists had predicted. It was established that, using this "de-coupling" method, surreptitious underground nuclear tests could be conducted in the Soviet Union. "This finding wrecked the [nuclear] test ban treaty, the Soviet Union returned to its nuclear tests in August 1961 and the Cold War and its arms race dragged on for many miserable years," said a panel.

Who would have thought it?

All due to Eddie's old lead mine down by Ullswater.

The Threlkeld Quarry and Mining Museum turned out to be full of intrigue, with grainy black-and-white pictures of miners from the good old days as well as faded newspaper cuttings from the time. Cabinets overflowed with drills, surveying equipment, slabs of slate and chunks of quartz gathered from the depths of the fells. One display covered the work of German miners brought in by Elizabeth I for their underground expertise and who, in the 1570s, introduced a very early, simple form of railway to transport their underground harvest, known as "rowle wagons". These Germans were also said to have made another, more lasting, local mark: the recipe for Cumberland sausages.

Add in the 70-plus excavators dotted around the grounds outside, the largest of which weighed more than 180 tonnes, and the Threlkeld Quarry and Mining Museum was all delightfully eccentric. No over-slick presentation. Nothing slick at all. Just a ramshackle metallic mess in a series of old yards, plus all the higgledy-piggledy museum displays. The collection of excavators, Ian says, is the largest of such vintage quarry vehicles on the planet. The vast majority still work, amazingly, and each summer there is a display for the public.

It is not every day you stumble upon the world's largest collection of excavators, I could not help reflecting. The Lakes was not all "beauty and grandeur" and playfully swaying daffodils at Threlkeld. It was rough round the edges and made no bones about it.

* * *

I returned to the Horse & Farrier, ate an excellent chicken madras curry, looked up my route for the next day – and gulped a bit at the prospect. The weather was turning and high winds were forecast. Was I about to bite off more than I could chew?

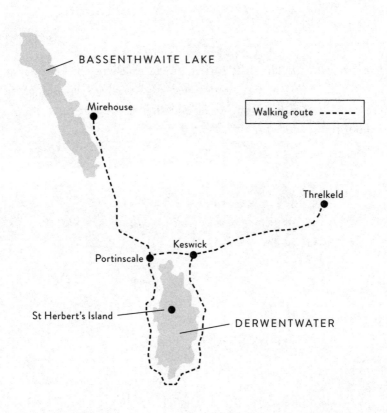

BASSENTHWAITE LAKE

Mirehouse

Walking route ------

Threlkeld

Keswick

Portinscale

St Herbert's Island

DERWENTWATER

CHAPTER THREE

THRELKELD TO BASSENTHWAITE LAKE, VIA KESWICK AND DERWENTWATER

CLOUDS AND PINTS

Possibly, was the answer to that question – possibly. In the morning I did what fell walkers are meant to do when concerned about conditions in the hills and asked a local what they thought. This local was the receptionist at the Horse & Farrier inn. Looking out from the Horse & Farrier, the weather did not exactly appear great. A thick, creamy band of cloud had descended and the top of Blencathra, at 868 metres, had disappeared beneath it. Across the way, beyond the granite quarry, the path along the Old Coach Road had vanished in this thick, creamy cloud too. The entire village of Threlkeld felt besieged by thick, creamy cloud. The mountains all around seemed to have closed in.

"To be honest," said the receptionist. "You will get wet. I wouldn't go. It will be windy. You may not like it."

"Will anyone go up today?" I asked.

"Yes, others will go. There are always people up on Blencathra. So yes, you could go. It will be slippery, but it's easy really."

She paused and added: "To be honest, if you went and didn't like it, you could always turn back."

The receptionist said that the round trip normally took her 2 hours up and down. If I wanted to go, she recommended taking a path up Hall's Fell, just behind the Horse & Farrier: "It's best from Hall's Fell."

She paused once again. "But to be honest, it's very slippery."

I thanked her and ate my well-cooked poached eggs served with a generous portion of smoked salmon. If you are going to head up into the clouds in the Lake District, you may as well do so after a decent breakfast. As I was thinking these thoughts, a man on a neighbouring table shared with three companions turned to me.

"You're going up, are you?" he said; he must have heard me talking to the receptionist.

"Yes," I replied, deciding for certain there and then that I would.

"We went up yesterday," he said. "The visibility was perfect. Sorry to say that." He did not want to rub it in too much. "Six hours going in a circle [around to another peak and back through the valley]. We went straight up from here. You should be fine. You just go straight up, don't you?"

With that, he wished me good luck and he and his companions began discussing earplugs. They were middle-aged and sharing rooms; snoring had been an issue in the night. "These ones I've got are great," said one of them. "They were tested on the loudest snoring known to man and they were successful."

The woman in reception, who doubled as the breakfast waitress, came to collect my plate, as she did so kindly handing over a printout of the day's Mountain Weather Information Service. This said: "Walking will be difficult on higher terrain and gusts may throw you off balance. Considerable wind chill, little sunshine all day, extensive hill fog. Will feel like −7°C in the wind at above 750 metres."

The peak of Blencathra, as I have mentioned, was higher, but neither the receptionist/waitress nor the four middle-aged snorers had actually said: "Do not go." I went upstairs to prepare – two fleeces seemed in order – after wishing the guys on the next-door table a good day's hiking: they were keeping to the lowlands, they had said. "Will you be around for beers later?" asked one of them. Another said: "*Hope* to see you later," in a tone of voice that suggested they might not. *Ha ha ha.* As I walked out of the breakfast room, I heard them snickering about this parting comment.

Wind, scree and boulders
Threlkeld to Blencathra and back

Given that my intention was to take a casual stroll around the Lakes, you may wonder why I was so determined to go up Blencathra. This had something to do with re-living the old days of when I had been in Threlkeld years before. I also again wanted to test myself early on, as I had as far as distance was concerned from Penrith to Patterdale.

This would be an altitude challenge. Could I make it up one of the big ones? There it was, supposedly up and down in 2 hours. If I could do that in iffy weather – though it was far from stormy conditions – then I would be better prepared for whatever came later on, plus I would not have the backpack, which I could leave at reception.

That was my thinking. I left at 9.15 a.m. and headed up Blease Road toward the foothills and the clouds. A local in an orange waterproof jacket pointed to the precise point where the footpath up began: "See that seam and buttress," he said. He appeared to be pointing at a part of the fell that protruded.

"Yes," I replied, as though understanding exactly what he was saying.

"See that tree at about eleven o'clock and the zigzag path going up above it?"

"Yes," I replied, having worked out by then where he meant.

"Go up there."

"Yes," I replied.

"And have fun!" he said, sounding dubious about the likelihood as he looked up at the clouds.

"I'll try," I replied, thanking him and noting that he was yet another person not to have said: "Do not go."

The man in the orange waterproof said the round trip would take 1 hour 30 minutes. I set off along a drystone wall toward Hall's Fell and turned left up an extremely steep scree path.

The cloud was not so thick and creamy close-up as I scampered through the scree, enjoying the plummeting heathery mountainside and the view across the valley beyond the quarry. The air was fresh and the sense of adventure liberating. I was bagging a Wainwright! A tricky Wainwright at that. I was doing the fells like a proper Lakeland walker.

It was then the wind picked up. As though funnelling through the valley at a precise height, a wall of fast-moving air suddenly struck. The wind was soon so strong that gusts were indeed "throw[ing me] off balance", as the Mountain Weather Information Service had said. I was far from the point of falling over, but certainly being buffeted. These gusts proceeded to turn from strong to very strong. I crept forward, crouching low, and came to a boulder that offered shelter, where I sat and ate a protein bar and drank some water. I had already gone a long way and could just see the village of Threlkeld through the haze below. Lorries, which looked like toys from way up above, spun along the A66.

No one said don't go, I reassured myself, as I continued further upward into even stronger wind that had me hunching down and facing into it to maintain balance as I walked on in an awkward crab-like motion. Then, almost as abruptly as the wind had begun, it abated, leaving me hiking through the still air covering what turned out to be a granite ridge. A persistent drizzle had replaced the gusts and I followed a path to a granite slope that appeared to be the way forward to the summit. I clambered up this, quickly realizing that this granite slope was not a brief blockage but the start of a serious climb over yet more sharp-edged granite boulders. I looked back. I had ascended a considerable distance up the granite slope. This was, I decided, *not quite right*. I returned to the path, having gingerly descended the way I had come, and crept along a side path that seemed to offer an alternative way to the top.

No one else was up Blencathra to ask advice on what to do. I did not see a single other soul, despite what the receptionist had said.

It became extremely misty. No view whatsoever of the valley below was to be had. I seemed to have entered a white-out. Realizing I had better retrace my steps and head back down to Threlkeld, I did so, only to discover I had taken a different path that was leading through a narrow gap between boulders, heading who knew where. Realizing I had better retrace my steps again, away from these new boulders, I did so, somehow finding the original path. This led to the zigzag track down through the scree of Hall's Fell, where a pair of sheep were munching on the highland grass. They turned and regarded me with what seemed to be highly sceptical expressions. Then they returned to eating the high-fell grass.

The strong wind began further down the zigzag scree path. By this stage I was soaked through. I hunched low once again through the especially windy patch of the mountain, came to a path through a deserted farm and returned to the Horse & Farrier, drenched. The journey had taken 3 hours and was quite exhilarating, though, I will also concede, slightly mad, if not verging on dangerous. I changed out of my wet clothes and looked at my map while warming up. I must have come quite close to the top of Blencathra, but I do not think I bagged it. Not that I was bothered. Not in the slightest. It had been quite a morning, and I had learned something about the Lake District's fells, at least I thought so. What had sunk in was: *if in doubt* – as I had been right at the top (three times, no less) – *turn back*. Retrace your steps. Do not push on, especially through narrow gaps between boulders leading to places you have never been before.

Blencathra in the wind and the mist had taught me a valuable Lakeland lesson.

Bar crawl with the mayor
Threlkeld to Keswick

It was with a light heart and a sense of relief at the fact that I would be going along the flat that I set off to Keswick, the largest northern Lakes town (population: 5,240). This was a particularly relaxed walk of 5 miles along a dotted orange line on the trusty Ordnance Survey map that indicated a "permissive footpath" – not a right of way but a pathway along which "landowners have permitted public use", although this agreement could be withdrawn. I would also be following the larger orange dots of a "traffic-free cycle route".

These orange dots of various sizes followed the route of the old Cockermouth, Keswick and Penrith Railway, which snaked alongside the river Greta, darting across bridges and into tunnels. The pathway was rough and muddy close to the granite quarry, before turning into a slick Tarmac surface that looked recently laid, on the edge of Threlkeld. At this point, the old railway line ducked beneath the noisy A66 and continued beside the wild boulders and the rushing water of the Greta in a secret valley that wound quietly onward and culminated by the old platforms of Keswick Station, next to the grand facade of the Keswick Country House Hotel, just to the north of the town centre.

It made for a fabulous stroll. The smart Tarmac part of the path ran for about 3½ miles and was smooth enough for a roller skater. A sign said the route was officially known as the Threlkeld Railway Trail, established with the help of public and private money in the aftermath of Storm Desmond in 2015, which had caused great damage to the former pathway and to some of the bridges. Every few hundred metres or so, further information signs cropped up. By this means, the walker discovered that the decline of mining in the early twentieth century, coupled with a growth in lorry transportation of freight and tourist preferences to drive to visit the Lakes, meant that by 1960 the railway was losing £50,000 a year, resulting in its "inevitable" 1972 closure. The line had opened in 1864, covering a total of 31 miles, and was key to transporting locally mined coal – unsuitable for iron ore smelting – to blast furnaces in the north-east of England where it was turned into coke effective for smelting and then returned. It seemed that any hopes Ian back at the Threlkeld granite quarry might have had that the railway could one day reopen to trains had been quashed by its recreation as a "leisure" route.

The river widened as the trail unfurled, with boulders and logs strewn on its banks. In the swirling water below were brown trout and otters, according to yet another sign. The trail wound into and out of a long tunnel, coming to a field of impossibly cute lambs. A bit further on came a holiday camp with pistachio-coloured holiday homes similar to the ones near Pooley Bridge. Soon after those, I cut down some side steps before the path reached the town centre, joining a road that led to Denton House hostel, where I had booked a bed in a dorm for two nights at less than half the cost of a stay at the Horse & Farrier. This was an attempt to economize, but I had a last-minute wobble: *did I really want to be in a shared dorm?* Close to the hostel, which I could see just down the way, was a pub-with-rooms called the Twa Dogs Inn. I went in to see if there was availability and how much a room for two nights might cost, just in case the hostel was packed/uncomfortable and I decided to find somewhere else.

Inside, a man was fixing a fruit machine and partially blocking the entrance. I dodged past him and went to the bar, where a smartly dressed woman who appeared to be a manager replied to my enquiry: "We haven't got any rooms till 14 April."

I asked about food, maybe this would be a good place to eat later. "We haven't got any food either," she said.

Then she took a phone call, muttered into the receiver and ended the conversation.

"That was one of our barmaids. Her car's broken down, so we haven't even got any staff now," she said.

I said I might pop round for a drink later and the woman replied sharply: "It's pay as you drink," looking me up and down.

I had mud all over my waterproof trousers from sliding about on the top of Blencathra. My boots were equally filthy. My hair was like a bird's nest after the wind of the mountain, and I was hauling a backpack that looked as though it might just contain my entire worldly possessions. I would have said it was "pay as you drink" pretty sharpish too if I ran a pub and saw a character such as myself amble in.

I walked onward to Denton House hostel, just round the corner, ready for whatever came my way. The hostel was a former stationmaster's house from the old railway, and it was in a prominent grey building close to a Royal Mail depot. Inside a porch, I found an envelope addressed to me pinned to a board. Inside this envelope was a code for the lock on the hostel's door. This code did not work, so I called the emergency number of the incredibly friendly manager who said that "this has never happened before" and that she had just gone home for the day but would come round and sort things out.

While I waited, another hostel guest named Pete turned up. He too could not get in. He was from Glasgow and a serious walker on a week off, having left his partner, not such a serious walker, at home. He was returning to Glasgow the next day. We stood outside the hostel, and he told me about his recent hikes, rattling off various Wainwrights he had bagged.

"There was High Rigg. Then Dodd," he said. "Also Carl Side, Longside Edge and Ullock Pike. Dodd was my favourite. It was the smallest [502 metres] but I caught a wee glimpse of an osprey."

Pete was in his twenties, a hulking figure wearing a hoodie, yet with a soft and gentle voice. He told me he enjoyed "the buzz of hiking, the views and just getting away from work and everything. I find it good for my mental health, especially with inflation and the rise in the cost of living." This had been getting him down of late: "I got four letters recently. All were about payments going up. Rent. Gas. Electric. Council tax."

He sighed. Pete said he worked as a carer and that money was tight due to the low wages: "My partner and I are hoping to get a house, but the prices of houses are going up as well, just like everything else. Suddenly we're back to square one: houses we looked at last year have gone up £10,000. We are going to have to save more. We don't want to spend all we've got on a house. We want to have money for emergencies, too."

Pete said he had been working "non-stop since September" and that his week's hiking in the Lakes had "really helped mentally". The mountains seemed to have come to his rescue, with so many troubles in his life.

Christina, the Denton House manager, arrived with an energetic terrier puppy on a lead. She apologized for the code problem and let us in, fixing new numbers for the entrance lock. The hostel was almost empty, and she kindly found me a room with four bunks that I would have to myself; Pete was staying in another room with a dozen bunks and no other guests either. The hostel had 64 beds. Most were unused, with just a small group of teenagers who were on an orienteering course sharing another dorm.

My extremely cheap, private room came with a window that rattled in the wind, a sink and a chair; the bathroom was down the hall. Christina walked me round the hostel's many confusing corridors showing me the lounge, where the teenagers were studying maps, the laundry room, the two kitchens ("take your pick") and an honesty fridge with sodas, water and slices of flapjack. She told me there was no need to follow the one-way system that was still marked on the floor from Covid-pandemic days or to wear a face mask, despite the many signs saying this was required. All in all, I had landed on my feet: Denton House was a bargain.

Christina headed home. Pete passed by saying he was going to get some fish and chips. And I called my old friend who had once lived in Threlkeld. He and his family had since moved out of the area, but I thought he might still be in touch with some of the people we once knew from Keswick. Christy answered the phone, we had a catch-up chat and he said that he had one old contact he thought might be of interest, who was not someone I had known.

"He's called Alan Dunn," Christy said, "And now he's the mayor of Keswick. Take him for a pint. He can talk his arse off."

With this glowing recommendation, I called Alan Dunn, the mayor of Keswick.

"Would I like a pint?" said Alan in the manner of someone asking: "Do one-legged ducks swim in circles?" We arranged to meet in an hour's time at a pub called The Crafty Baa.

* * *

The Crafty Baa was easy to find, just up from the river Greta, beyond Fitz Park where a bowling competition was in full swing, and down Bank Street, close to the offices of the town council. Its exterior was adorned with a mad-looking mannequin dressed in a tweed jacket, trilby and dark shades, next to a model of a sheep. An acoustic guitar was nailed to a panel above the door beside a pair of old flip-flops, an ironing board and some crutches. A board stated that more than a hundred "crafted world beers" were on offer as well as a selection of "fine wines". Only the "best soul, funk, blues and jazz" was played inside and a sign above the door pronounced: "NOBODY GETS OUT SOBER".

Inside, a singer was crooning away in a corner of the front room. I went to the back room where a board by the bar listed the hundred beers, which ranged from Cucumber Hippy sour ale from New Zealand to Blackberry Lambic beer from Belgium, Mango Unchained IPA from Salford and Brooklyn Lager. Beside this board was a large stuffed toy in the shape of a sheep, which was wearing a fluorescent jacket printed with the words: "THE CRAFTY BAA SECURITY". Beside the stuffed toy sheep was Alan Dunn, the mayor of Keswick.

Alan was, in old-fashioned terms, a jovial cove, beaming brightly with laughter lines on his face and an easy manner. He was evidently a popular mayor; several drinkers came up to say hello while we talked. He wore a jumper with the Route 66 highway symbol from the United States on it. He was in his early seventies. Attached to the wall above his head was a car number plate that said: "TWO 4 ALE". This had belonged to an old car of Alan's and he had given it to the owner of The Crafty Baa, who had decided to use the number plate as decoration; the interior of The Crafty Baa was as eclectic and unusual as its exterior. My old friend Christy's description of his old friend was spot on, in the nicest possible way.

After Alan told me about the number plate, he said: "I virtually live here." He was referring to The Crafty Baa.

I bought us pints of Crafty Baa lager and we stood by the stuffed toy sheep discussing this and that.

Alan had been mayor for almost a year and his term ran out in a month's time. After I explained I had walked along the Threlkeld Railway Trail to reach Keswick, Alan said there had been "a lot of controversy" over it as many councillors had wanted a special surface that was better for running on, but because some of the public funding had been from Highways England, "it had to be Tarmac". The trail had, nevertheless, been a hit with locals, walkers and runners alike. Alan, a retired businessman who had once run a roller-skating rink as well as a "cash and carry" service, was himself a walker: "I'm doing the Wainwrights, I only have eight left." His quest to complete the 214 peaks had begun after he had hiked up the fells at Dodd and then Skiddaw in January 2015: he announced to friends at the George Hotel, an old Keswick inn, after having had a few, that "I might as well do the rest", which his friends had kept him to. Proof that beer can sometimes (if very rarely) help keep you fit.

The two big issues of his mayorship had been a furore over a fox-hunting gathering on the Market Square the previous Boxing Day – fox hunting was made illegal in the UK in 2004, although "trail hunting", involving merely following a scent, continues (but outsiders are suspicious that actual hunting goes on under the guise of trail hunting) – and "second homes and holiday homes".

This really was the big issue in the Lakes and Alan spoke passionately on the subject. "Of the houses that are sold here, eighty per cent are turned into holiday and second homes," he said. "It pushes up prices. We've got Mayfair prices here and we're in the Lake District. It's crazy. It takes away homes from local people." To counter this, rules under the Town and Country Planning Act 1990 were being invoked to develop new housing specifically for "local occupancy", i.e. those born in the region. "It's done under section 106: that new builds must only be for people from Cumbria. But there aren't that many new builds as we're in a national park." Being in such an area meant planning permission could be difficult to obtain. Speaking of his own children, he said: "We've got four kids and only one has a house." To give an idea of the pressure on prices created by outsiders, Alan added that a new build under section 106 selling for £195,000 would be £260,000 if it was available to all comers. "That's at least thirty-five per cent more."

Alan called over a couple standing nearby. They were in their late twenties, bright and friendly and, also, stuck. "I still live with my dad," the man said. "It's impossible to buy a property. I checked with a mortgage advisor and found that, although we have reasonable wages, we can't afford the cheapest house in Keswick. Not even a terraced house in a flood-risk area." His partner simply said: "It's so frustrating."

Friends then called them back. The Crazy Baa was buzzing with chatter, laughter and music.

Aside from fox-hunting protests and the housing shortage, Alan said the other priority of his mayorship had begun two months earlier: "The Ukraine war. Yes, we've put a flag on the town hall, but we've also decided to raise money – so far eight thousand pounds. We've decided to go with medical supplies: specialist equipment, special bandages for burns. We're going to drive it to the border. We've taken the seats out of a Citroën and we're going to go via the Harwich ferry with the supplies on Saturday." By "we" he was referring to himself and a fellow councillor. "We'll try to bring a Ukrainian family back as well. Four of us on the council have all registered but we've not heard anything back yet about this [from the authorities]. My wife and I have got a spare room. It's one of the things that, practically, we can do. Not just put up a flag."

As he said all of this – and when he discussed the second- and holiday-home problems – Alan's demeanour completely changed: the *jovial cove* was replaced by a politician who clearly understood when serious and urgent matters needed to be addressed. Just as quickly, though, he switched back once again, grabbed my arm and said: "Come on, let's go to another bar I know."

I was about to go on a bar crawl with the mayor of Keswick.

Walking through the town centre, via a little lane into Market Square, involved a procession of greetings to passers-by as Alan took on the role of tourist guide. "See that," he was pointing at a Barclays bank. "That's our only bank now. We used to have a Lloyds, an HSBC and a NatWest." They had gone due to online banking and the old buildings had been converted into clothing shops. Alan showed me a new whisky shop. "I don't drink spirits," he said. "Which is just as well." We passed a Cornish Bakery shop. "*Cornish* Bakery," he said, jokingly. "What's that doing here?"

We turned down a lane toward Derwentwater, passing the Wainwright pub and a vegan café, outside of which a local walking in the other direction said: "Are you out patrolling?" To which Alan replied: "Yes, the licensed premises."

We entered the door of one of these, The Pocket Café Bar, a new licensed premises run by a 22-year-old woman named Kerry Regan. Alan was impressed by her drive and skills as a businesswoman. He wanted me to meet her.

Kerry came round from behind the bar. She wore glasses, a lilac beanie and a necklace made of beads. She played the fiddle and part of the selling point of The Pocket Café Bar was regular live music with "open mic nights", acoustic and folk music "jams", reggae nights and Friday gigs with talented local musicians. "I've always had an open mind to music and creative things," she said; Kerry had studied music at Newcastle University. She wanted her bar/café to be a community hub, not just a place to go for a drink and a pizza (there was a pizza menu). "Keswick has a good young community, and I hope it continues. I get the impression there is more of it here than in other parts of the Lake District." She was referring to Bowness and Ambleside by the shores of Windermere to the south, where tourism drove many local businesses rather than accommodating local interests. Keswick had more of an alternative streak, she said, although she admitted her recent experiences of running a business had personally involved "a steep learning curve".

Setting up her "pocket of music and culture" so soon after graduating from Newcastle had been tough.

Kerry's other hobby, aside from playing the fiddle, was "ghyll scrambling". I had never heard of that, and Kerry explained that "basically you slide or scramble or jump down streams". Her boyfriend was a ghyll-scrambling instructor; a *ghyll* was a stream, quite often within a ravine, as I touched on before, deriving from *gil*, an Old Norse word. She had been out in a ravine doing some scrambling earlier in the day, and she showed me various pictures on her phone of people wearing helmets and wetsuits sloshing about in a freezing-looking stream.

New customers arrived. Kerry went to serve them. Alan and I drank pints of smooth and moreish Ghyll golden ale, produced by the Fell Brewery based in Flookburgh, a village in the southern Lakes, close to Morecambe Bay. We discussed this and that for a while longer with a mate of Alan's who had come to join us. *Discussing this and that* seemed to be all the rage in Keswick. Then I said goodbye and thanked the mayor of Keswick, wishing him luck with the drive to Poland. If only all local politicians – and national ones too, for that matter – were so open, friendly and dynamic.

I had liked Keswick for years, from well before this hike around the Lakes.

Now I liked it even better still.

History and a wet walk
Keswick, Derwentwater and Bassenthwaite Lake

"Keswick" is said to come from the Old English *cese wic*, which means "cheese farm", although there is debate about the name and some believe it is Old Norse or Danish and means "Kell's place at the bend of the river". This is despite the highly respected English Place-Name Society accepting "cheese farm".

Whatever the truth, the land close to Keswick had been, and was to be, occupied and populated across many a century by various motley assortments of invaders, as well as locals simply minding their own business.

The earliest signs of occupation go way back. A fine stone circle known as Castlerigg, which I visited the morning after my bar crawl with the mayor and was situated on a steep hill close to Denton House hostel, dated from 3200 BC. Land around Keswick was at that time (the Stone Age) occupied by local tribes, as it would be later on in the Iron Age. Then, later still, the Romans passed by. They completed the western end of Hadrian's Wall in 122 AD at Bowness-on-Solway, by the coast in north-west Cumbria, although there is no evidence of a settlement in Keswick, just parts of a road.

After the Vikings of the early Middle Ages, the Kingdom of Strathclyde, which had its capital in Dumbarton, in Scotland, took charge of Keswick and Cumbria in the tenth century. This was followed in the eleventh century by a powerful Scandinavian ruler named Siward, Earl of Northumbria, who was aligned to the English king Canute the Great, also of Scandinavian descent and who reigned as king of Norway and Denmark simultaneously, leading a coalition known as the North Sea Empire. This must have been quite a period: Oslo, Copenhagen, London, Keswick and Penrith forming a northern superpower never seen before.

In the twelfth century, monks arrived, with abbeys established in the valleys around and about Keswick. And in 1276 Keswick was granted a royal charter for a market by Edward I. This marketplace remains and was the fulcrum of the town's business, with a useful tourist information office in Moot Hall at one end.

During the time of Elizabeth I, copper mining in the fells thrived largely because copper was important for military weaponry. Lead mining prospered too; cannonballs could be made more smoothly in lead moulds, thus travelling further and being more effective in warfare. Local graphite was later used to make pencils, for which

Keswick became famous, hence its popular pencil museum. All the while, farming continued and after the dissolution of the monasteries in the 1540s a new class of wealthy landowners enjoyed healthy profits from wool making.

Tourism, as I touched upon in the "Preface", tentatively began at the start of the eighteenth century, with a few hardy souls – Daniel Defoe excluded – venturing into the fells and liking what they saw. When Thomas Gray, the Poet Laureate, gave Cumbria the thumbs up in 1769, having stayed at the Queen's Head in Keswick, now known as the Inn on the Square, even more visitors came. Gray had had a slightly rough time of it during his visit, one evening after dinner falling "down on my back across a dirty lane with my glass open in one hand" but he had "broke only my knuckles" (that "glass" was not for drinking, it was a device known as a Claude glass, a convex darkened mirror used to gaze on scenery with an enhanced perspective). Yet he spoke highly of Keswick and seemed to have enjoyed his stay overall, his first impressions being positively glowing: a "Vale of Elysium in all its verdure, the sun then playing on the bosom of the lake and lighting up all the mountains with its lustre".

Then, of course, the Lake Poets really put Keswick on the tourist map, with poet Samuel Taylor Coleridge leasing Greta Hall in 1800, wanting to be close to his friend Wordsworth, who had moved to Grasmere, a dozen miles south of Keswick, the previous year. Coleridge was later to be joined by yet another (eventual) Poet Laureate, Robert Southey, who took a room at Greta Hall in 1803 and lived there until he died in 1843. Southey was buried in the churchyard of Crosthwaite parish church, a 5-minute stroll west of Keswick, and Greta Hall is still a private residence, tucked away near the river Greta behind the Lakes & Dales Co-Operative supermarket.

Next up came the trains... and a hero. When the railway arrived from Penrith in 1864, tourism boomed in Keswick like never before. Luckily, however, yet another famous resident of Keswick, Canon

Hardwicke Rawnsley (1851–1920), came along too, having been appointed vicar at Crosthwaite. He was to found local schools, greatly improving educational opportunities, as well as the National Trust, along with Octavia Hill and Sir Robert Hunter. The National Trust, of course, went on to acquire large tracts of land around Keswick and, eventually, across the entire Lakes.

This meant that the scenery that was attracting so many visitors could be protected against overdevelopment, the result being fewer extravagant houses owned by Industrial Revolution bigwigs of the sort Wordsworth so despised, built beside the loveliest stretches of water and guarded by prominent "private" signs. The formation of the Lake District National Park in 1951 was a natural progression from Rawnsley and the co-founders' earlier work. At the time of my visit, a staggering quarter of the park's land belonged to the National Trust. The trio of founders, with Rawnsley in Keswick such a key player, had left a big local mark.

If you looked at the history of Keswick, I was finding, it was as though you were peering into the past of the entire Lake District, all the pieces slotting into place.

* * *

Mulling this over, I went for a walk around Derwentwater. The journey was to be 10 miles, said a trusty tourist-office map. It was pouring down, grey and miserable.

Before setting off, I had described this scenario in a text to a friend, who happened to be on holiday in Seville.

His reply had been: "Good for the soul in its own way."

Ha ha – while he basked in southern Spanish sunshine on a trip with his son, as his accompanying picture showed.

Maybe a little of Gray's "sun playing on the bosom of the lake" would come along later, though that really did not look likely: the sky was moody and unmoving, a leaden grey that seemed set for the day.

Into the rain I strode, quickly coming to a boat landing beyond a pitch-and-putt course at Hope Park and the grey stone bulk of the Theatre by the Lake, opened by Dame Judi Dench and her late husband, Michael Williams, in 1999. The lake matched the sky, with waves whipping up in the breeze and purple-tinted fells brooding in the distance. Ferrymen milled about on one of the piers by a varnished wooden ferry *discussing this and that* in true Keswick style. Various varnished wooden rowing boats lay by the shore. No tourists around. Just a couple of ducks.

Hood on my waterproof jacket up, I began my circuit along the east side of the lake, soon coming to the first point of interest: Friar's Crag, a little headland with a bench and a beautiful view, despite the weather. Across Derwentwater, a series of small islands poked up like pointy little hats through the morning mist. On one of these, not much more than a rock, a Ukrainian flag fluttered on a pole. Yet another sign of local solidarity.

A further island, lying straight ahead beyond the Ukrainian rock, was of particular interest. It was named after St Herbert, and this was where a hermit saint of that name had once lived, catching fish to survive and growing his own vegetables in the seventh century. The story of St Herbert had captured Wordsworth's attention and become the subject of one of the Lakeland Bard's poems. St Herbert had become friends with another saint, St Cuthbert of Holy Island off the north-east coast of Northumberland, whom he greatly respected. Such was his admiration that, upon discovering St Cuthbert faced a terminal illness, St Herbert had prayed to the Lord he would die on the same day as his friend. That, so it went, was precisely what happened next. St Herbert died at the very "same hour" as St Cuthbert, as Wordsworth's vivid poem ends.

St Herbert's Island was also the basis of Owl Island in Beatrix Potter's *The Tale of Squirrel Nutkin*: Squirrel Nutkin, in the company of his squirrel friends, sailed across Derwentwater to the island on twig rafts, using his tail as a sail.

Another local historical connection was that Friar's Crag was gifted to the National Trust on the death of Canon Rawnsley in 1920. Also of interest, close by, tucked amid some trees, was a bust of the nineteenth-century social reformer, philosopher and art critic John Ruskin. He recalled loving the view as a child, which he said was his first memory, and was to move to live not so far away by Coniston Water in later life.

A busy little spot, Friar's Crag.

I kept going in the downpour, traversing a pebble beach and marshland and listening to birds cawing, squawking, quacking, trilling, shrilling, tweeting, cooing, pecking and generally making a racket. There seemed to be an awful lot of birds making an awful lot of noise in the rain beside Derwentwater: goldfinches, thrushes, gulls, woodpeckers, crows, blue tits, robins, long-tailed tits.

The imposing grey stone facade of Lodore Falls Hotel arose ahead in the afternoon mist, while further on, the river Derwent swirled in eddies beneath the Chinese Bridge, so named as it was shaped in a long slow curve in an oriental style. This led through reeds below a fell with a craggy ridge and then to a pine forest with tall mossy trees.

At a gate beyond the forest, an elderly man with his wife let the gate slam shut although I was a couple of steps behind them. He had definitely seen me; no doubt about that. This was not, I considered, good walker etiquette. When I passed them a moment or so later, however, I said: "Good afternoon!" as though nothing had happened, partly, I will admit, simply to gauge their response. The elderly man, without turning my way even a fraction, replied very quietly indeed: "Hi there."

This was said with such a flat, dull tone that he seemed deeply despondent, as though utterly defeated by life.

The woman did not look up either.

What an odd duo.

After passing a pair of adventure centres, a canoe depot and a paddock of alpacas, I soon found I was crossing a field known as the Howrahs, which had once been owned by Edward Stephenson (1691–1768). Stephenson had, earlier in his life, been the governor of Bengal and had lived in a suburb of Kolkata named Howrah, hence the name of the fields, before returning to England and retiring locally.

You never really quite knew what was coming next on a walk round Derwentwater, or so I was finding.

The same was true in Keswick. Across the field I went, returning to the centre of the market town and entering a newsagent's named Youdale's of Keswick. Inside, I bought *The Westmorland Gazette*, the *News & Star* and a copy of a crime thriller entitled *The Ambleside Alibi* by Rebecca Tope. Youdale's turned out to be a jamboree of a newsagent's, old-fashioned with its wall of books, displays of pipes and hip flasks, and side section devoted to fishing. Ultimate Mayfly, Dabbler and Bumble fishing flies were sold alongside nets and rods. There were dozens of different floats, wires, reels and types of bait, too. Everywhere you looked there was either something to read, something to smoke or something to help you catch a slippery creature swimming below the shimmering waters of the Lake District.

Bob Youdale, the owner, was standing behind the counter. He was bald, bespectacled, kindly and another Keswick talker. He was about to retire, he said, and sell his business, but he was worried he would not find a suitable person to take it on. "In 1959 my dad bought this place," he said. "It is not a usual shop. Any fool can sell Kendal Mint Cake, walking books and newspapers but you've got to have a little bit of knowledge of fishing to sell tackle and bait and to know where to send people and tell them what permits are required."

Bob was looking forward to retiring and going to fish festivals in Ireland and perhaps playing golf in Portugal and Spain. He lived above the shop. When he retired, he said, "I won't have to get up at 5 a.m. and deal with the damn newspapers. Newspaper sales are in decline. People under forty don't buy newspapers any more. That's what I've found. It's all this now." He pointed to my phone, which I happened to be holding. "When my father started this business, there were four places selling newspapers in Keswick. Now there are petrol stations, supermarkets and corner shops and they're all at it."

I praised his shop and told him I was about to eat lunch at the Old Keswickian fish-and-chip shop, famous in local culinary circles. Bob said: "My cousins twice removed run that place: we're all related in Keswick." And he recommended the plaice. Another top fellow. The more time I was spending in Keswick, the more the market town was growing on me.

* * *

So I found myself tucking in to battered plaice and chips in the Old Keswickian, while reading in the *News & Star* all about a man who had fled a lorry crash leaving £630,000 of cannabis in the back. Stalking cases had, sadly, "hit a record high" locally, said another story. In other news, local firefighters were raising money for Ukraine, and Cumbria County Council was dropping Gazprom supplies from Russia. Meanwhile, *The Westmorland Gazette* reported on a "march for Mariupol" in Kendal, also to raise cash for the beleaguered country. Another piece focused on parking "chaos" across the national park, and yet another covered the busy local MP Tim Farron and his calls for a doubling of council tax on second homes. Oh yes: the plaice was excellent, not greasy at all, and the chips – "Double fried," said the waitress – were crisp and perfect with plenty of salt and vinegar. Recommended.

So I found myself in Keswick's famous Derwent Pencil Museum, which was surprisingly busy, next to the river Greta. You enter a "cave" as though walking through a mine and then there were many displays in cabinets: all featuring pencils. The highlight, near the end, was "the world's biggest pencil", which jutted at an angle toward the high ceiling, placed on a plinth. Pencils sold in the shop beyond seemed very expensive – they must be very high-quality pencils – though you got a "free" one with your ticket.

So I found myself at Keswick Museum by Fitz Park, where I inspected its famous stone xylophone, a collection of 340-million-year-old fossils, a picture of skaters on a frozen-over Derwentwater in 1895, another (brilliant) painting of Keswick's Market Square dating from 1870 showing local tradesmen going about their business, a stuffed otter and a stuffed badger. The museum was staffed by one person: Clare Poulter, chair of the trustees of Keswick Museum. She was doing a shift due to staff shortages. "Staffing is dreadful, even the café's shut," she said. Just like at so many other places, it seemed.

So I found myself returning to Denton House hostel, getting a good night's sleep in my private bunk room with its rattling window, before waking up and considering my next port of call: Bassenthwaite Lake, the Lake District's only official "lake".

And so I found myself the next morning, in more pouring rain, hiking past Crosthwaite parish church, crossing a short suspension bridge, following the remote winding banks of the river Derwent, skirting a field of molehills and another field of ewes and lambs with matching numbers painted on their sides (the days of the lambs literally numbered), and then passing along a short section of the A591 and a house called Dancing Gate (once a farm, now a holiday home), entering a wood beside a quarry, and reaching the shores of Bassenthwaite Lake and a very old mansion, whose owner was sitting quite contentedly in an armchair by the fireplace... with plenty of stories to tell.

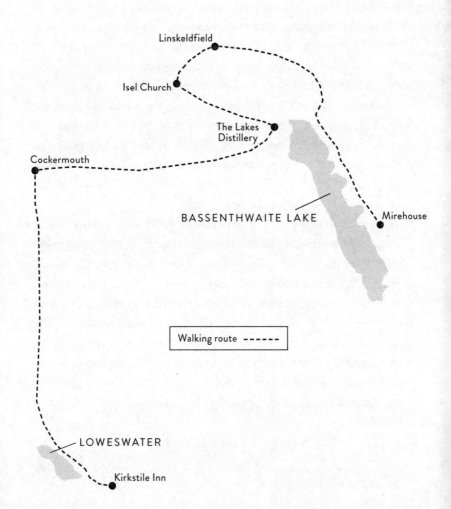

Linskeldfield

Isel Church

The Lakes
Distillery

Cockermouth

BASSENTHWAITE LAKE

Mirehouse

Walking route -------

LOWESWATER

Kirkstile Inn

CHAPTER FOUR

BASSENTHWAITE LAKE TO LOWESWATER, VIA LINSKELDFIELD, SETMURTHY AND COCKERMOUTH

"WHY DON'T YOU SIT ON TENNYSON'S CHAIR?"

Sometimes you just strike it lucky as a traveller. On this journey already, I had had the good fortune to meet Kathleen and Merv at the Station Hotel in Penrith, Beryl and Eddie in Glenridding and Patterdale, the talkative barmaid in Threlkeld, Ian in his quarry and Alan and Kerry in Keswick, among many others. Now it was the turn of a charming gentleman in possession of both a tweed blazer and a splendid country house, which had belonged to his family since 1802.

This heritage was just about the first communication made by John Spedding, who was in the lounge/drawing room/sitting room (or whatever such rooms are called in very grand houses). "Unlike the National Trust, this is a living family house," he said. "It hasn't been sold since 1688." A previous owner had left it to the Spedding family at the beginning of the nineteenth century.

The house, known as Mirehouse, faced Bassenthwaite Lake. It was 15 windows across, coloured salmon-pink and pistachio-grey and reached down a winding lane beside azaleas, Scots pines and a bumbling brook. The house was open twice a week on Wednesdays and Sundays from April to October between 1.30 p.m. and 4.30.p.m.; the gardens more regularly than that. I happened to be passing at the right time on a Wednesday. I bought a ticket from a kiosk at a tea room, entered a doorway flanked by Doric columns and showed the ticket to the smiling woman inside the front door, who turned out to be Clare Spedding, wife of John Spedding. Mrs Spedding seemed quite understandably alarmed by the size of my backpack, which was placed to one side (the house was full of delicate objects). I was swiftly led into the lounge/drawing room/sitting room and introduced to Mr Spedding, who "knows everything" about Mirehouse, Mrs Spedding said.

Mr Spedding wore a grey tweed blazer, a checked shirt and a navy-blue cardigan. His grey hair was slightly ruffled, and he clutched a cane. He had the manner of a kindly headmaster or perhaps an Oxford don. His second piece of communication came in the form of an invitation. "Why don't you sit on Tennyson's chair?"

How could you turn down an invite like that?

So I sat on the cane chair Mr Spedding was indicating and he showed me a framed sketch of Alfred, Lord Tennyson, on the very same cane chair. The sketch dated from 1835 and was drawn from behind; all you could really see was a shock of messy hair and the pointy collar of a jacket, with Tennyson's face buried in a book. The Poet Laureate had visited with his wife, Emily, on their honeymoon and had also written "Morte d'Arthur" at the house. Mr Spedding drew my attention to another sketch, this one on the wall close by. It depicted Tennyson yet again, with equally wild hair but on a different chair and from the side, capturing an extremely sleepy expression on his face as he rested before the fireplace, legs crossed and wearing a trench coat. This chair, I was informed, was not Tennyson's chair, but Wordsworth's chair, a sturdier affair originating from a place in Keswick where William, Tennyson's predecessor as Poet Laureate, and Dorothy Wordsworth had lived in 1794. Alfred, Lord Tennyson, had been sketched from more than one chair at Mirehouse.

I was, I must admit, becoming confused exactly as to which Poet Laureate sat where and when during the eminent literary history of Mirehouse.

Many others had come, including Robert Southey of Keswick, Wordsworth's predecessor as Poet Laureate. There was also a link between James Spedding and Francis Bacon (Spedding (1808–1881) was Bacon's editor and biographer), and a friendship between Thomas Spedding (1795–1881) and the Scottish philosopher and writer Thomas Carlyle, who visited many times. William Thackeray had dropped by too.

Poet Laureates and scribes in general seemed to have been a dime a dozen at Mirehouse during the nineteenth century.

Mr Spedding said that he inherited Mirehouse in 1961 and that three generations of Speddings lived there now across a series of buildings including the main house. He seemed pleased to have someone to join him to discuss *this and that*, just like the others in nearby Keswick. So we did just that. I asked him how things had changed around Bassenthwaite Lake and Keswick over the years.

"It's changed vastly in Keswick," he replied. "From small family shops to chains. I used to know nearly all the shopkeepers." He did not any more. "Of course, agriculture has changed enormously too. On this estate there used to be… I forget how many farms." Many of the farms were let out by Mirehouse Estate, which covered about 1,000 acres and several fells including Ullock Pike and Dodd. I was meeting someone who owned mountains. "But so many farms have been combined over the years and houses sold off and so on. At times I wish I'd just left everything as it was. But when I inherited this estate, it was the days of the Rent Act and a lot of the houses on the estate were costing considerably more to maintain than they produced from rents, so it was a net loss, the whole business. That was in the 1960s, Harold Wilson's day [as prime minister]. Then it all changed. Property now is very valuable and can produce quite useful returns. We sold a lot off." Was he regretful? "Well, you can't relive things. I'm very happy with what we do have."

The other big local alteration over the years was the building of the A66 on the west side of Bassenthwaite Lake: "This valley here has been greatly altered by the A66. There was a public inquiry about it in the early 1970s. I think it [the road] must have been finished in 1975 or thereabouts. I and others opposed it on the grounds that there were other ways of resolving the transport problems. The reason for the road being built was that Lord Stokes had persuaded Harold Wilson that his bus factory in Workington [Leyland Motors] would only prosper if there were good communications with the motorway from Workington and he needed a new road. So the A66 was built. That was the flagship reason for building it." He paused for dramatic effect. "But Lord Stokes' bus factory was closed within about seven or eight years afterward. Of course, we'd much rather have a railway. The railway had been closed by then." He was referring to the Cockermouth, Keswick and Penrith Railway, which had not been particularly well run in its final years, he said. "The trains to Penrith would arrive just after the London train had left and the London

train would arrive just after the Keswick train had left." He laughed at
the memory of this. "When they ran, people thought they were nasty
smelly things, trains. They produced such smut and soot, all over the
place. But Keswick station was always a nice place to go."

Mr Spedding, holding his cane in both hands as he sat, returned to
the subject of Tennyson, who had written a poem entitled "To J. S."
for James Spedding, whose brother Edward had died the year before.
It begins:

> The wind, that beats the mountain, blows
> More softly round the open wold,
> And gently comes the world to those
> That are cast in gentle mould.
>
> And me this knowledge bolder made,
> Or else I had not dare to flow
> In these words toward you, and invade
> With even a verse your holy woe.

We talked about Southey for a while – "a great scholar but unfortunately
not a very great poet" said Mr Spedding – and about opening up
Mirehouse to the public. Did he like the public coming in? "Oh yes!"
he said. "And we miss them when they go. It all feels rather pointless
if people aren't coming and enjoying it. You wonder what it's all worth
doing it for. I'm keen for the next generation to know what it's all
about. I've got all sorts of projects that I'm working on now. We have
largely, my wife and I, catalogued the library. We've catalogued the oil
paintings. We want to catalogue the prints: get that done."

Aside from this, Mr Spedding said he "was quite worried about the
bird populations round here. They seem to be changing. The lake here
belongs to the national park. There's a vast population of geese here.
My observation is there are many less of the other birds, the smaller
ducks, snipe and those sorts of things because the geese come in their

hundreds. They come down from the Solway. I don't know the answer to that really. The ospreys come in the second week of April."

That was in a few days, even though Pete back at Denton House hostel thought he had spotted one. Ospreys had begun nesting beside Bassenthwaite Lake for the first time in 2001, using a nest on a platform built specifically to entice the creatures, which had already begun to flourish in Scotland. The scheme, overseen by the Forestry Commission and the Lake District National Park Authority, had worked, and for the first time in 150 years the birds were back; a viewing platform had been set up in Dodd Wood and live CCTV coverage organized for enthusiasts.

Mr Spedding, a lawyer by profession and who had worked before his retirement as a barrister in Newcastle, turned to the subject of the war in Ukraine. "You always feel glad about it when you wake up in the morning in your bed and comfort and you know that there's going to be some nice breakfast for you. When you think about all those people in the basement in Mariupol, it really makes you feel quite guilty," he said. "The more that I think about it, well I'm devastated really. The lives lost and the cultural history, particularly of places like Odessa, which is so much under threat at the moment. I mean I've been thinking about the Russians all my life. I didn't really realize they were up to this. But they were. I didn't really believe they would behave like that. To be honest, they are out of control."

We both fell silent for a while. Events on the south-eastern edge of Europe seemed to put everything in perspective on this walk around the Lake District: distressing, terrifying events taking place not so far away really, when you looked at a world map.

After a period of us both simply staring straight ahead, Mr Spedding said: "When you go to the study, do sit on Wordsworth's chair; then you will have done the rounds."

We parted and I took a tour of the lovely old house, sat as instructed on Wordsworth's chair, listened to the pianist playing in another lounge/drawing room/sitting room, where a fire had been lit, and admired both an exquisite J. M. W. Turner illustration for a book of Lord Byron's poems and a painting of Hampstead Heath by John Constable. "He was a friend of the family too," said Mrs Spedding, who noticed me gazing at it. "But he never visited here." The Speddings had in the past, she said, sold another, larger Constable for £2,000 that "is possibly worth two million now".

After taking a photo of the Speddings in the reception and retrieving my backpack, I strolled around the "Poetry Walk" in the garden, with joyful lines from Wordsworth, Tennyson and Coleridge posted on little signs here and there. Then I made my way down a path behind Mirehouse to a peaceful fourteenth-century stone church, St Bega's Church, and continued on along the eastern side of the Lake District's famous only lake, which was quite deserted, with fells soaring up over the placid water and a feeling of having left behind the "bustle" of Derwentwater, even though it had been quite quiet back there, when not out on the town with the local mayor, that is.

Kebabs and whisky
Mirehouse to Setmurthy, via Linskeldfield

It was around this time that I realized I had better step on it. Using Airbnb, I had booked a "pod" on the grounds of Linskeldfield Farm and this was at least an 8-mile walk. Rain had begun once again and the lake was reflecting the clouds in the sky, turning into a great pool of milk settled between the mountains. The green dotted line on the map led through farming fields, along a path by a beck, across marshland, then a cluster of remote barns. The light changed toward sunset, with delicate pinks rising across the water by Scarness Bay, where some swans paddled my way, perhaps in the hope of being fed. The path wound onward past some houses with "STRICTLY PRIVATE, NO PUBLIC ACCESS" signs – message received! – and skirted round Armathwaite Hall Hotel, a four-star country house, leisure club and conference centre with a spa and a beauty salon. Around there, I called Linskeldfield Farm to say that I was running late and talked to Marion. I explained when I was likely to arrive and asked about food.

"Yes, there is food," she said. "In Cockermouth."

But wasn't that 5 miles on from Linskeldfield Farm?

"Yes," she replied.

I explained I was walking.

"Walking?" she asked as though she had not heard me right.

I confirmed my mode of movement.

"Do you have any food?" she asked.

"No," I replied, and I was starving, having only consumed a bowl of soup from the Mirehouse tea room since breakfast.

She paused. "You could order a delivery – there's pizza or kebabs," she said.

Marion texted me the number of the Alternative Takeaway kebab shop in Cockermouth, which I called and arranged for a chicken kebab and chips to be delivered to my pod at 8 p.m.; life had moved on somewhat since Wordsworth's days of tramping around the fells. Quite what the author of *Guide to the Lakes* with his elevated approach to the appreciation of nature would make of kebab deliveries to pods was anyone's guess (though I was fairly sure he would not exactly be impressed).

Culinary arrangements in place, I crossed a boggy section of field in the pouring rain. This downpour, however, soon ceased and the sky turned an ethereal apricot. It was quite unexpectedly gorgeous. Almost at Linskeldfield Farm, I passed Long Close Farm, where a large number of doleful dairy cows stared out at me from a barn and appeared let-down that I was not about to feed or perhaps milk them (judging by the racket they made). I continued down a lane with grain silos. Chickens clucked away somewhere close by. A squeal of what sounded like a parrot cried out across the yard at the back of Linskeldfield's farmhouse, where I located my pod and sat on its little terrace drinking one of two bottles of lager that Marion had kindly set out on a table as a welcome gift (thank you, Marion).

This wooden pod, shaped a little like a bishop's mitre, was beside a tarn with a deck for spotting birds on the water. It was tiny, with a bed squashed at one end and less space than the size of this bed at the other. The rain resumed lashing down, and I sat gazing toward the farmhouse as well as an unoccupied neighbouring safari-style tent. A series of cages containing exotic birds and owls lay beyond this safari tent, the source of the parrot's cries.

A small grey car soon pulled up and my kebab was delivered. Sitting on the terrace, I consumed the chicken kebab at a rate of knots, returned inside to listen to rain pelting on the roof and read about Bassenthwaite Lake. My *Rough Guide* was of the opinion that it "doesn't receive much attention, partly because of the difficulty in actually reaching its shores". This was due to so much of the lakeside being private land. In his entertaining book *Lakeland*, Hunter Davies, I discovered, considered the A66 on the lake's western shore to be "hideous". He also mentioned that Wordsworth had confusingly called Bassenthwaite Lake "Broadwater". Davies regarded Mirehouse to be "one of the most important literary homes in the whole Lakeland". He also pointed out that Bassenthwaite Lake was shallow, only 21 metres deep at its deepest point. Its waters, according to Christopher Winn in *I Never Knew That About the Lake District*, were also home to rare vendace fish, an endangered species. *I never did know that.* Winn went on to assert correctly that Bassenthwaite Lake was the most northerly lake in the Lake District, the fourth largest (4 miles long and ¾ mile wide). He continued by referring to a quote by Alfred, Lord Tennyson, regarding the lake, from "Morte d'Arthur":

> I heard the ripple washing in the reeds
> And the wild water lapping on the crag.

Useful having this little portable library at my disposal (if really quite heavy).

* * *

The purpose of this book, having thought about it a little more, is fourfold: 1) To describe a big circular hike around the Lake District that could easily be achieved by the casual rambler who is not set on bagging Wainwright peaks and who may have a taste for out-of-the-way spots, 2) To capture the gentle solace that is offered by the fells and the lakes, especially at a time when so many troubles rumbled on in Europe, 3) To paint a picture of the hostelry options along the way, and 4) Perhaps most importantly, to talk to people. A lot of people.

Regarding this final ambition, it was my intention, as you may already have detected, to record the language of the Lakes, rather than simply describe the dramatic landscape. To this end, I aimed to be social. I would not be a stranger sitting in a corner. I would put myself about. It was not my voice that mattered of course, an outsider from "down south". It was the many voices, and stories, of those I met on the trail.

I was more than ready, as Eddie back in Patterdale might have put it, as though addressing his whippet, to be a right nosy "boug-a".

This general policy having become well established by the time of my night in the Linskeldfield pod, I walked slightly backward, given that the day's destination was Cockermouth, to the north-western edge of Bassenthwaite Lake... to meet some people.

These people ran The Lakes Distillery and I did not have an appointment.

First, though, I called Marion, whom I was never to lay eyes on, to ask if she was around to talk about her tourism business – as well as the pod and the safari tent, she ran a campsite – but she told me: "I'm just collecting eggs. It's a working farm, you see." I thanked her for a good night's stay in her pod and for the beers. Then I made my way along a path beside a waterlogged field, not long afterward stopping at Isel church, close to the river Derwent. Like St Bega's Church, this was extremely peaceful and it was even older, dating from around 1130 and smelling of polish and incense.

A little church organ was on one side. Oil lanterns hung from the ceiling. A perfect little church, really.

After this, I continued on my way down a lane past a field of pheasants and rabbits to the distillery.

I had not come across another soul all morning.

At The Lakes Distillery, I turned into a courtyard of what looked like a farm and entered a snazzy shop with rows of glinting bottles. Standing by a counter was Ben Stuart, The Lakes Distillery's "experience manager", who was soon telling me about its whisky-, gin- and vodka-making operations. Already, I knew from reading *The Westmorland Gazette* back in Keswick, the distillery had recently received a massive accolade. Ben picked up the story.

"*Whisky Magazine* has a world whisky award each year," Ben said. "First, we won the English single malt category." Which had come as a "pleasant surprise", he said. He paused for dramatic effect, milking the moment. He was wearing a navy-blue Lakes Distillery jacket, a pale-blue shirt and black trousers. He had short grey hair and a short grey beard and looked like a man who understood what made a good tipple. He was from Christchurch in New Zealand, middle-aged and married to Rebecca Gibb, the award-winning wine journalist and author of a book entitled *The Wines of New Zealand*. "Then we won the best single malt overall," he said.

He paused once again.

From a pod in a field by a tarn, across a series of deserted fields and empty lanes, I had arrived at the source of the world's best whisky. By "overall", Ben had been referring to *the world*.

"All the judging was based on blind tastings," he said. The awards had taken place the previous week. "Even since then we've had more people come in than usual." The little distillery, officially opened by Princess Anne in 2015, had hit the global jackpot, whisky-wise.

"This is an old cattle farm," Ben said. "We get about twenty thousand visitors a year. Most people buy a bottle at the end. Because whisky takes a long time to produce, and a lot of capital upfront [for the stills in which it is made], it takes time to generate income. Whiskies must age at least three years in Scotland to be called a Scotch. We have adopted the same method, even though we do not have to."

The distillery employed 45 people at the site by Bassenthwaite Lake and at a "back office" in Newcastle. Ben said that the Scotch Whisky Association had other rules that "must be obeyed to be a Scotch, including that the product must be from one distillery and must be forty per cent proof... we follow the guidelines to the letter."

Ben switched tack and talked for a while about a controversy in the distilling world: the Stolichnaya vodka brand, produced in Latvia, had been stressing its Latvian roots of late rather than its original Russian background because of the conflict in Ukraine. The irony was that, previously, the Russian Standard vodka distillers had been upset that Stolichnaya might seem to be Russian, even though it was Latvian. Vodka wars were seemingly going on while real battles raged.

I asked Ben what it was like living in the Lakes after being brought up in New Zealand.

"The north and south Lake District are quite different," he said. "The north is more for ramblers, people get there on the A66 from the northeast, Yorkshire and Scotland. The southern Lakes attracts more people from Liverpool, Manchester and London. Even though it is busy here, it's much quieter than in the southern Lakes. There are eighteen million visitors to the Lakes each year. Coming from New Zealand, where there's five million people in the whole country, it's incredible. English people are very quick to say the English landscape is rubbish, but this is a beautiful landscape. I really enjoy the serenity of the Lakes. Just step outside: I think the mountains offer that perspective."

I joined a tour of the distillery.

This was led by a wiry man named Simon, who took the group of a dozen of us into a room to watch a video showing the local area from above and referring to "brooding corners and deafening silence". He then told us that the distillery "worked 24/7", that the chief taster's nose had been insured (such was its value to production), the casks were handmade in Andalusia, and that the copper pot stills in which the whisky was made were named Rachel and Susan. Regarding the recent award, he said: "We are ecstatic! Over the moon! It was a real honour for us. We're very encouraged by it. We have sold out already! Within a matter of hours, companies that sell our bottles were sold out too. It's the collectors, you see," he said.

Our group was shown the stills and then taken to a tasting room at the back of the shop.

We began to drink whisky.

"Do you get the caramel and the coffee beans and the honey?" Simon asked as we tried the award-winner. We all nodded sagely and took more sips. "Anyone tasting honey? Anyone getting liquorice? Anyone?" We all nodded sagely and took more sips. "Yes? Good! Dry fruits anyone? Explore your palate! Be dynamic! My absolute favourite is a glass of whisky with some chocolate on the side. Or Galaxy cookie crumble ice cream. I personally have that with blended whisky: two drops on top. It's heaven on earth!"

Simon had become quite animated.

We had all become quite animated, discussing the flavours and taking more sips.

Then we began to drink gin.

"The greater the volume the greater the depth and strength," said Simon, off on another roll, adding, slightly mystifyingly, "Certainly, from a tasting narrative, there's a benefit there."

An elderly woman beside me commented: "Lovely and smooth, this gin."

Simon beamed at her. "Do you get the floral notes?" he asked.

She did. Simon beamed once more. Emboldened, the elderly woman asked Simon a question: "What do you think about pink gin and strawberry gin?"

This set Simon off on another roll: "Of the liqueur blends, I personally like the elderflower. Then there's salted caramel vodka, just pour it over ice cream. It's so easy, you forget that it's alcohol."

Then we began to try the vodka.

"It's straight from the fridge," said Simon, "Quite strong on the palate. It's good with a sorbet. It's slightly peppery, don't you think?" We all nodded sagely and took more sips once again. "Yes? Good! After the whisky and the gin, you might be a bit overwhelmed on the palate." Then he added, slightly mystifyingly again, "This vodka, I could try this vodka, sitting down in the afternoon, not feeling pushed in any sense." He paused, before asking: "Any impressions on the vodka?"

A few people agreed that it was "peppery" once again, and Simon looked very pleased; this was definitely the right thing to say.

The tasting was concluded, and we all shuffled into the shop.

The elderly woman fell into stride beside me as we left, enquiring about my interest in the distillery. I was wearing my filthy waterproof trousers, still suffering from my ill-advised activities on Blencathra, and my boots were muddy from the fields. I stood out a bit from the other well-healed whisky-distillery visitors.

"We thought you might be a workman," she said cheerfully (everyone was cheerful by this stage). She did not elaborate on what type of workman.

We talked about Lakes Distillery whisky for a while. She and her husband were from Dorset and staying a week for a holiday in Cockermouth. They were going to buy a few bottles of whisky and gin as they liked it so much.

I would have done the same, but not with the backpack, which seemed to be taking on a life of its own. By this I mean that it seemed to be growing at an alarming rate. This was, of course, all my own fault. Newly purchased booklets on Mirehouse and the history of Keswick alongside Lake District-based crime thrillers, tourist-office maps and various pamphlets for attractions such as the Derwent Pencil Museum had added considerably to my portable Lake District library. This was not to mention slabs of Kendal Mint Cake, several new hiking socks (bought partially to put off washing), copies of *The*

Westmorland Gazette and the *News & Star* that I was not done with and a heavy magazine named *Cumbria Life* that was full of all sorts of juicy insider stories on the region. In short, there was no room for heavy bottles of award-winning booze in my backpack.

The tour group dispersed.

In a downpour, I made my way from the eastern side of the parish of Setmurthy, where The Lakes Distillery was located, to Cockermouth.

Fairest of all rivers?
Setmurthy to Cockermouth

Dotted green lines were scant on the map for the 4-mile traverse across this section of the north-western Lakes. But little orangey-yellow lanes, classed as "generally more than four metres wide" by the Ordnance Survey people, seemed to link the way ahead.

Initially, perhaps still under the influence of all the award-winning whisky, gin and vodka, I took the wrong orangey-yellow lane, soon reaching the dreadful, hideous A66. No way was I walking along that. Leaving the roar of engines behind, I backtracked and tramped along a parallel, higher-altitude orangey-yellow roadway with hardly any vehicles.

Much better, though it was not exactly the greatest day. Rain beat down. Clouds hung low. The wind blew in billowy gusts. Disused quarries gave way to woods leading up a long, slowly rising hill clad with damp gorse and occasional fields of bedraggled ewes and lambs. I put my head down and marched grimly on. After a while, the lane began to descend and eventually I came to a sign for Cockermouth stating: "Birthplace of William and Dorothy Wordsworth". Good to see both getting namechecks from the local council. Judging by "I Wandered Lonely as a Cloud", Dorothy had clearly had a big influence on her illustrious brother's works, as well as having left behind her vivid journals and her own poems. During her lifetime, though, she had not wished to be published, so William had got all the plaudits.

The rain eased a bit. Suburban houses with bluebells and purple pansies in their front gardens lined the streets on the hill down into town. The tall, elegant spire of All Saints Church arose, where William and Dorothy's father, John, was buried. So did Cockermouth School, an incongruous modern blue-and-white building. Then the road curved beyond a gate and driveway to Cockermouth Castle, a medieval castle with parts dating from the eleventh century. Some of it was in a state of ruin though many of the later buildings were maintained. This, although you might expect it to be an "attraction", was privately owned with a notice at the front making this abundantly clear: "PRIVATE, CLOSED TO THE PUBLIC".

From there, I crossed a bridge over the river Cocker. Jennings Brewery, famous in these parts for its Cumberland ale, was to the right, while ahead was Main Street, a wide avenue that was home to a great many pubs and independent shops including butchers, bakers, cafés, bookshops, the Alternative Takeaway (my kebab saviour at the pod in Linskeldfield) and several quirky gift shops. Good to see so few major chains. Straight away, it felt less touristy in Cockermouth than in Keswick.

One of the pubs was called The Wordsworth, but of course. On its facade, the Cockermouth Rotary Club had posted banners with verses from "I Wandered Lonely as a Cloud". The same banners were attached to the plinth of a statue of a grand yet severe-looking man grasping a scroll, just across from The Wordsworth on an "island" in the middle of Main Street, which was particularly wide. The statue was not of Wordsworth, however. It was the Earl of Mayo, who was a member of parliament for Cockermouth before becoming viceroy of India in 1869 and being assassinated in the Andaman Islands in 1872. He stood proudly, almost defiantly, on the island with flower beds of daffodils planted close by. Larger plastic daffodils were also "planted" next to the real ones, seemingly also the work of the Cockermouth

Rotary Club and designed to celebrate both the renowned local author and the arrival of spring. Which was very nice of them.

Having discovered that my guest house did not open its doors till 4 p.m., I went with my backpack to the Black Bull pub and asked a burly man wearing camouflage trousers, who was standing in the doorway smoking a rollie, whether the pub was serving food. "None of the pubs round here do food at lunchtime to be honest," he replied. He gave me a blank look as though suggesting I would like to challenge this statement. I did not. Then, dropping his hard-man act, he said: "There's a lovely place in The Old Kings Arms Lane, just turn right past Bootsies [sic]." He was referring to a side alley with yet more independent shops in the former stables of a coaching inn just beyond the pharmacy Boots, one of the few big chain shops. Which was very nice of him, too.

I followed his instructions and came to the Lanes Bistro & Café, where I ate a generous portion of chilli con carne at a table with a plastic tablecloth depicting owls and frogs, while listening to pop music. The polite waitress served me despite the café being about to close for the day. Which was very nice of her as well.

I was getting good vibes from Cockermouth.

But then I had a setback. Wordsworth House was closed on Thursdays and Fridays. This was a Thursday and I aimed to make my way south to Buttermere on the Friday. I was going to miss Cockermouth's biggest tourist draw; no way round it really, I had already booked and paid for a room in Buttermere. I thought about this for a while, staring through a locked gate at the grand, slightly damp-looking terracotta-coloured Georgian building. Then I reasoned: **** *it, there's nothing that can be done.* Later, I would be visiting Dove Cottage, in the village of Grasmere, and Rydal Mount, in the hamlet of Rydal – Wordsworth dwellings further south in the Lakes. I even had an appointment with the director of the Wordsworth Trust in Grasmere. There would be plenty of Wordsworth down there. Anyway, no need to try and cram in everything on this hike around the Lakes. My intention had always been to go with the flow and see what popped up… it was the random as much as the obvious that I wanted to capture.

Wordsworth House, which everyone says is so marvellous with its period furniture and portraits of Wordsworth and painting of Cockermouth Castle by J. M. W. Turner, would simply not be popping up. I would have to satisfy myself with knowing, thanks to my portable Lakes library, that William (in 1770) and Dorothy (in 1771) were born in the grand, slightly damp-looking Georgian terracotta-coloured house along with their three siblings. By the time of the death, in 1783, of their father, John, who worked as a steward for a wealthy local landowner named Sir James Lowther, the children were already mainly living with relations or sent to school (William to a school in Hawkshead in the southern Lakes). Their mother, Ann, had already died (in 1778) and their father travelled a lot for his job, hence the children being dispersed all about; Dorothy was in Halifax in Yorkshire living with her mother's cousin. John had been provided with the house by his employer for the family to live in, so on his death it was no longer part of the family's life.

The river Derwent flowed serenely behind Wordsworth House; Cockermouth is at the confluence of the river Derwent and the river Cocker. Wordsworth experts including David McCracken, author of the excellent *Wordsworth and the Lake District: A Guide to the Poems and their Places*, believe the Derwent left an indelible mark on the poet's life. He had, after all, lived in Cockermouth until the age of nine before being sent to Hawkshead. Lines from his famous 1805 poem "The Prelude" refer directly to it:

> – Was it for this
> That one, the fairest of all Rivers, lov'd
> To blend his murmurs with my Nurse's song,
> And from his alder shades and rocky falls,
> And from his fords and shallows, sent a voice
> That flow'd along my dreams? For this, didst Thou,

> O Derwent! travelling over the green Plains
> Near my 'sweet Birthplace', didst thou, beauteous Stream,
> Make ceaseless music through the night and day
> Which with its steady cadence, tempering
> Our human waywardness, compos'd my thoughts
> To more than infant softness, giving me
> Among the fretful dwellings of mankind,
> A knowledge, a dim earnest, of the calm
> That Nature breathes among the hills and groves.

It was indeed a splendid spot.

With these thoughts percolating, I left the "beauteous stream", dropped off my backpack at the guest house and went to the pub.

As mentioned earlier, and just as in Keswick and Penrith, there were many from which to choose: The Bush, the Black Bull, the Swan Inn, The Huntsman, The Wordsworth, The Bitter End, among others. Not bad for a town of 8,800, though not quite up to Penrithian levels of boozers. That said, the northern Lakes in general seemed well served by a particularly good, wide-ranging selection of pubs. My feet led to the Fletcher Christian inn, named after the mutineer on board HMS *Bounty* back in 1789; a strange hero, perhaps, but he was brought up locally and even went to school in Cockermouth with William Wordsworth (although William was much younger when they were both there).

Inside, it was busy, you might say raucous, the spirit of Christian seemingly alive and well with a cacophony of chatter, laughter and music. A football game played on several TVs. A barmaid was serving pints faster than I have ever seen a barmaid serve pints; many in rounds of five or six drinks for groups of friends who stood around taking up just about every space. A man in front of me ordered two pints and two accompanying "fireball bongs" (involving some form of potent liquor) and I got my request in for a pint of ale, discovering the price was *less than half* of the cost in my local in London.

Talk about the north–south divide: fantastic. I took this amazingly good-value pint to the quietest corner near the front – the music was reaching disco-level loud at the back – and proceeded to pass the time of day with a middle-aged man wearing a crumpled Barbour jacket. He somehow managed both to talk and take in the West Ham game playing on the TV, simultaneously, while also reaching faithfully for his pint whenever he felt like a sip, without even looking for it: he just knew where it was, his hand slipping round the glass perfectly each time. Quite a skill.

This man said: "Cockermouth is more of a working, business town than other towns in the Lakes. You can live a more normal life here." By "other towns" he was referring to other touristy parts of the Lake District. "But there's still beautiful scenery. It's a good base for visitors to the less-busy western Lakes." These included Loweswater, Crummock Water, Buttermere and Ennerdale, all to the south. I was due to see the first three of these the following day.

The man in the crumpled Barbour jacket reached for his pint, grabbed it (without looking), took a sip, put the pint back and told me about the awful floods in Cockermouth in November 2009. "It was pretty dramatic," he said. "Water was charging down Main Street. It was pouring into cellars and lower floors." The Fletcher Christian inn, like so many other businesses and homes, was "wrecked". Water in town had reached 8 feet deep in places, he said. The statue of the stern-looking Earl of Mayo had poked up above the swirling muddy water, stranded amid the torrent; it had not been Wordsworth's "fairest of all rivers" that day. Luckily, however, although Wordsworth House was affected by the flooding too, the main first floor had been built on a raised level, probably to avoid long-ago floods, so artefacts were saved. "Whoever designed it knew what they were doing," said my neighbour.

He grabbed his pint once again, eyes still glued to the game and told me flood defences in the town had been "much improved" after the 2009 flood, but for a long time afterward "there was an emotional cost as well as the financial cost, it was a living nightmare". Almost a thousand locals had been affected. "Then it all happened again in 2015."

Despite almost £5 million having been spent on walls, embankments and floodgates, the town was devasted once more by rising waters, this time the result of Storm Desmond. Nearly 500 properties had been damaged as waters overwhelmed the defences introduced after 2009. Since then, yet more millions had been spent on shoring up flood barriers, but local concerns remained, especially after high waters in 2021 that almost brought a repeat.

Hand to pint. Sip. Pint back to table. Eyes on screen.

"It's climate change," the man in the crumpled Barbour said. "That's all it is."

He paused as West Ham almost scored; they were playing Lyon in a European game. "Waters were really high just the other week too," he added. "We had to get the floodgates out and the Environment Agency said to take cars to park on higher ground. By the river, glass screens were moved up from within the river walls. So that was scary."

Hand to pint. Sip. Pint back to table. Eyes on screen.

"All the locals by the bridge were out by the brewery," he said. "They knew that if it was OK by 4.05 p.m., it would be fine." If the banks did not break, that is. "It was all OK. There was a collective sigh of relief, but there was some damage to the flood defences."

All of this was related quite matter-of-factly.

Then West Ham had a player sent off.

"Never, never!" said the man in the crumpled Barbour, suddenly extremely animated. "Simulation! Referee!"

He went to the bar to get another pint from Britain's quickest barmaid. I returned to my guest house; a long walk lay ahead tomorrow.

Mean sheep, dropping south
Cockermouth to Loweswater

During this story of a long hike in the Lakes, the hope is to provide a series of snapshots; the telling of the journey was never intended to be comprehensive. Included among these snapshots, or glimpses, are to be descriptions of the various forms of accommodation: it is to be, after all, a traveller's eye view, a *travel* story, with the nitty-gritty of getting about and staying in places all part of the tale.

With that in mind, the Croft Guest House in Cockermouth deserves a special mention. It was in a row of old terraced houses on Challoner Street in the town centre, comprising seven reasonably priced smart rooms, and was run by Dave and Glenis Gibson, a quiet couple.

They had faced a tricky time during the pandemic but had been fortunate to attract a guest who was on official Covid-related business and allowed to stay, a pharmacist. "We were the 'three Os' back then," Dave said. "The only ones open." Bigger hotels were forced to shut due to the struggle to cover the costs of staff with so few customers.

They had bought the guest house five years ago after moving from Leicester. Dave was a former milkman and painter-and-decorator in his mid-sixties. He served the (first-rate) breakfast, stood nearby and talked. "We'd never heard of Cockermouth or heard of the floods. We were ignorant. We just googled 'B & B for sale'. It was going to be either here or Blackpool," he said. "It's a cut-throat business there though [in Blackpool], and it comes down to what's the cheapest. It must be very hard work."

They had taken to Cockermouth: "We both love it. I can guarantee that if I go to the shop, people will say hello and good morning. There's a strong community. We feel a part of that. You've got everything you could possibly need within five minutes' walk. We do get our eggs from Scales Farm though – it's the only time we really need the car. If you want to do poached eggs, they must be fresh."

Dave showed me a few of the rooms. In one, a bed leg had been attached to the ceiling as though it had crashed through from the floor above. "Where a couple got too energetic," he said, chuckling at his own joke. He showed another room where a fake mousehole had been created in a corner, with a little figure of a mouse poking out. "People like little eccentric things, that's what makes a B & B. You can go to a Travelodge or a Premier Inn if you want anonymity. They're excellent for that," he said.

Because he and Glenis did all the work, they had not suffered from staff shortages, but he had strong opinions on the problem that was sweeping the Lakes: "We are only allowing skilled workers into the country, but we need porters, waiters, road sweepers. These jobs are not appreciated enough. It doesn't matter what you do as long as you do it well. If you sweep a road well, that's great. There's an awful lot of snobbery. When waiting yourself, as I do here, you realize: *oh blimey: be nicer to the waiters.* You only need so many brain surgeons," he said. "There's no getting away from it, Eastern Europeans work hard and look like they are pleased to greet you, at least most of them." But many had returned home, and no one was coming to replace them now; the knock-on effects of Brexit, yet again.

* * *

The sun shone brightly the next morning. The day was as "crisp as a good biscuit", as J. B. Priestley once said during his trip for his captivating 1934 travel book *English Journey*, and pleasingly cool, too. The sky formed a canopy of perfect royal blue. I took a hilly road out of town and shortly afterward a car paused in the street and an elderly woman inside rolled down the window and yelled a question: "Did you have a nice evening?" It was the woman from the distillery. I yelled back that I had. She drove on and I soon arrived at a large roundabout with a Premier Inn on a corner. This was at the junction of the A66. Behind the Premier Inn, I picked up a dotted green line and walked in the direction of Waterloo Farm. Earlier I had posted home precisely 1.2 kilogrammes of booklets, pamphlets and other assorted papers to lessen the load and the backpack felt much better. A faded footpath sign pointed the way to a field, which I crossed, coming to another field with another sign, this one warning there was a "bull in field". Not sure quite what to do as it was a long way back, I walked swiftly across this field, which did not have a bull in it. Arriving at a stile into yet another field, I relaxed and strolled on, following the dotted green line as shown on the map. No bulls about there either, just ewes with newly born lambs, which were gambolling about cutely.

These, however, were not your average Lakeland ewes with newly born lambs gambolling about cutely. These particular Lakeland ewes decided to follow en masse whichever hiker arrived in their field (in this instance, me), the front runner being an especially mean-looking Lakeland ewe with a fine set of lungs. My presence in their field was clearly far from appreciated. I picked up my pace. The mean-looking ewe picked up her speed. I had about 40 metres on her. I began to jog up the hill, the ewe quickening further still, catching up. I arrived at a stile and smartly leaped over it. The mean-looking ewe regarded me from the other side of the stile with fierce, intense eyes. I waved at the mean-looking ewe, blew it a kiss and walked on down a lane, following a sign for a place called Brandlingill.

It had been quite a start to the day.

Snow-dusted mountains towered on the horizon to the north-east, one of which I took to be Skiddaw, a classic Wainwright climb (931 metres) close to Lake Bassenthwaite. I crossed a beck near Sneckyeat Farm, continuing onward beyond How Farm, Blea Bank Farm and High Mosser Farm. I was following a series of remote paths and lanes, passing a small set of yurt-style holiday homes, a farmer in a field who saw me and steadfastly ignored me, another farmer who said "Morning," and yet another who was on a quad bike in a field and being chased by sheep, rather as I had been.

Perhaps the mean-looking ewes had just wanted to be fed, though it had not seemed that way. The sheep following the farmer were making an awful lot of noise. "What the hell!" the farmer yelled at them. "Be quiet!"

A woman on a horse asked where I was heading. I mentioned Loweswater. "Ohhh, nice!" she replied. Dogs barked at me by Mossergate Farm. Crows cawed in treetops. A ragged sheep that seemed to have escaped ventured on to the path, regarded me and hobbled away. I reached the top of a hill and, looking back, Cockermouth appeared far in the distance: a thin line of buildings way below. A cyclist struggled by on a rough track by Mosser Fell. "This gets worse every year," he complained, talking about the potholes on the track. I moved up into the sun-drenched hills as Loweswater began to unfurl in a glimmering metallic pool below. Occasional clouds drifted above, casting shadowy patches of mauve on the landscape beyond the lake, where bare slopes above led to lizard-green woodland by the shore. Reaching the water's edge, I followed a path between towering conifers. Lapping water trickled. Birdsong trilled in the trees. It was all quite dreamy. I went up a hill in the direction of a fell shaped like a sphinx or maybe a pyramid, depending on which angle you viewed it from. This was Mellbreak (512 metres), according to my map.

Then I arrived at perhaps the Lake District's most peaceful, perfect inn. Aside from being chased by the Lake District's meanest sheep, it had been an excellent morning's hike, covering 9 miles. I took off my backpack and rested my feet. I had clearly arrived in some kind of hikers' paradise.

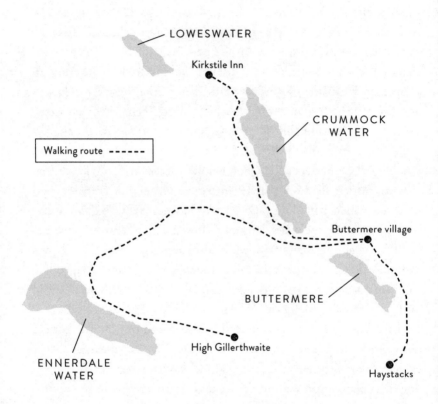

LOWESWATER

Kirkstile Inn

CRUMMOCK
WATER

Walking route -------

Buttermere village

BUTTERMERE

High Gillerthwaite

ENNERDALE
WATER

Haystacks

CHAPTER FIVE

LOWESWATER TO ENNERDALE, VIA CRUMMOCK WATER AND BUTTERMERE

THE WILD WEST

George Orwell once wrote about what makes a perfect pub, colourfully describing a hostelry named The Moon Under Water that was "uncompromisingly Victorian" with sturdy wooden fittings, a stuffed bull's head above the mantelpiece and all the "solid, comfortable ugliness of the nineteenth century". As well as serving bar snacks such as pickles, mussels and "liver-sausage sandwiches", pints could be ordered in "pewter pots", while "a creamy sort of stout" was available and children were tolerated throughout. No music played. There was also, crucially, a good beer garden with shade offered by plane trees and plenty of tables and chairs.

This pub, as Orwell admitted at the end of his essay, did not exist. It was simply his dream of how a perfect pub might be. However, as Orwell was writing this piece in the *Evening Standard*, his description of the imaginary Moon Under Water was pitched at Londoners/city dwellers. So, toward the end, he made an important qualification. "The qualities one expects of a country pub are slightly different," he wrote. Though he did not go into them.

The Kirkstile Inn in the tiny village of Loweswater might just, however, have met with his approval. From the outside, the building itself does not promise much: a plain white exterior like so many Lakeland cottages/farmhouses, with a simple sign pointing to a "Bar" (there was a separate entrance for overnight guests). Inside and out at the back, though, it was as though you had stepped into what might have been Orwell's dream country pub.

Through a doorway beside a water keg and bowl for dogs, I entered a room with a low ceiling and beams with a small bar on the left serving pints of craft beer from a local brewery, including the widely acclaimed Loweswater Gold. A large fireplace lay ahead. Polished horse brasses and higgledy-piggledy pieces of old farming equipment decorated the walls, as did fading black-and-white pictures of blacksmiths hammering horseshoes into shape and long-ago village gatherings featuring fine assortments of frilly frocks, floppy hats and tweed. Crooked stone walls had been whitewashed and simple wooden tables were spread across two principal rooms covered by a wine-red carpet. No music played.

As well as the locally brewed beers and an extensive list of wines, the menu offered ploughman's lunches of game terrine, pickled eggs and chutney, as well as steak and ale pies (in two sizes) and a selection of soups and sandwiches including locally smoked salmon with lemon sour cream, and beef and horseradish. I ordered the latter and a pint of Loweswater Gold and ventured through the back door to discover the Kirkstile Inn's biggest selling point: its wide beer garden stretching across a grassy slope above a beck and facing the fells of Mellbreak.

Hundred-year-old oaks lined the beck and picnic tables were dotted here and there on rectangles of paving, thoughtfully laid so tables were level on the grass. There was a terrace beside the main pub building, which was where I sat on a bench eating my beef and horseradish sandwich and drinking my beer while gazing across the gorgeous scenery. All around were fellow hikers as well as cyclists taking a rest. In the sunshine on the Kirkstile Inn terrace, I could not, for the time I was there, have imagined a place I would rather be. Not just in the Lakes. Anywhere.

The inn was more than 400 years old and remote, tucked away between Loweswater, the Lake District's shallowest lake (18 metres at its deepest), and Crummock Water just to the south. There was nothing whatsoever fancy, flashy or gimmicky about it, which is why Orwell, at a guess, might have liked the place. The sandwich was good. The beer was good. And so was the company.

"It's amazing how constantly busy it is. We're in the middle of nowhere here," said Gareth Hussey, the pub manager. Gareth had joined me at my bench after I had asked him about the inn as he passed by with a tray of empties. He was a tall cheerful man with a broad smile, seemingly unrushed despite the crowded tables; a perfect publican to match the perfect country pub. "It has always been busy. It's probably the best beer garden in the Lake District, especially when the sun is out."

I said that I bet it must be.

"Even when it's raining, we're busy," Gareth said. "Yesterday was a prime example. It was all wet dogs and clothes, people seeking refuge by the open fire."

I complimented him on the Loweswater Gold.

"Well, we brew the beer ourselves," Gareth said. "It was originally produced here from 2003 to 2009 in an old outbuilding. Now Cumbrian Ales makes it [on the pub's behalf] in Hawkshead. Our steak pies are famous, too. We've served the same steak pie for twenty years. They're our biggest seller. We sold a hundred and twenty-two pies last weekend and we sell a hundred and forty-four pints a day at peak. Over a weekend we get, say, three to four hundred customers."

Gareth was from Cornwall and had lived in the Lake District for eight years, having worked previously at The Punch Bowl Inn in Crosthwaite in the south-east Lakes, another renowned Lakeland pub. His wife, he said, was a dietician. Like so many others I had been meeting in the Lakes, he was more than happy to open up about his work and life.

"The core staff have been here a long time [at Kirkstile Inn]," he said. "The chef alone has been here twenty years." Which was why the steak and ale pie recipe had never changed.

"It's unusual in hospitality for people to stay such a long time. It's a more relaxed life here. It's gridlock in Cornwall. Yes, it can be as busy here, but the tourism is spread out. In the western Lakes it's a little bit more niche." Loweswater counted as being in the heart of the western Lakes. "When you are in Windermere or Bowness or Grasmere, those places do get crowded," Gareth said, adding that at Loweswater and Crummock Water, my next lake, it might be busy at times but nowhere near as overrun as in those tourist honeypots.

Three lakes in a day
Loweswater to Buttermere, via Crummock Water

Gareth disappeared to deal with a pie order and I hiked down a lane flanked with delicate yellow wild flowers, soon arriving at the northern tip of Crummock Water. It was a mere half-mile between Loweswater and Crummock Water, the latter being the larger of two lakes, 2½ miles long, more than double the length of Loweswater.

The new lake looked sumptuous in the sunshine, with gentle ripples on the surface as though disturbed from below by little fish rather than from above by the soft breeze. Being so placid, the mirror effect on the water was almost perfect, capturing the fells of Grasmoor across the way. I stopped for a while, simply enjoying the quiet and this double-vision view.

Beyond a gravel beach, the path along the western shore was springy and hardly anyone was about. Woodpeckers rattled in the distance, their drilling echoing across the valley. Lichen-covered boulders lined the shore and streams cascaded in streaks of white from damp brown bracken slopes above. I stepped aside for a fell runner coming by at a rate of knots. "Thanks, man," he said.

A narrow peninsula jutted into the lake. This was known as Low Ling Crag and was flanked by two more gravel beaches beside which ran stretches of grass so neat and tidy they might have passed for mown lawns. This peninsula was about 80 metres long and 20 metres wide with a curious rocky section at the end: a tranquil spot. Delightfully hidden away. Glorious, even, with all the mountains rising around. Was I gushing about Crummock Water? Yes, and why not? Hunter Davies once said this was his favourite lake for being "beautifully quiet and sedate". High praise indeed.

Clouds closed in, the sun disappearing and turning into a looming white disc through the gathering grey. The path became boggier and boggier. A man with a long beard, a flat cap and gaiters appeared from the direction of Buttermere. He looked as though he belonged to another century – the nineteenth or eighteenth, perhaps. I wished him good afternoon and, at first, he said nothing, seemingly lost in thought. After a pause, however, he replied: "Oh, hello," as though he had just spotted me. We were, quite possibly, the only two hikers on the western shore of the lake, passing right by one another.

Absent-minded? Eccentric? Grouchy? In a *walking zone*? Hypnotized by the scenery?

Or perhaps I had just witnessed a ghost.

The path became boggier still, boots almost disappearing below. Tiny Scale Island emerged, with its cluster of scraggly trees. Countless thin streams ran down the hillside, none marked on the map. It was as though the landscape was so saturated, it was leaking. Which, I supposed, it was.

Clouds lowered and the wind picked up. I checked my phone for reception for a weather forecast. A 40 per cent chance of rain was predicted for 5 p.m. I stepped up my pace and, at precisely that hour, while crossing a narrow strip of land between Crummock Water and Buttermere, the heavens opened. I hastened into the village of Buttermere at the northern end of the lake and found my room for the night at yet another hostel, just up a lane from the village centre, in a stark stone building.

In quick time I had bagged no fewer than three lakes: Loweswater, Crummock Water and Buttermere. This equalled the total of all the days previously: Ullswater, Derwentwater and Bassenthwaite Lake.

Fine progress was being made in the western Lakes.

* * *

Then I went to church (and another very good inn).

It is always a pleasure on long hikes with a heavy backpack when the moment arrives to *take off your heavy backpack after your long hike*. That feeling of light-footedness. That realization you may just, but not always, get a second wind. By this stage of a long run of long hikes with a heavy backpack, however, coming up to a fortnight, you tend to have fallen into the rhythm of the daily marches and this second burst of energy becomes much more likely. At least, that was what I was finding. There was another factor, too: Buttermere village was full of intrigue, and I wanted to learn all about it.

So, having deposited the backpack in a narrow private bunk-room with two bunks and a fine fell view, I returned along the lane toward the village, soon coming to a halt beside a field of sheep behind a drystone wall. I had not noticed them on the way up and they were striking creatures, quite different to the ones that had chased me earlier.

These had long white faces with curious, contemplative expressions and tight little smiles that seemed to curl up from their mouths as though they were in the middle of a particularly wry thought. The older sheep had grey coats, while the younger ones' were dark brown. They appeared cool, calm and collected, many having decided to lie down for an afternoon rest to watch the world go by – i.e. all the strange folk in waterproof clothing clutching backpacks of various sizes, of which there were a fair few in Buttermere.

These sheep were, I later learned, having compared pictures with the ones I took, Herdwick sheep, the best-known Lake District sheep and particularly hardy at higher altitudes. Judging by the photographs of other types of sheep found in the Lakes, of which there were at least half a dozen – and there are 3 million sheep in all roaming about the region – it seemed the mean-looking sheep of the morning were possibly Swaledales or, most likely, Texels, tougher creatures by far, in appearance at least: rough-and-ready looking, no wry, thoughtful smiles there. Though, I will admit, this was all speculation; maybe it had been another breed of sheep altogether that had come after me and Swaledales and Texels in reality were the gentlest of creatures – in which case I apologize for my slur.

Sheep thoughts over, I carried on down the hill and, a little further on, arrived at St James's Church.

This was a tiny stone structure with an elaborate iron gate decorated in the shape of a shepherd herding a sheep. The church was notable in Lake District walking circles for a touching memorial plaque to Alfred Wainwright on the windowsill of the first window on the right as you enter. This slate plaque bore the inscription: "PAUSE AND REMEMBER ALFRED WAINWRIGHT[,] FELLWALKER, GUIDE BOOK AUTHOR AND ILLUSTRATOR WHO LOVED THIS VALLEY. LIFT YOUR EYES TO HAYSTACKS[,] HIS FAVOURITE PLACE. 1907–1991".

I did so and through the leaded window could see the jagged contour of Haystacks fell, where Wainwright's ashes were scattered. Tomorrow, I intended to climb Haystacks, which, at 597 metres and with fine weather forecast, was much more doable than Blencathra's 868 metres in cloud and wind. If I was going to bag just one Wainwright, it should at least be Wainwright's favourite Wainwright, my reasoning went.

At the foot of the small hill, near the hostel, a cluster of buildings huddled where the lane twisted round Wilkinsyke Farm. From a barn, the smell and sounds of cattle emanated. The engine of a tractor whirred and a sign on a gate said: "CAUTION THIS IS A WORKING FARM. YOUR COMMON SENSE IS GREATLY APPRECIATED" – making me consider the point of the word "working" in this message. Yet with so many farms in the Lakes turning to static holiday homes and so on, perhaps the distinction was needed.

Pedantic thoughts over, I continued past Wilkinsyke Farm into the village centre with its tea room, café, a handful of holiday cottages, pair of bars and pair of hotels. A veritable hive of hiking-holidaymaking was in full swing in this remote corner of the western Lakes.

I made a beeline for Buttermere Court Hotel – smaller than the Bridge Hotel, its main rival – as I understood this to be at the heart of the "intrigue" I mentioned earlier.

Buttermere Court Hotel was formerly the Fish Inn and it was the scene of a great early nineteenth-century scandal. This had centred on the barmaid Mary Robinson, daughter of the innkeeper and a renowned local beauty who had begun to attract gentlemen visitors keen to gawp at her. Word of her good looks had spread after an author named Joseph Palmer, who wrote under the pen name of Captain Budworth and who visited Buttermere in 1792, had described Robinson in an article: "Her hair was thick and long, of a dark brown and though unadorned with ringlets, did not seem to want them. Her face was a fine oval with full eyes and lips as red as vermillion. Her cheeks had more of the lily than the rose…"

Et cetera, et cetera. The "Beauty of Buttermere" legend was born. Gentlemen visiting Keswick on Lakes tours would pop over to Buttermere to glimpse Robinson, the Beauty. Local gentlemen went too, including William Wordsworth, who visited in 1799 with Samuel Taylor Coleridge. Robert Southey of Keswick was also to drop by. Interestingly, none of this trio was moved to pen a verse in her honour at the time, though Wordsworth later, when she had become really famous, praised in poetry her "modest mein", "unexampled grace", "retiredness of mind" and "patience".

No doubt she had needed quite a lot of that.

As her fame grew, in stepped a certain "Colonel, the Hon. Alexander Augustus Hope", or so he was calling himself, claiming to be the member of parliament for Linlithgow and brother to the Earl of Hopetoun. In other words: loaded. Or so it would seem. The "colonel", who had recently been swanning about in Keswick arousing the suspicions of Coleridge (who was unconvinced of his background), was enchanted by Robinson.

He courted the Beauty and was granted permission to marry her. This went ahead on 3 October 1802, only for it to be discovered soon afterward that the "colonel" was a bankrupt fraudster named John Hatfield, who was already married with children. Hatfield was arrested, charged on the technicality of having franked his post as an MP – such forgery was then a capital offence – and hanged in Carlisle on 3 September 1803. Bizarrely, during his spell behind bars in Carlisle, Wordsworth, who had been passing the city, visited Hatfield. Such was the notoriety of the case it seemed the Lakeland Bard simply could not resist.

The affair was the talk of the nation, recreated in newspapers (including several prominent accounts by the vindicated Coleridge), books, prints (many merely depicting the Beauty, upon whom so many had become fixated), poems and even plays in London. Wordsworth was to refer to Robinson in "The Prelude" as the "Maid of Buttermere" and this name stuck; the Beauty turning into the Maid. Meanwhile, Robinson, perhaps sick of the limelight, moved from Buttermere after marrying a farmer who lived in Caldbeck in the northern Lakes. There she lived a quiet life to the age of 58 and bore five children.

Not many inns can claim such juicy tales. I asked the receptionist about the hotel's new name, and he replied: "It was owned by the same family for fifty years and it got changed two years ago. Some people still call it the Fish. We're more than happy to let that happen." He pointed to a yellowing cutting from *The Cumberland News* in 1973, framed on a wall in the reception, helpfully outlining the scandal. He also said the former name of the hotel came from the popularity of char fishing, both in Buttermere and Crummock Water, that there were 13 rooms and that the bar had just been renovated.

This turned out to be called the High Stile Kitchen, acting as both a bar and a restaurant, and was at the back, overlooking Haystacks in the far distance and High Stile fell, after which it was named, in the foreground. Mill Beck, a small river feeding into Crummock Water, flowed calmly beyond a car park.

I ordered a pint of Signal Peak beer from yet another local brewery, the Great Corby Brewhouse in Carlisle, which was served by one of the current barmaids of Buttermere.

She had very long blue nails, so I asked her whether it was easy to pull pints with them? "No problem," she said, proving so with gusto and adding: "Yes, they're a bit bright aren't they – a bit of fun."

The High Stile Kitchen bar/restaurant was in a cacophonous room with a low ceiling and various Lake District maps on the walls. Windows were large, allowing good fell views. Bob Marley crooned on the stereo. I sat at a tartan booth reading *The Ambleside Alibi*, which had got off to an immediately murderous start, and eavesdropping.

A man with his son, sitting on one side, was drilling his boy on football knowledge.

"Name three teams Brendan Rodgers has managed."

"Leicester City and Liverpool," said the boy, failing to recall a third.

"Not bad," said his father.

"Name a Scottish city rivalry."

"Rangers versus Celtic," said the boy.

"Well done, son! Who does Roy Hodgson manage?"

"He has white hair," the boy replied.

"I'm not asking you what he looks like!" the father said.

"Name a north-London rivalry."

"Arsenal versus Spurs."

"Well done, son!"

"Name a team that got relegated from the Premier League last year."

"Sheffield United."

"Really well done, son!"

The boy would certainly grow up to do well on the BBC's *Question of Sport*, the way things were going.

On the other side, a group of young American hikers, in their twenties, were discussing their dreams.

"When I was a kid I was asked what my biggest ambition was: I said to play baseball on the moon," a man with a Stanford University jumper was saying. "Well, no one has done that yet." Then, as though passing on the baton of dreaminess, he asked a woman in their group, "What would you do if you had money to buy anything?"

"I'd buy pandas," she replied.

"How many would you buy?"

"A hundred," she said.

"What about a Lamborghini? Wouldn't you want that instead?" he asked.

"Yeah, maybe you're right," she conceded.

They looked like happy hikers, letting their hair down after a long day on the fells – happy to talk nonsense for a while with their drinks after pounding the trails. Not so much après-ski, more après-scree.

A couple joined me. I had noticed them earlier at the YHA Buttermere hostel. They were staying in a pod in its grounds. Steve worked in "software service for the oil and gas industry", and Penny was a housekeeper. They were in their fifties, from Richmond in the Yorkshire Dales. They told me they were extremely pleased with their pod.

"We've got logs to have a fire," Penny said. "So cosy."

"You don't have to do the Wainwrights," said Steve, when I mentioned Haystacks. "We've been to the Lakes maybe a hundred times. As we've got older, we've got to know the lower walks." They said they had particularly enjoyed a hike around Derwentwater earlier on their trip and were going round Buttermere tomorrow: 4½ miles.

Penny said: "Haystacks was Wainwright's favourite fell, his ashes were scattered there."

Just about everyone was keen to tell you this in Buttermere, already the receptionists at both the hostel and the hotel had said the same.

I mentioned the Fish Inn and the Maid of Buttermere. They had not heard of her. So I told the story.

"It all happened here?" asked Penny.

"In theory," I replied.

Then we had a good chat, hiker to hikers – boots, waterproofs, socks, maps, plastic coverings for maps, compasses, all of that.

Fraudster colonels, legendary maids, inquisitive romantic poets and gentlemen voyeurs may not have been around, but there was plenty of life in the old Fish yet. Another great spot.

Wainwright's favourite fell
Haystacks from Buttermere

Finches twittered. Water slapped on the stone-strewn shore. Fish flipped through the surface of Buttermere as though taking morning exercise. Fells rose all around in bands of scree and grass and woodland and granite, blending like carefree strokes on a watercolour painting as soft yellow light enveloped the valley.

A pair of photographers had set up tripods by the footpath, making the most of it. "So much beauty, you hardly know which way to look," said one as I passed. They had been by the lake since 5 a.m. to capture the best of the dawn sky. They had chosen a great location: there was an elemental splendour to Buttermere, the mountains gathering around the little lake somehow watching and waiting.

Thin streaks of snow dusted the peaks of High Stile (806 metres), High Crag (745 metres) and even lowly Haystacks. It was cold, 0°C as I set off around 8 a.m., and the temperature had dropped to –3°C at night though the forecast was for 7°C later. Wrapped up well, none of this bothered me as I followed the path along the lake's eastern shore, backpack-free as I was staying another night in Buttermere. That always lifted the spirits. As far as taking on this Wainwright-of-all-Wainwrights was concerned, I had picked the easiest way up Haystacks; High Stile and High Crag required tough-looking ascents. No point in being overambitious.

At the end of Buttermere, a German couple asked for directions. I entered and exited a damp tunnel in a crag. A man fishing from an orange kayak, possibly for Arctic char, waved at me. I waved back. I arrived at Gatesgarth Farm and followed a track round the edge of the lake. Then I went up, up, up: I had reached the Scarth Gap Pass.

A few others ahead were going up, up, up too, which was pleasing to see: just follow them. This required ascending a series of boulders crafted into steps. It was tough going, like climbing a never-ending broken escalator. Halfway up, I met two thirty-something male hikers who were taking a break.

"Knackering," I said.

"Yep," said one.

We stood around staring at the twisting pathway plunging into the valley.

"Long way up," I said.

"Yep," said the other.

And that was as far as the conversation went, for a while.

We stood around a bit more staring down. Some fell walkers, I was more than aware by that stage, preferred to let the scenery do the talking.

I asked for directions to the summit, showing one of them my Ordnance Survey map. Was I going the right way?

He looked at the folded paper for a second, took out his phone, switched on an app, pinpointed exactly where we were and said: "Yep."

I was amazed by this technology, which of course I should not have been. Having decided to take a traditionalist's approach with maps and a compass, I had simply turned a blind eye to what was possible.

The walker suddenly became talkative. He was a big fan of the app: "I tell my brother where I'm going, so he can check if there's any trouble." This could be done via the app. "And I can follow other people's routes, which makes it easier." Routes were collectively shared on the app. "You can point it at a peak and it will tell you which one it is." He did this and "Haystacks" popped up on the screen.

Amazed, I thanked them for their help and the walker withdrew into himself again. "Yep," he replied.

Then I ascended the rest of the stone stairway of Scarth Gap Pass, reaching a plateau. There, another pair of walkers, this time a man and a woman, were taking a break too. While pointing to a lofty ridge, the woman said: "That's Innominate Tarn up there." Then she added: "Wainwright's ashes are up there too." She paused. "Haystacks was his favourite fell, you know."

These facts, I predicted, would probably be lodged in my memory forever.

The route ahead required clambering over boulders using hands. I followed the helpful woman's directions and shortly found myself at the summit, enjoying the most awe-inspiring views of the trip so far.

Buttermere glistened way below, framed by the contour of High Crag, which tumbled wildly to the shore. Beyond, Crummock Water formed a hazy "C" of slate grey. The village had become a few white specks of habitation, while rogue clouds had gathered above looking like strange sea-ships in the sky.

You could understand why Wainwright approved of it all round here so much.

Anyway, I had bagged a Wainwright! I had even stepped over to the correct place, where an iron bar had been hammered into the rock to mark the top.

Patches of snow lay beside a small frozen pond. I put on a woolly hat. The path led to craggy ridges sprinkled with an overnight dusting of white. A pair of walkers passed in the opposite direction, and I heard one say: "So what are we having tonight, Thai?" Hospitality had moved on somewhat since the days of the Maid of Buttermere and the Fish Inn.

I tried to spot famous peaks such as Scafell Pike and Great Gable but it was impossible with all the clouds. Innominate Tarn, by which Wainwright's ashes were so famously scattered, came into view, looking like a pool of mercury.

It was a moving spot. The master hiker had once written: "If you dear reader, should get a bit of grit in your boot as you are crossing Haystacks in the years to come, please treat it with respect. It might be me." Beside the trail at this point, I noticed some rocks had been piled. I went over to look and found an inscription: "CHERISHED MEMORIES OF MY LOVING WIFE CAROL, AT PEACE ON HER MOUNTAIN, ALWAYS IN MY THOUGHTS BUT FOREVER IN MY HEART." Wainwright was not the only hiker to have adored this fell.

I joined a long green dotted line that led to the lake, winding toward Fleetwith Pike. As I did so, I fell in step with David and Ronan from Chester-le-Street in County Durham.

They were in their early forties, clad in Mountain Warehouse gear and had left that morning at 6.30 a.m., driven for 2 hours across the north of England, ascended Haystacks and were planning to drive back in the afternoon, having first had lunch at a deserted bothy and gone for a dip in a mountain stream (they had brought swimming trunks for that).

David was a Lakes regular; during the pandemic he would leave his home at 4 a.m. to come and bag a Wainwright. Blencathra had taken him three attempts as conditions had been tricky the first two times (I was pleased to hear it was not just me who had struggled). He had once, he said, had a job making small electrical components for Henry vacuum cleaners: "Oh, they're indestructible they are, probably the only thing that will survive Putin's holocaust." But he had since become a carer for his mother while inventing and patenting handy devices that he hoped might break through and make him a fortune: the latest was a cupholder that fitted on to the dashboard of Volkswagen Transporters (he owned one of these, which had given him the idea). His friend Ronan, whom David was showing the Lake District for the first time, said he worked in "mindset nutrient therapy for weight loss – I do Zoom meetings with Americans, Canadians, Scandinavians, Dutch and French ladies." Previously he had been a personal fitness instructor. His Liverpool-based "mindset nutrient therapy for weight loss" company had 950,000 followers on Instagram and was doing well. You meet all sorts on a hike in the Lakes.

Stepping downward toward a spot called Little Round How, one breathtaking view after another opened out with delicious glimpses of the valley below between sheer cliffs and crumbling crags. Great boulders lay on heathery slopes. It was an uncompromising rough-and-tumble landscape, with few hikers around.

David said that it had not been like this during the height of the lockdowns, especially at Scafell Pike, which had attracted swarms of day visitors. "Last year," he said, "people were going up Scafell with their pocket dogs."

Ronan, it turned out, was even more of a mountain novice than me: "It's the first ever hike in my life. It's amazing. I love it. I work on a computer at home all day. And then there is this! This!" He waved an arm toward the crags above.

They followed a fork in the path to the bothy, a simple grey stone structure up a slope – and I returned on a long snaking trail to the lake.

Follow the path!
Buttermere to Ennerdale

From Buttermere to Ennerdale Water, my next lake, was about two and a half miles as the crow flew. Easy-peasy, a short one, or so you might think. The problem was that Red Pike fell blocked the way, measuring 755 metres.

To avoid Red Pike required retracing my steps to the edge of Crummock Water, turning left near Scale Island and traversing isolated valleys slicing between Scale Knott, Blea Crag, Hen Comb, Great Borne, Floutern Cop, Herdus and Banna Fell. The landscape of the Lakes enjoyed some truly unusual place names.

After Banna Fell, I would turn left again at Whins and go down a hill to Ennerdale Water beside Bowness Knot and proceed eastward along the lake, skirting the forests of Latterbarrow and Cat Crag before reaching the eastern edge of Ennerdale. This was where I had booked another bunk room, at YHA Ennerdale, which was so remote it was off-grid. The hostel was about half a mile beyond the eastern shore of Ennerdale Water. The entire route was 9 miles, more than three times the direct Red Pike way.

It was the morning after my ascent of Haystacks. A small, wiry, helpful receptionist at the hostel in Buttermere, a proficient climber and fell walker himself, was manning the front desk. I asked him about the route ahead and he said the longer way was fine, though he had a couple of caveats: "You'll go through a bog in that valley and then you've got to avoid a grumpy farmer."

What did he mean by *grumpy*, I asked. I had visions of a red-faced man clasping a shotgun speeding across fields on a quad bike to confront "trespassers" who were merely following a public right of way.

"Let's just say he's not the greatest fan of hikers," the receptionist said. "Last year, he wrote 'GO AWAY: LOCKDOWN' on a road over there." The receptionist paused and added: "Actually, it was a much more colourful expression than that."

The benefit of the longer route was that it would rise to a mere 300 metres, much lower than Red Pike. "It will be clear today," the small, wiry, helpful receptionist said. "It can get a bit slippery there on the way down," he was pointing to a spot on the map near Floutern Cop, "And the path is not clear in places, but you should be OK."

If only all receptionists could be as helpful as the small, wiry receptionist at YHA Buttermere. I thanked him profusely: a little bit of local knowledge in the Lake District went a long way.

Before I left, however, I phoned Kasia, my other half, aware that there might not be reception by Ennerdale Water.

In my absence, Kasia was in the middle of a scheme, one I was immensely proud of her having undertaken.

As mentioned previously, Kasia was Polish although she lived with me in London (we met in a bar in Cracow when I was writing a city guide for *The Times*). When the war in Ukraine broke out and refugees began to flee the country, not long before I departed for the Lakes, she had immediately had an idea: to offer her unoccupied apartment in the city of Siedlce, about 60 miles east of Warsaw, to Ukrainian refugees who needed a halfway house while UK visa applications were processed, which had been taking a disgracefully long time.

To this end, she had contacted an agency that was arranging for British hosts to house refugees, discovered that a mother (Lena) and child (Anna, aged 14) needed somewhere to stay; they were from Kiev and their husband/father was in the army fighting the invading Russians. Kasia had agreed they could stay at her apartment as long as required and the agency had put her in touch with the pair. By that method, arrangements had been put in place and Kasia was about to fly to Warsaw to meet them at the Polish capital's main refugee reception centre. This was happening the very next day, when I would be at the off-grid hostel by Ennerdale Water. Kasia was due to meet her parents at Warsaw airport. They would then drive to the reception centre, collect Lena and Anna and take them to the apartment, which Kasia's parents had ready with fresh laundry and food.

"They're on the train from Kiev now," Kasia said, and it was an extremely worrying time as the Russians had been attacking railways and reports of Russian atrocities in Bucha, a small city on the northwest outskirts of Kiev, were beginning to filter through; men, women and children massacred, their bodies dumped in streets.

Kasia had just talked to Anna, who spoke some English, by phone and also to Lena in Russian (Kasia knew some Russian). Lena and Anna, she learned, had been staying in bunkers during raids in Ukraine's capital city although their apartment remained intact. Kasia had explained to the Ukrainians that a United Nations/Polish government cash allowance would be available to them via their phones on arrival. Worried her flight would be delayed, as it was due to arrive 2 hours before the train from Kiev, she had also asked her parents to collect the Ukrainians and take them to Siedlce first, should that be the case.

Far away events suddenly seemed much closer.

It was all quite fraught, as well as potentially dangerous for Lena and Anna on the train. Kasia said she would give me an update later from Poland.

* * *

A little preoccupied, I set off for Ennerdale Water after buying a steak and ale pie for lunch from the Syke Farm Café on the edge of Wilkinsyke Farm.

Most hikers were taking circuits of Buttermere that morning. After crossing the gentle swirling eddies of Mill Beck, I did not see another soul all the way to Ennerdale Water. I was increasingly surprised how swiftly you could "disappear" like that if you fixed your own way around the Lake District, off the beaten track.

Across the bog I went.

It was damp. It was empty. The plains ahead comprised golden grass, peat and not a whole lot more. Stumbling onward and often upward and sometimes downward, I followed the path, lost the path, zigzagged, corrected myself, zigzagged again and fell into a trance in the deserted scenery. It hardly felt like Britain: too immense, too open, too untouched. The impression, just as it had been on Matterdale Common on the way to Threlkeld, was of somehow being transported many thousands of miles away. Another prairie in Wyoming or Montana, perhaps, hidden in the Cumbrian hills.

Fells billowed all around. Stones from old sheepfolds lay scattered like ruins of an ancient civilization. Sunlight bleached the grassland beneath an electric-blue sky as skylarks squealed, rising up from among the reeds and hovering, alert, as an outsider passed: *who is this human with his olive-green 65-litre backpack from Mountain Warehouse squelching by? And could he please squelch onward pronto!*

Obeying their wishes, I came to a stile where a dried-out skull of a creature, presumably a sheep, had been placed on the fence. *Welcome, if you dare*, the skull seemed to suggest. I kept going, arriving next at a small gathering of cattle by a stream. Like the skylarks, they too seemed surprised by an intruder, though not especially perturbed.

The boggy landscape undulated to the heady height of 300 metres before descending slowly. Near the "summit", such as it was, I stopped for water and a rest, taking the backpack off for a minute. As I did so, I heard the voices of a man and a woman behind me, or at least I swore I did. Yet when I turned, the landscape remained as empty as ever. This "back route" to Ennerdale Water was both evocative and (slightly) eerie: so far removed from the hurly-burly of Buttermere.

I marched on. The Ordnance Survey map was teaching me things. Firstly, keep an eye out for bields, these were a form of den where you could take refuge during a storm (if I have this right, which I may not). Secondly, watch out for sheepfolds, as knowing to go right or left of both bields and sheepfolds helps keep you on track (sheepfolds, like bields, were marked). Thirdly, count the fells, even the small ones; not only does this help you know where you are, it also keeps your brain ticking over when crossing a long bog. Fourthly, whatever you do, stick to the dotted green lines around farms near Ennerdale Water. The small, wiry, helpful receptionist had me on high alert regarding that.

Ennerdale Water gleamed below, the most isolated lake yet and the only one in the Lakes without a road by its shores. As I came down the hill, it opened out quietly with brooding purple fells on the southern side; piebald slopes of scree sliding downward amid folds of granite. In this final section of the "traverse" from Crummock Water, there were many signs by gates, providing much advice for walkers: "YOUR DOG CAN SCARE OR HARM ANIMALS: STAY SAFE – USE A LEAD AROUND LIVESTOCK, BUT RELEASE YOUR DOG IF CHASED BY CATTLE", "TAKE YOUR LITTER HOME", "LEAVE GATES AS YOU FIND THEM", "CLEAN UP AFTER YOUR DOG: BAG IT, BIN IT", "NO FIRES OR BARBECUES", "PRIVATE PROPERTY, KEEP OUT", "FOLLOW THE PATH", "FARM ACCESS ONLY", "NO THROUGH ROAD", "NO ACCESS TO LAKE".

With extreme care, I made my way down a narrow lane with a couple of cottages. Some people were eating sandwiches at a table by one of these. They said hello and asked where I had come from. I explained my route and that I had not seen anyone else, to which one of them said: "Yes, it's nice isn't it?" I agreed, and then they offered me a sandwich.

Yet more charming Lakeland folk.

The lane led to a car park below Bowness Knot, a rocky outcrop that rose sharply. This was as far as cars could go that were not owned by the Forestry Commission, the National Trust or United Utilities, each of which had an interest in Ennerdale Water. The various bodies had gathered resources and joined forces to create a local group known as Wild Ennerdale that was busy rewilding the countryside around the lake, with projects to reintroduce beavers, monitor growing red-squirrel populations (not that I ever spotted one), encourage marsh fritillary butterflies and remove blockades in the water, such as old bridges on tributary rivers. This would allow salmon and Arctic char to breed.

A campaign had been launched to counter the devastating effects of a tree disease called *Phytophthora ramorum*, which attacked larches and had been identified in the forest plantations around Ennerdale Water. Thousands of volunteers were involved and there was a project centre called The Gather in the village of Ennerdale Bridge, just to the west of the lake, with a café. This was designed to be a headquarters for both those getting involved in the campaign and walkers taking trails that were highlighted on a local map produced by Wild Ennerdale; one of these was the loop around the entire lake (6½ miles).

From the car park, a dirt track led along the edge of a conifer forest by the shore, where I stopped to eat the steak and ale pie (first-rate) at an isolated picnic table by the water. The table had been dedicated to Ian Bliss (1943–1983), "who loved these hills", as have so many others over the years. Look around in the Lake District and dedications of this sort are all over the place. Refuelled, I completed the last bit of the dirt track to the hostel, the odd hiker passing by the other way. But really there was hardly anyone about. Ennerdale Water felt almost off the map.

Meeting the Germans
YHA Ennerdale, by Ennerdale Water

Then I met the Germans, well one of them. On arrival at YHA Ennerdale, at around 2 p.m., initially no one was about. The front door of the old stone building, tucked away on a slope amid trees, was locked; check-in was not possible until 5 p.m. I went round the back to a veranda, where I found the back door was unlocked. So, I went in and slumped on a sofa in a lounge with a panoramic view through large windows: the slopes of Steeple (819 metres) to the left and a pine forest across a valley with a winding river straight ahead, the river Liza. In this position, I closed my eyes for a while, listening to the birdsong. When I opened them, a man wearing a waterproof jacket was regarding me through the window.

He seemed keen to talk. I went outside and he asked: "Are you manager?"

He was, I could tell from his accent, German.

I explained I was not the manager.

"Ah ok, ok," he said. "Okee doke. Cuuul, cuuul, cuuul." (Cool, cool, cool.) He paused, and then explained himself. He was indeed from Germany, from near Hamburg, and was hiking with a couple of friends accompanied by their sons on the coast-to-coast route created by Alfred Wainwright, as described in his 1973 book *A Coast to Coast Walk*. They had begun at St Bees, on the coast, that morning but he had had trouble with his knees, so had caught a taxi to the hostel, where his friend had booked beds. He had transported the backpacks for his fellow walkers, which he brought into the lounge. He slumped in an armchair. "Limping. Ah yes, limping. Twenty miles! No way!" He laughed. "Ha ha ha!" He checked his phone. There was no Wi-Fi at the hostel and he wanted the internet for some reason. "Oh sheeeet! No Wi-Fi. Oh sheeeet!" He paused. "This phone is offline," he said. "Sheeeet." There was no reception for his, or my, phone. "Absolutely offline. Absolutely. No way. This is not good. No network. Sheeeet,

sheeeet, sheeeet. This is not adventure. This is absolute sheeeet. No Wi-Fi. This is sheeeet."

His name was Stefan and he had short, cropped hair, a pink complexion, clear blue eyes and a boyish manner though he was in his late forties. Although not having Wi-Fi was "absolute sheeeet", you could tell he did not really mean it; he was just playing around. He began to tell me about an epic hike he had once made on the famous E5 route from Oberstdorf in Germany to Merano in Italy: "One hundred and fifty miles. Very hard. Highest peak three thousand, five hundred metres. You go in the sun in the morning and you get to the top and it's…" Stefan shivered to indicate cold. "Ha ha ha!"

Through the window, we noticed a woman in multicoloured clothes in the back garden of a neighbouring building. Stefan and I went and talked to her. "We are waiting for check-in person," said Stefan.

"That's me," she replied, with a note of irony in her voice. "I'm doing the chainsawing now." She indicated a pile of logs. "And then I've got a staff meeting."

Stefan asked about Wi-Fi. "It's on the website: there isn't any," the woman replied, raising an eyebrow and assessing us with a look of: *you're not in the city now*. A lovely black-and-white collie ran up with a stick in her mouth and began whining at my feet. "That's Poppy," said the woman.

Stefan and I returned to the deserted hostel with Poppy following us. "It is catastrophe," said Stefan, referring to the lack of Wi-Fi again.

Then I noticed there was a payphone attached to the wall in a corridor. I wanted to find out from Kasia whether she had been successful in collecting the Ukrainians. A sign by the phone, however, said: "Unfortunately this phone does not take new £1 coins, apologies for any inconvenience caused." The "new" pound coins had been introduced five years previously and the old ones were no longer legal tender.

I relayed this to Stefan and he said: "Oh, ah, ah, sheeeet."

We sat on the veranda beneath some Nepalese flags with Poppy watching us and whining. After a while, I started throwing the stick for Poppy, who fetched it with great alacrity, returned it and whined. So went the afternoon playing with Poppy, until a cheerful member of staff named Suzanne, not the woman we had met earlier, arrived, earlier than 5 p.m., and checked us in – Stefan's friend, it turned out had booked the next night, but luckily there was room: "He has booked every hostel one day late on the coast-to-coast. Oh, sheeeet! This is absolutely adventure. Absolutely!"

Stefan seemed to have changed his tune on whether his coast-to-coast experience across the north of England was proving to be an adventure or not.

Suzanne exchanged a £5 note for 50-pence pieces and I called Kasia, establishing that she had collected the Ukrainians and was driving with them and her parents to Siedlce, just before the time ran out and the line went dead.

I got talking to Kirsty, the woman with the chainsaw from earlier. She was the hostel manager and she had come and joined Stefan and me in the lounge. "We make our own electricity and source our own water here," she said. "We don't have kettles, microwaves, toasters or water boilers." These would use up too much electricity. "We have to adapt out here. I love it because of that and because I live in a beautiful valley with the longest-running rewilding project in England. It's an interesting valley to live in. Five years I've been here. It's not without its challenges. Making sure there's a stable water supply. Fixing the electric – we have our own dam on a beck. You go back to basics, with the risk of sounding as though I'm John Major." Kirsty chuckled at her own joke; she had an offbeat wit. "The dam has two one and a half-kilowatt turbines. I love all that techy stuff. We do have to top it up with solar. And we have a dirty diesel generator." That was for backup in an emergency. The hostel had a capacity of 24 guests and there was room for 13 more in a camping barn close by. Kirsty sported a tattoo of a red squirrel on one arm, among many others, and had piercings in her nose and lips. She wore a multicoloured skirt above multicoloured leggings and had an alternative style to match the alternative living. The perfect host out in the Lakeland sticks of Ennerdale.

Stefan asked her: "Beer please. Can I have a beer?" Kirsty regarded him coolly for a moment and replied in the affirmative. Beers were for sale at the reception. She fetched one for him. "Wild place! Wild! Ha ha ha!" said Stefan. "Wild!" He took a sip of the beer, which was named Wild, an ale from Ennerdale Craft Brewery – yet another local brewery. "Ah perfect!" He explained to Kirsty and me how a friend of his had dreamed up taking Wainwright's old coast-to-coast route. "He couldn't come. He got Covid. Absolutely sheeeet! Absolute! Sheeeet! Not nice!"

Kirsty went to check the score in a key Premier League game for the German and me via the single internet connection in a back room: Liverpool versus Man City had ended two–two. I got a very early night reading *The Ambleside Alibi*, hearing the other Germans arrive around 8 p.m. amid much yelling and "ha ha ha"s. Stefan was right, it was "absolutely adventure" on the edge of Ennerdale Water, a wild (and wonderful) place indeed.

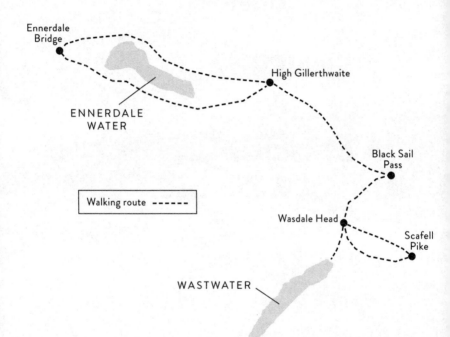

Ennerdale
Bridge

High Gillerthwaite

ENNERDALE
WATER

Black Sail
Pass

Walking route ------

Wasdale Head

Scafell
Pike

WASTWATER

CHAPTER SIX

ENNERDALE TO WASDALE HEAD, VIA ENNERDALE BRIDGE AND BLACK SAIL PASS

HIGH JINKS, HIGH MOUNTAINS

There is a camaraderie among hikers in the Lake District that comes from shared interests – and the first and foremost of these is the weather. You become obsessed by it and, in particular, weather forecasts. Should the weather "turn", after all, you could find yourself in all sorts of bother – potentially life-threatening bother. After swiftly backtracking from Blencathra – realizing I had bitten off way more than I could chew – I had gone online at the Horse & Farrier in Threlkeld to check whether there had been any recent accidents there and had read of a tragic fall a mere six months earlier. Further fatalities were to come elsewhere in the Lakes soon after I had completed the 379-mile hike for this book. According to Lake District Mountain Rescue teams, deaths on the fells ranged from about 15 to 30 annually. So being weather-aware was important: wind and clouds could make the fells treacherous. This was why the Mountain Weather Information Service website was so revered. The hostel at Ennerdale printed out its Lake District report each morning and posted this hallowed document in the reception. The latest summary predicted a dry day ahead, with "mostly small" wind, a 70 per cent chance of cloud-free summits, rising to 90 per cent in the afternoon, and a high temperature of 3°C. Nothing much to worry about there.

Another shared interest was obviously the route you and others you met were taking. This formed a common currency of conversation. In the breakfast room, the Germans were quick to lay out their map and show me their route ahead, which was to take in Rosthwaite, Patterdale and Shap before heading onward to Whitby on the North Sea coast in North Yorkshire; they were intending, they said, to catch a few taxi rides to speed things up. I showed them where I had been and what I aimed to do that day: a loop walk to the village of Ennerdale Bridge and back (about a dozen miles).

The Germans were down early for breakfast, as was I. "May we have eggs. Fried eggs," Stefan asked of Kirsty, having peered round into the kitchen.

This had elicited a series of muffled comments and seeming gasps from Kirsty and Suzanne, which emanated from the depths of the kitchen before Kirsty had emerged, assessed the Germans with a raised eyebrow and said with some aplomb: "At 8.30 a.m. you can have fried eggs, that is when breakfast is served." The hostel was run like a tight ship, with dos and don'ts and timings – all helping maintain order.

Stefan's friend, who wore a lumberjack shirt, cargo trousers and a blue gilet, told me: "It is me! It is me who is guilty!" He was referring to booking all the accommodation across Britain on the wrong days for their occasionally taxi-assisted, cross-country hike. "It is classic catch-22 situation," he continued. Getting the starting date wrong was going to mean a lot of calls and emails, once they got reception on their phones. Yet he and the others did not seem especially bothered. They returned to their maps, and I sat at a table with a mother and son, guests who had arrived yesterday evening.

They were Kristin and Finlay Grant, from Derbyshire and on a week-long holiday, with some "light training" for Finlay thrown in. Finlay was aged 18 and one of Britain's best fell runners. Their plan for the day was for Kristin to go wild swimming in Ennerdale Water while Finlay would run for 2 hours to meet a fell-running pal near Buttermere, run a further 3 hours with his friend and run back, taking another 2 hours: so *7 hours of running in the mountains of the Lake District* lay ahead. I was flabbergasted. "You should try feeding him, he's expensive," said Kristin. Finlay competed for the under-twenties national fell-running team, the cross-country team of Chesterfield & District Athletics Club and the fell-running team of Buxton Athletic Club. "He was about ten when we realized he could run," Kristin said. "There was a huge crowd of ten-year-olds who went off on a cross-country school run. They set off and I was wondering how long it would be before he came back crying. Then two of them came back ahead of all the others and one of them was Finlay and he was in the lead. I thought: *oh my God, the others are on the other side of the lake, miles away*." He was noticed by someone from Chesterfield Athletics and scouted there and then.

There was not a lot of money to be made in fell and cross-country running, but Finlay said: "I get a lot of free stuff." This was when he won races, which he often did; the "free stuff" might be shoes or other running kit. He said he expected to cover 16 miles today. He was building up to a 2-mile sprint-race in June in Windermere and "should have been in Thailand for a race in February", but the pandemic had cancelled that.

"The amount of trophies he's got," said Kristin. "All the sideboards in the living room are full. The big one is on the kitchen table. It's a terrible size: three feet by three feet, a silver shield dating from 1870. It's the Northern Central team trophy. It weighs an absolute tonne and came with a big wooden case. It's so big it has to go on the kitchen table. There's no other place for it. Looking at the names on it is like a history of cross-country running." Finlay looked bashful about his mother's discussion of his trophies. He agreed to talk later about the joys of fell running. He was off for his 7 hours and I was too, a little less strenuously.

"We've got to do things while we still can"
YHA Ennerdale to Ennerdale Bridge and back

It was a chilly overcast morning with high milky clouds and no one else around. A bridge led over the shallow, rocky river Liza to the silvery southern shore of Ennerdale Water, where a narrow path crossed sections of scree and wound between tangles of silver-birch roots, with thick clumps of gorse and banks of heather all about. With no vehicles around the lake, an extra sense of peacefulness and remoteness hung in the air.

On a walk somewhere round Ennerdale, Bill Clinton proposed to Hillary in 1973 on a holiday after they had graduated from Yale

Law School. This knowledge came courtesy of the ever-inquisitive Hunter Davies, who had heard a rumour that it was so and had the opportunity to ask Hillary in person at an event at the US embassy in London. As Davies reports in his book *Lakeland: A Personal Journey*, she confirmed that Bill had popped the question somewhere on the lakeside, though she could not remember the precise spot (and said she had not initially accepted).

Winding along, I began to wonder where the most romantic place and likeliest location for a proposal was on Ennerdale, perhaps the dramatic rocky section toward the western end known as Robin Hood's Chair. It was around there that I bumped into Peter and Helen from Belper in Derbyshire, who were doing the coast-to-coast walk too. Peter wore an olive-green Craghoppers jacket – a newer line than my blue one, I could not help noticing (I was beginning to spot such hiking-clothing things) – and Helen a thick grey fleece. They had stayed at Ennerdale Bridge last night and their bags had been sent ahead to Rosthwaite. I mentioned the Germans and they knew all about them already; the Germans seemed to be blazing a prominent trail across northern England. Peter explained that they were doing the coast-to-coast because "a friend got cancer and I realized: *we've got to do things while we still can*. I'm about to turn fifty." He was a geography teacher and his sister had bought him a suitable present for Christmas – the coast-to-coast walk maps – hoping to encourage them. It had worked. They had set aside a fortnight to complete the 195-mile trek. We parted wishing each other luck. Yet more camaraderie.

Soon afterward, a fell runner (not Finlay) ran past quite fast with a distinctive crab-like side-to-side movement as he negotiated the trickiest boulders, almost floating along despite the careful steps and the awkward terrain. Soon after that, I arrived at the end of the lake, where I crossed a weir, turned inland and bumped into an elderly man with a woolly hat and a sheepdog: "Are you coast-to-coast?" he asked. I said I was not. "A fair few get lost round here." He was speeding along with his sheepdog at twice my pace – I could hardly believe how quickly he was moving – and I remarked on this. He replied: "Aye, she takes me for a walk really. If I don't take her out, she goes bonkers."

Beyond a damp field with a fine draught horse, the village of Ennerdale Bridge appeared. I made a beeline for The Gather community centre/café, which was in a small wooden building. It was a cosy place with a small shop selling items handy for walkers, such as plasters, "toe protector tubes", heel shields, arm slings, "instant ice packs" and ankle supports. Just looking at all the different problems that might crop up made me nervous. I went to the counter and ordered a can of Coke and a coffee.

"Eat in or takeaway?" an assistant asked.

"Drink in," I replied.

The assistant looked at me, as if considering this reply very carefully. "Do you have a table number?" she asked.

"Sorry, I don't," I replied

"I can't give you a coffee if you don't have a table number," she said.

"Do I really need one?" I asked – I would be just over there, I indicated, in a corner with a handful of tables.

"Yes, you do," she said.

"I'll just have the Coke then," I replied. I did not want to walk over between all the tables and return with the table number while holding up others in the queue.

She handed over a can of Coke but would not give me a glass for my Coke. This was because I did not have a table number. I would have to drink it from the can. These appeared to be the rules.

"Could I have a receipt, please?" I asked, just to keep her on her toes, as she was certainly keeping me on mine.

She could not manage this straight away, being unable to work out the till. So I went and sat in the corner where I said I would sit, drinking my Coke from the can. A few minutes later, the assistant came over and wordlessly handed me the receipt.

A peculiar episode.

After drinking my can of Coke, I read a panel on a wall about excellent local conservation work being conducted to encourage freshwater mussels in the river Ehen. Water polluted by fertilizer, silt and leaking septic tanks had been threatening the endangered species, which was not found anywhere else in England and had declined by 90 per cent during the past century. By helping to keep the river water clean, conservationists from the West Cumbria Rivers Trust were protecting both mussels and Atlantic salmon populations. Meanwhile, the salmon also had an intriguing (positive) link with the life cycle of the mussels: larvae released from the river mussels attach themselves to the gills of young salmon, living in the gills for a period before dropping away and eventually becoming fully grown mussels in the depths of the riverbed. Freshwater mussels could live for 100 years, grow to be 15 centimetres long and could filter (and therefore clean) 50 litres of water a day: "More than you use in the shower."

I was learning all sorts about Cumbrian freshwater mussels.

Prince Charles (as he was known at the time) had officially opened The Gather exactly five years to the day before my visit. Signs in big letters on the walls said that Ennerdale was a "LIVING, WORKING, BREATHING LANDSCAPE". And a motto said: "SHAPING THE LANDSCAPE NATURALLY". It was clearly a fantastic scheme (if a little fussy on the table-number front).

Round the corner I stopped at the Fox and Hounds, yet another collaboration among residents of Ennerdale Bridge. The local community had come together to buy the inn in 2011 after it had been closed – raising £67,000 in a remarkable eight days to take over the lease, refurbishing the old interior and, in doing so, saving it from potentially becoming a holiday home or second home. There had been great concern at the time after the closing of a village shop and post office; the community was in danger of dying away. The boarding-up of the pub had been the final straw. Since then, the Fox and Hounds had thrived, exceeding annual targets and benefiting from the steady stream of coast-to-coast walkers dropping by. The pub had become a vibrant community hub, bang in the heart of the village with its distinctive whitewashed facade and old sash windows.

At noon, however, it was empty. Polished wooden tables were laid out on a simple tiled floor beneath a beamed ceiling as a coal fire glowed in the front lounge. I ordered a (very good) ham and pickle sandwich that was a couple of pounds cheaper than any I had bought so far on the hike and a pint of lime-and-soda, also at a good price (and a sure sign you are in a "decent" pub, in my experience). Catchy old pop hits played: "Walk on the Wild Side", by Lou Reed, more than suitable for these parts, "Atomic" by Sleeper and "Bad Moon Rising" by the Creedence Clearwater Revival. No phone connection, but there was Wi-Fi.

Still the only customer, I sat by a window near the fire and called Kasia in Poland. She answered and provided an update on her activities with the Ukrainians. After meeting Lena and Anna at the Warsaw reception centre, where the pair had been given a SIM card with 10 gigabytes of data by the Polish government and where Kasia had handed them £150 in cash from their host in the UK, they had made it to Siedlce. "Lena has a credit card," Kasia said. "I sent them a link to get money from the Polish government and a United Nations fund. She seems a very international lady. She travels a lot, goes on holiday to Egypt often and went to Cuba for a month once. She's fifty-eight years old and an entrepreneur [though Kasia had not yet established what kind]. I don't want to babysit them." They already had itchy feet in Poland. "They want to know where they can go from Siedlce. I told them they could catch a train to Warsaw, and they can go for free on that train and on public transport in Warsaw. They just needed to keep tickets from when they arrived [from Ukraine] and show these and their documents to ticket inspectors."

Poland was leading the way in Europe with housing refugees and also accepting them across its border for travel elsewhere. The country was to go on to accept more than 1.2 million refugees, having around

5 million people from Ukraine pass through (the United Kingdom with its Homes for Ukraine visa scheme lagged way behind).

Kasia said her parents had filled the fridge; her mother had made them soup. "They said they need independence," she continued, hence not wanting to babysit them. "Lena is very self-sufficient. They need to feel they have control over their lives. I'm just leaving that to them. It came together really well. My flight was half an hour late. We went straight to the reception centre. They said they were waiting by the white tent. There were lots of white tents, but it was very well organized actually. I went into a huge tent and called her and she walked over. It wasn't crowded. At the border crossing they had not had to wait. It all went smoothly. There could be another wave from eastern Ukraine, Lena said, as people are realizing the Russians are so brutal. There is already plenty of movement from east to west. She is very determined for Anna to get a good education. Anna used to do ballet every day and she went to an IT school. She knows all the programming languages. She seems really smart. She had really good grades and everything. She was set to go to university in the Netherlands. She's determined. She needs internet for classes. A lot of things could have gone wrong [on the journey from Kiev] but they didn't."

While I was hiking round the Lakes, Europe was turning upside down. With Ukrainian flags in just about every village and so many local newspaper reports on schemes to raise money to send, the troubles were a constant backdrop, even so far away. The world was watching what went on, from every corner. The scenery may have been idyllic in the Lakes, but that was not an adjective suited to events in south-east Europe.

The pub was filling up.

The table opposite, by the fire, had been taken by two women accompanied by a Labrador. The younger woman, middle-aged, was with her mother and she introduced herself. Her name was Mel Comley. I had taken some of the Lakes portable library as well as my laptop and notebooks to the Fox and Hounds to do some research ahead of the next stops in Wasdale Head, Scalderskew and Eskdale, down in the south-west corner of the Lakes. Mel had asked what I was up to. I explained and she said: "I release a book a month and have written over two hundred titles. I've got one coming out later this week." This was entitled *To Make Them Pay*, about "a DI in the Lake District who has a marriage breakdown".

Then she added: "When people ask, I say I kill people for a living [in her crime thrillers]. That's usually a conversation stopper."

She was kindly eyed and casual (jeans, baggy jumper and parka jacket) and lived close to the beach in the village of Seascale, near the enormous Sellafield nuclear power plant, which had ceased making electricity in 2003 and was being decommissioned. This was about 9 miles due south. She and her mother were drinking tea. Mel, who published as M. A. Comley, explained her incredible productivity by describing her working day: "I tend to write from 6 a.m. to 10 a.m. as well as from 8.30 p.m. to 10 p.m." In between, she cared for her mother and took the dog for walks. "I've sold over four million books," she said, having only taken to thriller writing at the age of 35 after working as a supermarket manager for a while. She was self-published and one of her favourite crime writers was Ian Rankin. Her best-selling Justice series had been set in London, accounting for 19 of her titles. "When I became successful sixteen years ago, we lived in France," Mel said, almost shuddering at the memory. "But there was eighty per cent tax. People think the tax here is bad! We had just done up our house, but we sold it, taking a reduction on the value, and just got out of there as soon as we could."

It is not often you sit down in a pub, or anywhere for that matter, next to someone who has written 200 crime thrillers – characters seemed to be lurking just about every place you turned around Ennerdale Water: madcap Germans, champion fell runners, best-selling novelists. I said I would pick up a copy of *To Make Them Pay*. Mel said: "Oh no, please don't!" She seemed shy about her works (and one more sale was not going to make a big difference to her 4 million total, I suppose,

Arrival at Penrith North Lakes Station.

Station Hotel, Penrith.

First glimpse of Ullswater.

Interior of the White Lion in Patterdale.

Daffodils at Glencoyne Bay, inspiration for William Wordsworth's poem "I Wandered Lonely as a Cloud".

Path from Aira Force to Watermillock.

*Red squirrel
protection sign.*

Old Coach Road between Dockray and Threlkeld.

"Pod" for the night at Linskeldfield Farm.

*The award-winning Lakes Distillery,
near Bassenthwaite Lake.*

The River Derwent, Cockermouth.

The Wordsworth pub, Cockermouth.

Kirkstile Inn, Loweswater.

Crummock Water.

Sheep's skull on fence by bog between Crummock Water and Ennerdale Water.

The Innominate Tarn on Haystacks, where Alfred Wainwright's ashes were scattered.

Summit of Scafell Pike, England's highest mountain (978 metres).

The Screes at Wastwater.

Ram near Nether Wasdale.

On the edge of Devoke Water.

Civil Nuclear Constabulary sign on way to Eskdale.

Sheep on platform at Irton Road Station, Ravenglass and Eskdale Railway.

Battered phone box at start of Hardknott Pass.

Encouraging graffiti on Hardknott Pass road.

Car mishap at Wrynose Bottom.

The Sun hotel, Coniston.

Remains of "Bluebird K7" at Ruskin Museum, Coniston.

Levers Water tarn above Boulder Valley.

John Ruskin's grave, Coniston.

Hawkshead village centre.

Hawkshead Grammar School, attended by William Wordsworth.

Beatrix Potter's study at Hill Top Farm, Near Sawrey.

Ukraine flag at St Peter's Parish Church, Sawrey.

Christian Motorcyclists Association annual general meeting at Rydal Hall.

Sunset over Windermere from YHA Ambleside.

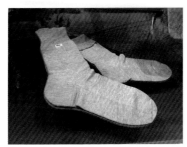

William Wordsworth's socks at Dove Cottage museum.

Bar at Old Dungeon Ghyll, Great Langdale.

View of Great Langdale.

Dam at Thirlmere.

Inside Mosedale Cottage bothy.

Mosedale Cottage bothy.

Outside of Mardale Inn, Bampton.

Sign between Shap and Penrith.

Author on top of The Old Man of Coniston.

though I did buy it anyway). And then I walked back in the rain along the northern side of Ennerdale to the hostel.

Hills, heroes and drones
Ennerdale to Wasdale Head and Wastwater

Characters, as I said, were not short on the ground in the environs of Ennerdale. Back in the lounge at the hostel, Finlay had already arrived. He was eating a lentil stew with Kristin – she had made it and brought it with them to heat up in the kitchen. He wore a fleece, tracksuit bottoms and sandals and told me he had covered 17½ miles running that day, including *3,227 metres of ascent* and *3,222 metres of descent*, taking 5½ hours plus a "thirty-minute break for a flapjack". Instead of taking 7 hours, as he had previously thought, he had gone *even further in 6*. Once again, I was flabbergasted: my 300 metres of ascent and 9 miles the other day, admittedly with a backpack, were put firmly in perspective. Finlay, who was unsurprisingly beanpole thin, talked about fell-running footwear for a while. The soles of fell-running shoes were all important, and complicated: "You've got super sticky, standard rubber and harder rubber, which don't wear out as fast. Then you've got five different types of stud pads: scree, rocky, really wet, boggy and normal." I asked him what he liked so much about running in the mountains and he answered carefully: "The ability to explore the fells without going on trodden routes."

It was this freedom that attracted him to the sport. He found running around tracks, at which he also excelled, dull. Kristin cut in: "At track meets I'll yell 'fifty-nine' at him or whatever when he comes round [59 seconds] for each lap on a five thousand-metre race. He'll be at the back. Then with two thousand metres to go, he turns into a different figure and overtakes everyone."

Kristin, a special-needs teacher, had a story to tell that had nothing to do with athletics and all to do with a very near miss. She had heard me talking to another of the hikers at the hostel earlier about straying into the field of cattle near Penrith. "I had a very unfortunate incident with cows last year," she began. "I was crossing a field and I heard thundering hooves. I looked up and what looked like bulls were charging up a hill. I panicked. I know you're not supposed to. These were long-horned cattle, and they were trying to get at my dog. What was I going to do? I ran away and dived into a shrub near a fence with my dog. I was terrified. If I moved from there, they'd get me. I was hitting them with a stick, poking their noses. They were completely like: *I'm having you.* Finlay had gone off for a run and I was in a field on the side of a hill. I called 999 and they said this is the second time in a week this has happened. Forty-five minutes later the police came with batons and cleared them away. I genuinely thought I was going to die – that I was going to be trampled to death. These things are absolutely horrific. They do say to let your dog go, but I was terrified. If I ever go into a field with cows again, I'll turn around. I don't do cows."

Finlay commented: "If I'm chased, I just run and jump over a wall."

Kristin said she was from farming stock so knew how lucky she had been, but then she added: "In fact more farmers get killed by sheep than by cows. They'll headbutt you really quickly and, once you are down, will trample you. Especially ones with lambs."

So maybe the mean-looking ewes near Cockermouth *were* chasing me off across the field and not seeking food after all. Whichever way, I was glad I had not discovered the answer.

Kirsty came in and served chicken curry to me and the other walkers, a group of three veteran hikers – former prison officers from Solihull – and three women in their twenties. Two of these women were following the St Bega's Way, covering 40 miles from St Bees Priory on the coast to St Bega's Church by Bassenthwaite Lake, and one was doing the coast-to-coast route solo and was an expert hiker who aimed one day to be a long-distance walking guide.

The ex-prison officers included an incredibly talkative man named Eddie, a younger ginger man named Andy (who hardly said a thing) and Steve, in his sixties and wearing a camouflage jacket. They were heading from St Bees to Shap and had cars parked at both ends so they could drive back easily. Eddie asked whether I had done the South Downs Way (then told me and everyone in the room all about it), the West Highland Way (then told me and everyone in the room all about it), the Hadrian's Wall Path (ditto) and the Great Glen Way (ditto). Andy, perhaps having heard the stories before, left the room. Anna, the coast-to-coaster, told Eddie she would be doing the West Highland Way next year, staying in bothies. Eddie shut up for a while and Anna explained that she was doing a Master's at Imperial College on "Environmental Teaching: Environment Assessment and Management", covering the effect of jet fuel on a wetland near Heathrow Airport, and wanted to work for the government or as a consultant for business, on top of being a walking guide. She was a firm believer in Kendal Mint Cake for energy as "that was what Edmund Hillary took up Everest". Anna paused for a split second, and Eddie – seizing the opportunity – began to tell everyone about the Speyside Way Whisky Trail in Scotland. This went on for some time. Then, seeming to have run out of trails to describe for the time being, he went to fetch a beer.

The other two younger women got a word in. One, Emma, was a teaching assistant. The other, Christie, was a National Lottery Heritage Fund employee. They were covering St Bega's Way in three days and had learned about it from the website of the BBC programme *Pilgrimage* after googling "long walk in the Lake District". "Neither of us is particularly religious," said Christie, but they had been attracted to the story of the saint from the early Middle Ages: "She reportedly fled from Ireland as she was avoiding an arranged marriage. She lived in St Bees on the coast for a long time but there were raids from the sea so she moved inland [to the chapel by Bassenthwaite Lake]." Crossing from St Bees to Ennerdale, they had entered a deep forest and Emma said: "We got lost a couple of times and had to climb over barbed-wire fences. Then we saw a dead Herdwick sheep on the track, its face half eaten. The light in that forest was orangey. It felt like there was a haunted energy." They seemed to have enjoyed themselves greatly, nevertheless.

* * *

It was day 14 of this Lakeland circumnavigation. A mist had descended overnight. The hike up to Black Sail Pass (587 metres), on the way to Wasdale Head on the edge of yet another lake, Wastwater, was hazy the next morning. I followed a slowly rising track through conifers and silver-birch trees with the river Liza burbling contentedly to the right. This trail twisted up to Black Sail Hut, a smaller YHA hostel that had been fully booked when I had checked and was even remoter than the one at Ennerdale. Black Sail Hut is the YHA's least-accessible hostel of all in the whole country.

This tiny stone structure was tucked on a rolling hillside close to a narrow section of the Liza. A plaque on the wall said that the Olympic athlete, mountaineer, journalist and YHA benefactor Chris Brasher (1928–2003) had spent his last night of "hostelling" at Black Sail the year before his death. His group of hikers was known as OBOE, which stood for "on the back of an envelope" – the best way to plan mountain expeditions, the members believed. The night Brasher and OBOE had spent at Black Sail Hut in 2002 was "a disgraceful episode at which we devoured fourteen curries and consumed nine bottles of good Australian wine". It seemed to be quite the party hostel with a tiny main room filled with a fireplace and tables squashed together. Board games filled shelves and a little bar was on one side. The hostel dated from the late eighteenth century and was originally a shepherd's bothy before being leased to the YHA by the Forestry Commission.

Rex was among a boisterous group just checking out and setting off down the hill to Ennerdale. "It's genuinely my favourite place anywhere: welcoming, fun, calm and inspirational," he said. Rex had stayed before.

"Last time I came there was a singing group here from Yorkshire. When they had finished their sheet of music, they asked if anyone else had any songs. I found myself singing 'The Wild Rover' and they all joined in. That was just spectacular, the place was full of atmosphere, it always is." These parts were clearly legendary hiker territory.

Beyond the hostel was the steep part to the top of the pass.

Hands were required to negotiate boulders, the toughest obstacles I had faced while carrying the backpack. Wispy clouds drifted about the summits with the famous peaks of Pillar (892 metres) and Great Gable (899 metres) rising through the haze. The path levelled off before reaching stone steps downward into the misty swirl of Mosedale Valley. There were no other hikers. I followed the narrow path down beside drystone walls, passing through the odd gate. The landscape had turned into grassland and coppery bracken. Stepping stones had been arranged across the occasional rock-strewn beck. Cattle grazed on the plain beyond. I stopped for a while simply to admire the immensity of the valley: so awe-inspiring and quite empty. Then the path curved round and reached a cluster of farm buildings and my first fellow walker since Black Sail Hut, a solitary man wearing a cap bearing the message: "NUMBER ONE DAD". This top fell-walking father nodded at me, I nodded back, and I passed a small mossy stone bridge over Mosedale Beck that looked centuries old and about to collapse, arriving at the Wasdale Head Inn, the Lake District's unofficial fell walkers' HQ.

* * *

Being so close to the crags and cliffs of Great Gable, Pillar and Scafell Pike, Wasdale Head Inn was perfectly located for exploration of all the best peaks and ascents, with the big attraction being one of the easiest paths to the top of England's highest summit, Scafell Pike (978 metres), just across the road. I had a room for two nights at this famous resting spot for mountain explorers.

The inn was not exactly a looker: a rectangular beige building over three floors with brown window frames and a prominent car park at the front. Upon entering, you arrived in a ramshackle hall with a collection of dusty old hiking boots on a shelf and a cluttered reception kiosk. Backpacks were heaped on one side and a doorway by the kiosk opened on to a gloomy, deserted dining room featuring a collection of old ropes and pickaxes. A further doorway by the dining room led to a cramped "coffee room" with varnished wooden tables, wooden panels and a few more old boots. A lounge for guests only, with brown sofas, brown curtains and an old grandfather clock (not working), was beside the creaky staircase up to the rooms, which were aligned along a dingy hallway.

I loved it and the reason was simple: nothing much had changed for years and it was all the more impressive for it.

This was no super-slick boutique hotel of the sort that makes the "hip hotel" columns in weekend travel supplements; it had obviously not been done up much for years, beyond the odd splash of paint. What got you though, straight away, was an almost intoxicating sense of mountain-climbing history.

Along the walls just about everywhere you looked were evocative old photos from the early days of mountaineering. There he was in a corner, Walter Parry Haskett Smith (1859–1946), considered by some to be the father of rock climbing in England, an old Etonian who was the first to conquer a terrifying pinnacle of granite known as Napes Needle, on Great Gable, without the use of ropes (in 1886). This was deemed a key moment in popularizing the pursuit, and Haskett Smith then went on to make many other notable first ascents. Captured in profile, hunched over and wearing a trilby, it was hard to catch his personality from his shadowy expression. The picture frame, stained around the edges and not in the best of states, said he had been president of the revered Fell & Rock Climbing Club of the English Lake District from 1913 to 1917.

Close by was a grainy shot of another early British climbing champion, Owen Glynne Jones (1867–1899), who established many other famous Lakeland ascents and was author of the influential book *Rock-Climbing in the English Lake District*, published in 1897. Jones had preferred to refer to himself as O. G. Jones, saying the "O. G." stood for "Only Genuine". In his picture, his back was ramrod straight and ropes were slung around his shoulders as he clutched a climbing stick. He wore a pair of wire-framed glasses and looked more like a bank clerk than a daredevil climber known for his risk-taking prowess and enormous strength (sadly, he was to die in a fall in Switzerland, hence his short life).

Elsewhere, William Cecil Slingsby (1849–1929), another legend who conquered many summits in Norway, peered out from an old frame, with a faraway look in his eyes and wearing a flat cap. Meanwhile, a photograph of Will Ritson (1808–1890), a former landlord, dominated a corner of the coffee room, depicting him smoking a pipe, sporting a cravat and appearing both whimsical and quite content with life in general; this picture was also used as the sign for the Wasdale Head Inn's drinking hole, which was named Ritson's Bar. Ritson was famous for his tall tales and liked to describe himself as the "World's Greatest Liar". His stories told of huge turnips that were so big they were hollowed out to make sheep sheds, coffins being taken to graveyards and being knocked off carts on bumpy tracks to reveal the inhabitants quite alive inside, and eagles mating with hounds. Such was his skill at spinning a yarn (never done with malice) that an annual competition, the World's Biggest Liar competition, is still held in his honour each November at the Bridge Inn at Santon Bridge, just to the south-west of Wastwater.

Ritson's photograph was taken by G. P. Abraham (1846–1923), yet another well-known local from that era, who was a pioneering mountain photographer, proficient climber and also an early postcard maker. He had lived in Keswick and his two sons, George and Ashley, were to take early mountain photography to new levels, providing pictures for Jones' book that were a sensation at the time. These photographs, among others, were all around the reception and the dining room, taken from the mountaintops and showing early ascents of the likes of Eagle's Nest Ridge, the Sphinx and Napes Needle.

Climbers rested atop perilous shafts of stone, nonchalantly gazing down. Others shuffled along edges of sheer cliffs, looking as though someone in the village had asked if they wanted to give it a go and they had replied: "Oh jeepers, why not?" Some wore shirts with sleeves rolled up, others were in waistcoats, ties, tweed jackets, plus fours and flat caps. Ropes seemed casually tied around waists as summits were reached, which required risky passages across narrow snowy ridges in colder months. Back in those days, mountain climbing had been predominantly upper middle class, with some upper-middle-class women climbers among the (mainly) men, plus a few hardy local enthusiasts who helped with both assessment of conditions and by providing their own mountain knowledge.

Many of the latter, however, were rather confused by the influx of posh folk with ropes who wanted to explore the most dangerous parts of the fells. "Eh mon, nobbut a fleein' thing'll ever get up there!" one shepherd said as Haskett Smith prepared for an assault of Scafell Pinnacle. Why risk treacherous cliff faces when there were easier ways round? But back then it had all been jolly japes and high jinks at the Wasdale Head Inn, which was known as the Huntsman's Inn in the mid-nineteenth century. Plenty of whisky was consumed and there was much bravado, by all accounts. After a day clambering up Napes Needle, climbing parties would return to boast about their exploits and also – sometimes – show off their skills and strength by literally climbing about the walls of the inn, especially in the billiard room (as strange as that may sound).

Add to all this a muddy old rucksack that had belonged to Winifred Wood-Johnson (one of the best early female climbers, active from the 1930s to the 1950s) hanging in the dining room, a pair of binoculars from that period, a nineteenth-century camera and dusty books with titles such as *The Fell & Rock Journal*, *High in the Thin Cold Air*, *Lake*

District Rock and *The Best of Ascent* – you had a veritable fell-climbing treasure trove at the Wasdale Head Inn. It was like stepping into a mountaineering museum.

Best of all, though, for a guest checking in, was a picture taken of the reception hall of the hotel from those early days, showing a messy pile of boots, alongside old sticks and ropes dumped on the very same checked tile floor. Not so different from now, give or take a boot and rope or two (plus a few cardboard boxes of deliveries). The connection with the glory days of the past at the Wasdale Head Inn was inescapable.

* * *

Wastwater was my eighth major lake, halfway through the 16 big ones. From Wasdale Head, it was a 20-minute stroll along a damp path through a spot marked on the map as "Down in the Dale". I went to look at the view from the water's edge, such a good one that the Lake District National Park uses this perspective as its logo. The fells plunged into the water on all sides with banks of terrifying-looking scree, known simply as The Screes, to the south (where I would be going in two days). The landscape may have been dramatic and wild, but the water was gentle. Herdwick sheep roamed on the stony beach, poking about in search of food with their wry little smiles and thoughtful countenances. Coots investigated the reeds. The sun was obscured by towering vapours of wispy mist. A peaceful place.

Then I noticed a buzzing. This was coming from a drone and it was hovering above Wastwater. Its owner was strolling my way, a man named Martin from Leeds. He wore a blue jacket that was too big for him and floppy waterproof trousers that looked too big too. He was balding, in early middle age. I was ready to disapprove of Martin and his drone, I will admit, but we got on well enough and he told me all about his (slightly annoying) hobby.

"I can train this at any object and it will follow," Martin said. "It has a battery life of thirty minutes and it will come back if it is about to run out. Legally, it should be in line of sight. I set it to the legal height limit of a hundred and twenty metres of altitude." He aimed the drone, which had returned to its owner like a faithful dog, toward me. "Don't worry, it won't hit you!" The drone tilted my way and purred in a curve around me. "I could put it on 'brake' mode and it would have stopped in front of you, now it is on 'swerve' mode. I have set you as its 'point of interest'."

Martin's drone had had to be registered on the Civil Aviation Authority's website. He made it whizz away from us. "Now it's three hundred and seventy-five metres away and we cannot quite see it," Martin said. "Technically, legally, we should be able to see it." A haze was preventing this. "It could travel as far as five kilometres. I rode along on my bike with it earlier and set myself as the 'point of interest'. What I know about its functions now is just the tip of the iceberg. I've only had it six months. I'm still learning."

A curious pursuit.

Made you wonder what Wordsworth, with his "rules of taste" regarding visits to the Lakes, would have thought.

I walked back past a campsite and a guest house to the inn; aside from the tiny church of St Olaf's, there was not much else to the village of Wasdale Head. The inn was marked "INN" in prominent black lettering on one side, so any walker who happened to be passing by and not in possession of internet reception/an app knew it was there. I bought yet another book – *Hazard's Way* by Roger Hubank, a novel about the heady early days of Lake District climbing – from the inn's Barn Door gift shop, which was in a side building. This work had been recommended to me by the shop's co-owner Nicola, who told me that "last summer it was carnage" up on Scafell Pike as so many people had come, and that "a lot still got lost" despite it being a straightforward route. I ate chilli con carne in a plain wooden booth in Ritson's Bar, next to a table of people with forearms bulging with muscles. Climbers.

"There was one bit where there was quite a drop to the left-hand side. I mean it wasn't a cliff edge. You must have come the same way," said one. There was a buzz of similar discussion all around as well as plenty of après scree-style walker talk, of course. The ghost of "Auld Will", as the former landlord was known, seemed to have floated down and got people's tongues wagging. Wasdale Head Inn was the place to stay for anyone heading to England's highest mountain.

Into the clouds
Wasdale Head to Scafell Pike and back

Which was what I had come for. You cannot really go on a long tramp round the Lake District without tackling the biggie.

On Nicola's advice I started early, setting off at 6 a.m. with Wastwater dead still and woodpeckers echoing in the dale. The stone path rose across a slope that was not too steep at all, before the green dotted line traversed Lingmell Gill and curved upward, ever steeper, toward Hollow Stones.

There was no "carnage" on the way up (this was, after all, mid-April, not the height of summer). There was no anyone, for quite a long time. I had the path to myself, pacing upward into the clouds. The Mountain Weather Information Service predicted a 30 per cent chance of visibility at the top as well as "mostly small" wind and a low risk of showers. It was disappointing about the clouds, but this was the day I had set aside and that was just the way it was in the Lakes (you simply had to suck it up).

A handful of others on the trail were in the same boat, and most seemed to be attempting to complete the Three Peaks Challenge – to ascend the highest mountain in Scotland, Ben Nevis (1,345 metres), the highest mountain in England, Scafell Pike (978 metres), and the highest mountain in Wales, Snowdon/Yr Wyddfa (1,085 metres), preferably within 24 hours. This usually required a driver waiting at the foot of each mountain to whisk the hikers onward. It was often done to raise cash for charity, though not always.

After almost an hour, I met my first fellow hikers. "It took us five and a half hours up and down Ben Nevis yesterday," said David. "There was snow on the ground and we had crampons. Lots of people just had trainers or boots and they had to turn round. You're risking your life there on the snow without crampons. There were five deaths last year. It was like being in the Arctic at the top." He and his friend Khris hoped to do the challenge in 36 hours, a day was just too quick for them, they said. They were taking a rest, so I passed them by.

Mist was slowly rising from a gully like steam from a bathtub. A man wearing shorts and a woolly hat strode down the path at Hollow Stones. He had woken at 5 a.m. and aimed to be back at Wasdale Head Inn for breakfast. I was the third person he had seen all morning. Shortly afterward, I was overtaken at a flat section near Pikes Crag by a man walking a dog. Then the trail veered up, boulders emerged and the path was a little tricky to follow. A pair of Three Peaks Challenge hikers from Poland were coming down an especially rocky section beyond which I arrived at a heap of rocks with a few steps to a plateau: the highest place in England.

No one else was there. It was cold, windy and the summit was above the clouds. Because of the clouds below, you could see *just about nothing*. For a moment a peak poked through the haze to the north-east. This might or might not have been Great End (910 metres). I surveyed the boulders for a while from this lofty position, then I retraced my steps down Scafell Pike, soon reaching Hollow Stones where it was less windy and warmer. A man named Jim Davies was coming up the trail and we stopped to pass the time of day. Jim was a local who worked in "health and safety" at the Sellafield nuclear plant. He said he had climbed Scafell Pike five times already that year. He was wearing a bandana, Lycra leggings and gloves – looking like a regular. Yet while this seemed like a lot, his partner, Lindsay Buck, had made it to the top of England no fewer than 243 times the previous year and 78 so far since January, he said. She was a fell runner, and she was doing it to raise money for the Wasdale Mountain Rescue Team. She was known locally by a nickname, the "Wasdale Womble", and she was somewhere on the mountain at that moment, going up via the tougher Mickledore route. The pair would meet up later and return home by 10 a.m. "for a pot of coffee and the paper".

Jim said both his parents had worked at Sellafield – his father had been a senior physicist – as did Lindsay: "We're a nuclear family." His job was "all about waste handling and cleaning up. There are lots of job opportunities for locals and, because it pays well, there are schools and shops and you can afford to live here". Jim was comparing his corner of the Lake District to the Lakes in general, where prices had been so pushed up by second homes and holiday homes. His house was in the village of Gosforth, just to the west of Wasdale Head. Around 10,000 people worked at Sellafield Ltd and in its supply chain, he said, while the BAE Systems ship and submarine building plant in Barrow-in-Furness also provided key local jobs. It was not all about tourism and farming as far as employment went in the south-west Lake District.

We stood there chatting for quite a while and David and Khris passed by on their way down to pick up their ride to Snowdon. I followed them after a while and returned to the Wasdale Head Inn, where I had a long hot bath.

During the 4-hour round trip, I had seen a total of 81 people, if I counted right. Most of these were at the end, beginning ascents around 10 a.m.

If you want to see Scafell Pike without the crowds… get up early (and try to avoid the summer carnage if you can).

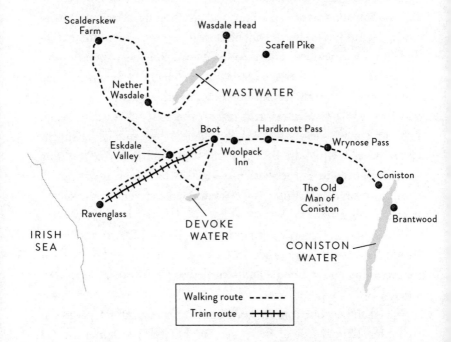

Scalderskew Farm

Wasdale Head

Scafell Pike

Nether Wasdale

WASTWATER

Boot

Hardknott Pass

Wrynose Pass

Eskdale Valley

Woolpack Inn

Coniston

The Old Man of Coniston

Ravenglass

DEVOKE WATER

Brantwood

IRISH SEA

CONISTON WATER

Walking route -------
Train route ++++++

CHAPTER SEVEN

WASDALE HEAD TO CONISTON, VIA SCALDERSKEW, ESKDALE AND RAVENGLASS

"ARE YOU SURE YOU DON'T HAVE A CAR?"

When staying at Wasdale Head Inn you might at times find the hotel short-staffed – and it would have nothing to do with any general shortage of hospitality workers that the Lakes was facing during your visit. The lack of people would be caused by hotel staff having been called into action for the Wasdale Mountain Rescue Team. By the old grandfather clock in the guest-only lounge, I talked to Tim, who carried out odd jobs at the hotel and who worked at Lingmell House B & B, a sister business to the inn. Tim was short in stature, skinny, bald and wore muddy boots, workmen's trousers and a blue-and-green checked jacket. He had pale blue eyes and was both softly spoken and full of stories (and opinions). The sort of person you cannot help but immediately like. He had worked for the local mountain-rescue outfit for 20 years but had retired recently from the service.

I asked him what changes he had noticed around Wasdale in recent times.

"In thirty years, the area hasn't changed at all: the mountains never change," he said. "It's just the number of people and the calibre of the people. In the old days it used to be for walkers and climbers, though you did get the odd casual visitor. Now it's not particularly dedicated to walkers or climbers." Perhaps my experience of the climbers/walkers during the evening at Ritson's Bar had been a blip. "Casual visitors don't really know what they are doing and they don't appreciate the history and geography," Tim continued. "They like to go to the shops in Ambleside and buy trinkets. They don't experience the Lakes at all." He paused, as though sadly considering this. "You just think: *what a waste of time*. The thing is, you're always going to get visitors to the valley who are not intrusive. But now some people have got no respect." He was referring to dog owners not clearing up mess and people dropping litter. "Just put litter in your pocket. Squash the bottle in your rucksack. It's definitely got worse."

Tim, aged 66 and originally from Bury in Lancashire, switched to the subject of mountain rescue: "Many people now depend on their mobile phones for navigation," he said. "Most problems are obviously when the phone runs out of battery and, anyway, it's not a good way to navigate. You've got to have a map and compass, but so many people don't know how to use their compass. I was taught geography in class, so I always did."

How big a problem were serious accidents/fatalities? "Well, I don't know the exact numbers," he said. "One time we might have six [deaths] in a year, other times none. Maybe thirty in the entire time I was doing it." He recalled one time having to talk down a young woman who was contemplating suicide. "I had to stay with her. It was at valley level by the lake. Police and doctors came." Call-outs at night were especially problematic: "Oh yeah, you need torches, and it can be a lot colder, and it can be bad weather."

There were around 40 people connected to the Wasdale Mountain Rescue Team. "You hope to get about twenty on a rescue. Sometimes more or less." Often help was needed on the most dangerous crags. "There have been various people who are not climbers and find themselves on a crag. It could be someone injured after losing their balance or maybe they've lost their bottle. It's a technical job. Any crag is a potential problem."

Tim used to visit from Bury as a teenager and go camping and climbing. This was when he fell for the Lakes: "We were lads. We'd go to Napes Needle. That's my favourite. Any region with mountains does attract me, but the thing about the Lakes that's unique is that it's so compact and it's not particularly high. But it's just as thrilling and dangerous. In Scotland and Ireland it's similar but it's slightly more spread out. I love New Zealand too, thirty years ago I went for four months."

I asked Tim, such a veteran of the mountains, what the most important advice was for any fell walker or climber. He paused and thought carefully once again. "Well, somebody said to me a very long time ago, just before I joined the team, when we were helping out the BBC carrying loads for a shoot: 'Never be afraid to turn back.' People often know they are in trouble, and they carry on and make it worse. If you're not sure, don't be afraid to turn back. Don't let pride take over. It's not a wuss thing to do."

Advice, perhaps, that could be followed on the mountains – as I had found through necessity on my rash ascent of Blencathra – as well as many other areas of life.

I thanked Tim and we shook hands by the grandfather clock.

It was time to move on.

Screes, sheep and a shepherd's hut
Wasdale Head to Scalderskew, via Nether Wasdale

As I did so, four peals of thunder passed above – at least they sounded like thunder. In reality, it was a squadron of four RAF Tornado jets on a training exercise, flipping on to their sides and curving round Yewbarrow fell in the flash of an eye. The first fighter jets I had seen in the Lakes (but definitely not the last).

I watched them go and was joined by Nigel Burton, the owner of Wasdale Head Inn, who had overheard me talking to Tim. He was a 64-year-old ex-banker who had bought the inn 20 years ago and decided from the outset that he did not want to create a "boutique hotel". He lived in Islington in London and came up to the inn once a month to check all was well. Like Tim – and like myself, for that matter – he had become a Lake District convert in his teens, when coming on scout trips. He was doing the Wainwrights and said he enjoyed many of the smaller peaks more than star fells such as Scafell Pike: "Even though they may be much lower, there are usually fantastic panoramic views all around you. It's only when going to some of the lesser-known parts of the Lakes that you realize you don't need such exertion. Everything round here is hard work!" He was referring to Wasdale Head.

The subject soon turned to staffing. "It's been a nightmare," he said.

"We can't have people coming off the mountain and we're saying to them: 'Tough, the restaurant's closed, the next one is nine miles away.' So, we've simplified the menu and added a catering trailer at the back." I complimented him on Ritson's Bar food portions and he replied: "Well, some bean counter would probably do it differently. But if you've just done a twenty-mile walk, you're hungry."

Regarding Brexit and the effect on Britain's workforce, Nigel said: "We can't rely on foreign staff permanently. A lot of foreigners have left here for London and the south-east." Staff shortages elsewhere meant that pay had improved and become more tempting. This was true for locals too. "They are sucked away to the central Lakes or to Blackpool." This was, he said, quite understandable, the desire to seek higher wages. "Chefs are particularly mobile. Two years ago, a chef's salary could be twenty-one thousand pounds, now the expectation is twenty-six thousand pounds. It might not seem like a lot but it's a big difference. The number of people through the kitchen is unbelievable, frightening." With such a fast turnover the problem was that "you get one order wrong, one bad order, and the Tripadvisor review is dreadful forever". Such was the staff shortage he had occasionally worked tables himself on his visits.

Seeing I was all set to go on the way to Scalderskew Farm about 10 miles away, where I had booked a converted shepherd's hut for the night, Nigel – who seemed quite happy to chew the cud all morning outside his inn (maybe he had Keswick blood in him) – popped inside and returned with a small informative book entitled *Wasdale Head and the Inn: A History* by Bob Bennett. I added this to the portable Lakeland library and thanked him, both for the book and an excellent stay.

* * *

Wastwater had a copper-grey sheen that morning, reflecting the crags and bracken of the fells. The surface had been turned into a million little ripples in the breeze and the effect was of an abstract painting lying in the lake. Around the southern shore, the path rose and became steadily rockier. The sound of car engines came from the opposite side, where the lane to the inn ran. No chance of a road by The Screes, which seemed to rain down from the fells in a waterfall of stone. The path was narrow but well-worn by hikers, and walking on the smaller scree produced a sound like shaking dominoes in a bag. Bumblebees buzzed in the gorse. Then, before long, heavier scree began with little vegetation at all, just endless boulders.

Tim had advised to "keep low" across the larger scree: "The temptation is to go up and look for a better route." That would be a waste of time, he said, as every way across was just about the same. So I entered the Armageddon of stone, carefully; each footstep requiring concentration. It was both a physical and mental workout. No switching off. At one section, where the stone was looser and I was close to the water, I slipped slightly, meaning I had to put a hand down to prop myself up. Just as I did so, a group of half a dozen men in their early twenties was passing above. One of them said: "This is the path." And, with that – no "Are you ok?" – he continued on his way. His voice was perfect-tone English public school. How he could know exactly where the path was, I could not fathom. The way ahead was just about impossible to discern.

At the end of the lake, The Screes finally navigated, there was a stone barn-like building and, across the way, a large mock-Tudor mansion of the sort that Wordsworth would probably not approve. Soon afterward, past a paddock containing two extraordinarily tough-looking sheep with mad curling horns – I took them to be rams – I arrived at the quaint village of Nether Wasdale and ordered a pint and a sandwich at the Strands Inn, a sister pub to the Screes across the way, although that was closed for renovations. The best part of Nether Wasdale (population: small) seemed to consist of pubs. I ate my hummus and red onion sandwich and drank my Scafell Summit pint (smooth, creamy and hard to resist with that name) beneath beams hung with dried hops and horse brasses. Scafell Summit was produced by Strands Brewery, making me wonder exactly how many breweries there were in the Lakes. An empty table close by had a little notice on it: "RESERVED FOR LOCALS". I finished my late lunch and went outside to look for a sycamore tree.

According to information on the Strands Inn menu, the poet Samuel Taylor Coleridge had come to the inn while on a long, nine-day walk around the Lakes in 1802. He had written in a letter to his lover, Sara Hutchinson, that he had enjoyed "a good dish of tea" at the quiet pub and was penning his words beneath "the shade of a huge sycamore tree" that was "twenty strides from the door". Coleridge, it should be noted, wrote what is believed to be the first account of climbing Scafell Pike during that trip, using his trusty portable ink horn and a stash of paper. Indeed, he had almost come a cropper crossing to England's highest mountain via a series of perilous ledges on a route called Broad Stand that most amateur walkers avoid like the plague. This is his gripping account, as told in a letter to Sara Hutchinson at the time, of his brush with death:

> And now I had only two more [ledges] to drop down – to return was impossible – but of these two the first was tremendous, it was twice my own height, and the ledge at the bottom was exceedingly narrow, that if I drop down upon it I must of necessity have fallen backwards and of course killed myself. My limbs were all in a tremble. I lay upon my back to rest myself, and was beginning according to my custom to laugh at myself for a Madman, when the sight of the Crags above me on each side, and the imperious Clouds just over them, posting so luridly and so rapidly northward, overawed me. I lay in a state of almost prophetic Trance and Delight and blessed God aloud for the powers of Reason and Will, which remaining no Danger can overpower us!

The author of the "Rime of the Ancient Mariner", also renowned for his opium eating (and for upsetting his friend Wordsworth due to that habit), was extremely fortunate to have survived.

His sycamore tree outside Strands Inn, however, was nowhere to be found.

As I was about to leave Nether Wasdale, having inspected a likely candidate of a tree near a wooden smoking booth, a man from inside the booth addressed me. His name was Peter and he was aged 82, a former a lieutenant commander in the Royal Navy. He had retired to the nearby market town of Egremont. He asked me why I had been looking at the tree and said: "I don't think it's two hundred years old and I don't think it's a sycamore." He seemed quite pleased with that statement, wittily delivered. He wore a baseball cap and was tall and skinny, with a bushy grey beard and a broad, gap-toothed grin. Then, seeming even more pleased with the prospect of what he was about to say, he added: "Perhaps it was poetic licence."

He paused and said: "Maybe if you wait here long enough, he'll turn up."

He was referring to Coleridge. He seemed especially pleased with that, beaming even further.

"So how are you getting about?" he asked.

I explained I was walking.

"But where's your car?" he asked.

I explained I did not have one. "So where did you start?" he asked.

I told him about Penrith. "Are you sure you don't have a car?" he asked.

I said I was sure.

"You're not Wainwright's son, are you?" he asked, especially amused with that joke.

Then he proceeded to tell me, at some length, all about how he would be visiting London soon to attend his 22-year-old granddaughter's graduation at the Royal Albert Hall. When he had finished, I wished him luck with that venture. We shook hands as we parted, and he seemed to be chuckling to himself as I plodded up the lane.

* * *

On the edge of Nether Wasdale the flag of the county of Cumbria, the Lake District's home of course, fluttered outside a house, the first time I had noticed it: green at the top, with three white flowers (Parnassus flowers found in the fells) and a series of blue and white swirls below (representing the lakes). Down another lane to the right and up a hill with a great many sheep and no lambs, thankfully – Kristin had me worried about psycho headbutting ewes – the path led beyond Yew Farm to a forest and a section of a low fell from which you could see the Irish Sea, a floor of grey beneath the cinnamon-silver afternoon sky. Looking the other way, The Screes rose in the distance, plunging into the vast depths of Wastwater, the deepest lake in the Lakes. It felt well off the beaten track round those parts.

Dogs barked in the valley as I entered a long track through a forest. For the first time, I tried a walking app for directions, but there was poor reception and it suggested a frankly weird route. I stuck to the Ordnance Survey map and came to a blockage of a fallen tree that required my scrambling down a steep bank by a stream, following the water and scrambling back up. Next came a larger obstacle: the river Bleng, a good 5 metres across. Although there were meant to be stepping stones, I could not find them, so I went extremely cautiously from one scattered boulder to another above the rushing water and was glad to reach a boggy plain on the other side. Across that plain and up a track next to a field with (gentle) ewes and lambs, I arrived at Scalderskew Farm and my converted pistachio-coloured shepherd's hut.

It was an extremely smart converted pistachio-coloured shepherd's hut with a key in a locker. I used the number I had been sent and retrieved the key and entered a space that was much larger than my previous pod – it included a tiny kitchen and bathroom on the right and a comfortable double bed on the left. In the middle was a cobalt-blue sofa with an excellent view over a deck with a table and two chairs to the empty fells, which once again reminded me of America's Wild West. A sign on the wall said: "HOME SHEEP HOME". By an egg-rack another sign said: "HAVE A CRACKING DAY". The instincts of tabloid journalism seemed alive and well among the sign-makers for the Lake District's habitable shepherd's huts.

Claire Whitaker, who ran Scalderskew Farm with her husband, Leigh, came to join me on the deck. She wore a burgundy jumper and had short blonde hair and an easy manner. She pointed out the fells, crags and moors ahead: Caw Fell, Gowder Crag, Seatallan and Stockdale Moor. And she told me she was not just a farmer, but also "a wife, a mother [of two children aged nine and two], a bookkeeper, a self-catering-accommodation provider and an auction-house worker". The latter job was at a farming auction house. Leigh worked both on the farm and as a machinist at BAE Systems at Barrow-in-Furness. The farm had just opened its solitary shepherd's hut, bought to order, to supplement its income, which was precarious due to uncertainty about what would replace the European Union's Common Agricultural Policy (CAP) once it was finally removed in the aftermath of Brexit (due to happen in 2024).

"Farming has always been subsidized so people can buy cheap food," she said, as her collie (named Mollie) joined us. "Because of Brexit there's going to be a new British agricultural policy. But in true British government style it all seems quite last-minute and has not been imparted yet. It looks pretty bleak at the moment."

Claire was critical of the pressure being put on farmers to become more eco-conscious when cash was tight and policies muddled. "The buzzwords now are 'carbon storage' and 'sequestering carbon' but that moor and that fell is all peat, it's massive carbon storage," she said, pointing ahead. "They want us to work out how much the landscape is storing and absorbing. But how do we do that? As farmers we feel as though we are being backed into a corner because people just seem to want to plant trees. They think that trees will absorb carbon. But sheep absorb carbon, they are eating the grass and encouraging more to grow on the fell, and that is sequestering carbon. Some activists want sheep off the fells. They have a magic number: half a livestock unit per hectare. Five sheep per hectare, I think. Vegans think they are going to save the world. I don't want to get into arguments with vegans, who say farming's cruel and evil and everything else. But we work hard and we put the care of the animals first and foremost. In their ideology animals should be free to breed as they want and run free." In practice, it could not work like that, she said.

Claire explained the hefting system by which the sheep went on to the fells and knew the terrain that "belonged" to them, ingrained in their memories and passed on from ewe to lamb. Scalderskew Farm was made up of 100 acres, leased from a private landlord, with 600 Herdwick and Swaledale sheep and 20 Aberdeen Angus cows (reared until 12 months old and sold on) and one bull. The farm was at 220 metres. Claire said that they sold wool, but it was "worth a pittance". Lambs had been born in the field by the hut earlier that day. "Because these are fell sheep, they're later lambing than sheep lower down in the Lakes," she said, explaining that while they ran free on the fells beyond the farm boundaries for much of the year, it was always difficult to gather every single one for the key period of giving birth. "There will always be a few out there on the fell, a handful. We get them ultra-scanned in February. If a sheep is barren, she is culled out, if over a certain age. Yearlings are taken to lower ground as there's usually better food."

Swaledale sheep were more productive than Herdwicks for lambs. "We 'finish' ours and sell them when they're fat for food," Claire said. "We weigh them here on the farm. At a certain weight, thirty-eight kilogrammes and above, they are 'ready'. If one feels skinny, it's not ready. If it's fleshy, it is ready and we go to the abattoir, who gives the lamb a grade and we are paid according to that."

She said their closest farming neighbours were 25 minutes away by car. "We see a few walkers, but not many," she added; but as she spoke, something strange happened. Two hikers were coming up the farm track.

"We've never been so popular!" said Claire. "I hope they haven't booked the shepherd's hut too!" Then she noticed that the woman coming up the track was holding a lamb, cradled in a scarf. She yelled across the field to Leigh, who was on a quad bike: "This lady's got a lamb off the fell!"

The woman came up to us and said: "It's so cold." The lamb's little black face was pointing out of the scarf, shivering. The couple, locals, had been on a walk and heard it "making a racket, bleating at the top of the hill, a quarter of a mile away you could hear it".

Within a few minutes the lamb was warmed up and saved, and the walkers went on their way. "Some mothers run away, traumatized by the birth," said Claire, before adding with a note of amused resignation: "I'm the lamb magnet! Another pet lamb to feed!" She looked across the field: "Maybe one of those ewes could have a dead lamb so there's a chance that it may be taken up."

I asked if Claire had ever had three people walk up in a day. "Nooooo," she replied. Scalderskew really was out on the edge of the Lakes.

Claire told me I had been her very first booking for the new shepherd's hut, reserved a couple of months earlier, although guests had stayed the previous week. Bookings had been steady; someone was arriving the next day to stay for two nights. Claire advised me to look out for jays, cuckoos, chaffinches, goldfinches, blackbirds, long-tailed tits, curlews, barn owls and snipe – and returned to the seemingly never-ending business of running Scalderskew, Mollie scampering by her side.

A farmer's life high on the fells in the Lakes was like no other. You got that straight away.

"The dark one" and a few inns
Scalderskew to Eskdale

Mist hung on the forgotten fells of Scalderskew the next morning. A dreamy-eyed ewe lay in the field behind a picket fence, chewing the cud and watching the local tourist (me). Long-tailed tits skipped here and there waking up worms. Sheep across the way clattered at a metal feeding station as a quad bike rumbled faintly in the distance and water trickled in a beck. I took off down the track leading to Eskdale. I had a long way to walk.

After Scalderskew you soon entered a conifer forest. Many of the trees lay collapsed by the side of the rough dirt track (the only access to Scalderskew), looking like a giant game of pick-up-sticks. This devastation was the result of Storm Arwen of November 2021, according to a notice warning to be careful. The damage had cut off the farm, which had been without power for 36 hours and a clear road for longer still, Claire had said. Yet more evidence of climate volatility in the Lakes.

The air smelled of resin. Startled wood pigeons flapped wildly. I crossed a bridge over the river Bleng, my nemesis of yesterday, following a path that necessitated ducking beneath fallen trees, and reached the village of Wellington. There, I turned left and went up a hill, passing Hawkbarrow Farm, from where a cacophony of moos emanated as though the cows were either in a state of great distress or having a bovine rave of some description. Near this farm, a sign had been posted on a fence by the Civil Nuclear Constabulary, which I had not previously known existed. It said: "ARMED POLICE PATROL THIS AREA AT UNPREDICTABLE TIMES". This must have had something to do with the proximity to the Sellafield nuclear plant, about five miles west.

I took a turn for Gaterigghow, moving along a lane lined with pretty Parnassus flowers. A cockerel crowed. A woodpecker pecked. I crossed the river Irt and came to another Civil Nuclear Constabulary sign near Hulling Farm, before winding onward to Santon Bridge and the Bridge Inn, where the World's Biggest Liar competition was held. Afterward, along a mossy path, I arrived at a bridleway where a woman on a horse named Joey – she said he was "a cobb horse cross with a fell pony" – gave me directions along a woodland path that required clambering around more fallen trees. After that, a lane passed a Union Jack on a flag post by the Bower House Inn, and then I paused for a while to watch a steam train rolling along the tracks of the Ravenglass and Eskdale Railway, a long white caterpillar trail of vapour evaporating slowly as the carriages rattled by. I had not seen another walker all morning.

My target for lunch was the King George IV Inn on the edge of the village of Eskdale Green. I sat at a picnic table on its terrace, gazing across at the fells and crags that led up to Devoke Water, another of the 16 main lakes although it is officially classified as a tarn; its name means "the dark one". A kindly elderly man at a table next to mine asked me about my walk and said of his own perambulations: "At my age it's always a leisurely walk. Nowadays the strong temptation is to do nothing. I used never to be able to sit still. That is no longer the case."

I ate a very good ham and tomato sandwich that was just as reasonably priced as the one at the Fox and Hounds at Ennerdale Bridge. I drank a lime-and-soda, again a decent price. Another local looked at my map when I asked about the best way to Devoke Water and then onward to the Woolpack Inn, where I was staying, close to the beginning of the Hardknott Pass. He said: "Aye, that would be the way I'd go." So off I went up a steep, long, twisting lane past a kennel of howling hounds, eventually reaching Devoke Water, a desolate spot where I took off my boots and socks and rested my feet in the water: highly refreshing after the long stomp.

A bird of prey swooped above; a little tree-covered island on the far side of the wide bowl of the lonely lake was shaped like a hedgehog. Devoke Water was mysterious, hidden up in the hills with just a couple of other hikers about. Evidence of Bronze Age settlements were said to be found hereabouts, but I did not spot any. I was soon heading down a fell with a fine eastward view of Scafell Pike and getting extremely lost on a craggy hillside, where I seemed to be following a "path" for a while, before this "path" abruptly disappeared and I was scrambling over boulders and apparently treading where few ramblers had wittingly trod before. Then the "path" would emerge once more, before disappearing once again and re-emerging – and going through this pattern at regular intervals. This path-no-path sequence had been keeping my faith alive in the "path". *Perhaps this was just a poorly maintained "path"*, I reasoned. The result was, eventually, a humiliating U-turn and a great deal more scrambling before following a stream in a woodland and arriving, exhausted and hot (it was the sunniest day yet), at the valley floor and the Brook House Inn. There, I ordered both a pint of lime-and-soda and a pint of Loweswater Gold and sat in the narrow front garden, with my pints next to one another on a plank-like table attached to a metal fence, gazing up at the golden sunlight on the crags where I had just been so off course, thinking: *never again thank you very much, dear God of the Lakes* (should such a God exist).

On a nearby table, a stag party had gathered, the groom dressed as a bishop. Quite a few walkers were out and about on the lane, where a Tesco delivery vehicle and an Amazon delivery vehicle for a while created mayhem trying to pass one another (the modern world intruding rudely on the idyllic setting). Feeling back to normal – the diversion to Devoke Water had taken it out of me – I walked the last ¾ mile to the Woolpack Inn, a large place ranging over a series of connected black-and-white buildings next to a campsite. An FA Cup semi-final between Liverpool and Manchester City was being shown on a big screen in the packed bar, with supporters of both sides yelling at the players from time to time and, at appropriate moments, applauding, cheering and groaning. I sat for a while next to a couple from Runcorn in Cheshire. They were Liverpool supporters and the man kept saying: "We've got this!" Liverpool was ahead. I commented that the Manchester City players looked tired after a big European match a few days earlier; he turned to me and said: "*Tired? Tired?* Excuses! On two hundred and fifty thousand pounds a week you can't be *tired!*" Liverpool went on to win three–two.

Out by the firepit in the garden, I called Kasia, who updated me on the Ukrainians. "They seemed better this afternoon," she said. A day earlier it appeared they had been crying when she had gone to see them, as their visas for entry to Britain had not come through yet. This was a major problem for many applying for asylum in the United Kingdom.

"I gave them a number for psychological help if they needed it," Kasia said. "They need to go to a visa centre now. They have already set up a Polish bank account. They have done some shopping in Warsaw and got some free stuff from a refugee centre. They seemed in better spirits, a better mood than the day before. My mum knocked to say happy Easter and give them some food and Lena said to her: 'Maybe we'll stay here, we like it so much.' She said it feels like a vacation to them right now. She would have stayed in Kiev if it wasn't for Anna, but she wants Anna to get a good education. They're not demanding and expecting us to do everything. I like them a lot."

Lovely valley, lovely ride
The Ravenglass and Eskdale Railway

The Woolpack Inn was a mile from the terminus of the Ravenglass and Eskdale Railway at Dalegarth Station on the outskirts of the village of Boot. With two nights booked at the inn, I had a day free so I went for an excursion on the 7-mile narrow-gauge heritage line to the furthest south-west point I would visit in the Lakes.

Yes, you might say I was cheating by taking the railway, originally opened in the late nineteenth century to transport iron ore. However, I wanted to experience the ride, I intended to walk back and, on top of that, the railway had a distinguished hiking pedigree: Alfred Wainwright no less had written a short book entitled *Walks from Ratty*, highlighting a series of hikes that could be made along the line. "Ratty" was the local nickname for the railway and Wainwright had been a big fan, describing the Eskdale valley through which it rolled as one of the "loveliest" in the Lakes, descending from "the highest and wildest mountains in the district to the Sands of Ravenglass in a swift transition from bleak and craggy ridges to verdant woodlands and pastures watered by a charming river".

I bought a ticket for the 10.30 train to Ravenglass from a ticket office close to a "bat tower" on the platform, home to a large number of roosting bats, though I never saw any. I ate a bacon sandwich and had a coffee at a table on the tranquil platform with a view straight ahead of Scafell Pike. Was this Britain's most peaceful and loveliest station? A shiny green locomotive called the *River Irt* chugged into view, puffing, rasping and hissing. The skinny, bearded driver wore a flat cap, a red bandana and overall-trousers. He repositioned the loco at the correct end of the carriages, ready for the return. He shovelled some coal into the engine, checked the oil and went to get a cup of tea, saying as he did: "Never set off without a brew!"

With a whistle and a hoot and more hissing of steam, we were soon off, clanking, clicking, ticking, tilting, juddering and clattering toward Ravenglass in our little toy train. I had a tiny compartment to myself. Sunlight bathed the fells and the rare sensation of moving without walking was quite splendid, as it had been back on the train into the quarry at Threlkeld. Cattle looked up from a field. The familiar facade of the King George IV Inn came into view by the winding lane up to Devoke Water. We stopped at Irton Road Station, where a sheep was running free along the platform and the conductor waved and whistled at it to go away (it must have got through a fence).

Onward we rolled through silver-birch woodland and alongside drystone walls and land full of reeds and heather. A Ukrainian flag hung by a remote cottage. Lambs gambolled about here and there, staring at the train as though hardly believing their eyes. An estuary was soon unveiled, with oystercatchers picking their way gingerly through the marshland, and shortly afterward we pulled into a station and I met Keith Herbert, railway controller of the Ravenglass and Eskdale Railway, with whom I had arranged an appointment.

Keith was in a signal box at the end of the platform and had a dark, bushy beard and rosy cheeks, looking more like a fisherman than a railwayman. He was aged 35, from Seascale and had been working for Ratty for a dozen years, originally as a driver. Inside the signal box room was a series of levers and a desk with a view of the tracks and a few old carriages that had been converted into unusual holiday lets. On a good year, more than 100,000 passengers took journeys on the line, being pulled by one of five steam locos or four diesel locos. "It's a pleasure to welcome that many people to this side of the Lakes," Keith said. "Ambleside and Keswick are rightly popular but there's plenty to see here for those who make the extra journey."

Did he enjoy his job? "Oh yes," he said. "Becoming a steam-train driver was the archetypal boyhood dream come true. I never imagined it would happen." Keith still got to drive the locos despite his promotion.

The line had 20 permanent staff, 40 seasonal staff and 100 volunteers. Keith paused in his explanation of the railway as a radio crackled and he said into it: "You may proceed to Irton Road!" Hearing the name of that station, I asked him about sheep on the line. "Yes, we do have sheep quite often. We try to keep cordial relations with farmers – and keep fences fixed." Did any ever get killed? "Very rarely." One a year? "Not even that often," he replied, before recalling his most unusual passenger ever: "I remember I stopped a train once at one of the stations and a sheep got off. I wasn't even sure when it got on."

Sheep seemed just about everywhere in the Lakes, even hitching free rides on heritage railways.

Nowhere seemed safe from the creatures.

* * *

A museum by the station, which was connected to a main-line station with trains running along the Cumbrian coast, went into the full history of the line (in some detail). I ambled into the little village of Ravenglass, the only coastal village within the boundaries of the Lake District National Park, where yet another Ukrainian flag fluttered – this time on a pole overlooking the estuary of the river Esk. The Drigg Dunes and Gullery Nature Reserve rose across the way, its sandy bumps looking like some sort of secret Cumbrian desert. Ravenglass was a quiet, charming spot with its tea room, couple of pubs by the water and pleasant-looking cottages.

To complete my increasingly comprehensive survey of the inns of the Eskdale valley (and the Lake District in general), I went for lunch at the Ratty Arms pub, which overlooked the platforms of the mainline station, and sat at a booth made of old train carriage seats. Good value yet again – decent bitter though the sandwich was a tad small. I was, I realized, becoming something of a connoisseur of the sandwiches and pints of the Eskdale valley (and the Lake District in general). This can happen to you on a long hike around the Lakes.

Then I walked back past the entrance to Muncaster, a "magnificent haunted castle" with "Himalayan gardens", according to a sign, though I was in my stride so did not stop. Beyond this castle, a dusty track led up a hill through Wainwright's rolling "verdant woodland". I followed the signs to the village of Boot, soon coming to the Eskdale Golf Course, where no one was playing golf. I bumped into Simon, the head greenkeeper, who said: "It's a short and tricky course. It's not as easy as people think as it's in a tight bit of land. It was built for one person originally. He did it on a floodplain, so the course does flood." The best golf course in the Lakes was Windermere Golf Club, on the east side of Windermere, he said.

Beyond, the path was long and mainly flat. I got a good pace going without the backpack, arriving at Boot and going directly to The Boot Inn, hidden down a lane behind the Brook House Inn. I sat at a picnic table in its gorgeous pub garden full of azaleas, daffodils, roses and birdsong, simply enjoying the moment.

Many fine pubs in Eskdale valley, it had to be said – perfect walker territory.

No wonder Wainwright was inspired to write his extra little book on the Ratty.

Romans, car crashes and a "good effort"
Eskdale to Coniston, via Hardknott Pass and Wrynose Pass

News from Ukraine in the morning was grim. A former official from Mariupol had described the Russian siege of the city as having effectively created a concentration camp in the remaining stronghold, a former steelworks. There had been early-morning missile strikes in both Kiev and Lviv, where black smoke hung in the sky above the old city as the reporter on the BBC's *Today* programme spoke. I had visited Lviv a few years earlier for my book *Slow Trains to Venice* and had loved it, such a peaceful, attractive city. What was going on in Europe? Kasia texted me to say that Lena had had her visa approved to enter Britain, but not Anna. They had become extremely anxious about what to do next. Kasia was advising them to hold on, not just turn up together at the border as this could cause a problem, a potential black mark on their records. The wait for Anna's papers went on, but at least some progress was being made.

Clouds had returned to the Lakes. It was not the best of days. The receptionist at the Woolpack Inn had asked me where I was going next. When I said Coniston, he had replied: "Wow, you are going to walk?" He was a skinny man in his twenties and seemed genuinely dumbstruck by the idea. The distance was 14 (hilly) miles after all. I asked about a Roman fort that lay ahead, just beyond the entrance to the Hardknott Pass, which led to Wrynose Pass and then to Coniston.

He said: "To be honest, I've never been. People say it's nice. It's a long way up there."

In half an hour or so, however, I was at the Hardknott Roman Fort, having crossed the quiet valley while admiring a field of Belted Galloway cattle and inspecting an almost destroyed old public phone box. This had a notice attached saying it was "available for adoption", should you wish to possess an almost destroyed old public phone box from the valley of Eskdale. A road sign next to this ruined phone box said that the slope ahead rose to a gradient of 30 per cent and was "unsuitable for all vehicles in winter conditions". I had not yet seen a car go past along the single-track lane.

The Roman fort, up a steep slope at the beginning of the Hardknott Pass, was impressive in position (with commanding views), but less so in what remained of it (unsurprisingly, given its age and exposed location). Much of the surrounding wall was there, 3 metres thick in places; the entire plot of the fort was roughly 150 metres by 100 metres. I entered and read the display panels by various foundation stones, explaining that they had once been the sites of a commanding officer's house, a headquarters and a granary. The Romans had concentrated their interest in the north of England along Hadrian's Wall and a series of forts along the Cumbrian coast. Within the wild and dangerous territory of the Lakes, they had not bothered much to defend the land as no one really seemed that keen on invading. I tried to cast my mind back in time: to imagine Italians posted to this desolate spot 2,000 years ago to create order and "empire". Human beings can sometimes be so determined (and odd).

Hardknott Pass was steep and exceedingly twisty, rising to a height of 393 metres before descending quite a bit and leading to a bridge over the river Duddon; here it ceased to be the Hardknott Pass any more and you hiked along the river for a while and entered a new pass, Wrynose Pass, rising once again to precisely 393 metres.

From the Roman fort, I intended to curve southward to Coniston Water, another major lake, where I had a room booked in a famous old Lakes hotel in the small town of Coniston for two nights. There were steeper shortcut routes to Coniston with names like Hell Gill Pike, Black Spouts and Wet Side Edge, but I did not fancy them with the backpack and the growing portable library.

* * *

So, I was taking the longer route via Hardknott and Wrynose. The single-track road zigzagged onward like a ribbon in a breeze. I tried to keep to the springy grass by the road as it was less gruelling than the Tarmac. There were no other hikers, just an occasional car. I would not have been able to complete this walk at the start of this hike back in Penrith, I realized halfway along; I seemed to have become slightly fitter, Lakeland trim. As though it had read my mind as I thought this, I came to a spray-painted message on the road that said: "GOOD EFFORT".

Thank you, whoever wrote that.

On the valley floor at Wrynose Bottom, a solitary walker with a stick was coming the other way. I asked him, hiker to hiker, if he had come far and he replied: "From that car." He pointed to a car parked 50 metres away. He was, however, about to do a long loop of the fells. He was in his seventies and it was inspiring to see someone that age who remained so enamoured by the scenery and so fit.

A wolf-like howl emanated from the direction of a fell called the Pike of Blisco. Along a river I followed the lane, stopping to inspect a red Ford Focus that had tumbled off the road into the water. The driver's door was hanging open and the vehicle was almost vertical, with its back wheels on the riverbank and bonnet in the stream. No one was about. It seemed to have been a recent accident. As I was looking at it, another car pulled up. "You all right?" the driver asked. She thought I had been in the crash. I explained I was just walking by and that the car must have come off the road the day before, to which she replied: "Yes, quite spectacularly. We'll be going slowly from now on."

The road wound up Wrynose Pass, the walk across the desolate valley every bit as exhilarating and satisfying as ascending Scafell Pike, in its own way.

A buzzard circled above Wrynose Fell. Chaffinches flittered in the grass. A cycling club of MAMILs (middle-aged men in Lycra) wearing yellow jerseys with "BARROW" written on them struggled up the fell to the high point, where a plaque explained that this used to be the meeting place of three counties: Cumberland, Westmorland and Lancashire. Cumberland and Westmorland had been amalgamated in 1974 and parts of Lancashire added to create Cumbria.

All of this, however, was shortly to change. The next year, extremely confusingly, the county of Cumbria was due to be split into two entirely new councils: Cumberland in the west and Westmorland and Furness in the east. This, dear reader, ought to have happened by the time of publication of this book. The current Cumbria County Council, deeming the change unnecessary (and fighting for its existence), had appealed twice to the High Court to prevent the central government-led move, but had failed; the action was, apparently, an attempt at "levelling up" the region as the economy lagged behind other parts of Britain, if I have this right. Many deemed the division to be politically motivated and likely to benefit the Conservative Party at local elections.

As I said: *extremely confusing*, though I do not think it will affect those going for a walk in the fells. The MAMILs passing by did not seem bothered in the slightest by it all, of course. And who would blame them? The sun had come out and it was a fine afternoon to go for a cycle in "Cumbria" as it was called, for the time being at least.

Beyond Fell Font Farm, half a dozen walkers in vests and shorts and with sticks came down the fell. They had a pared-down, almost feral look and were different from any other hikers I had yet seen. Each wore a blank expression. All were silent. I said hello brightly and the response was a feeble hi from the person at the front. What a bleak bunch. "The Misery Hikers", I dubbed them. Maybe you should not expect merry hellos from *everyone*, but they really stood out as being on the negative side of hiker-dom. Perhaps they were friends with the couple from Derwentwater who had let the gate shut on me. Quite possibly. Further on, by a disused slate quarry, the path was lined with bluebells and Parnassus. A mountain biker coming in the other direction on the narrow way waited to let me by. I thanked her and she said: "I'm faster than you, you have right of way." What a very pleasant cyclist... no Misery Cyclist, for sure. Then she said: "Look at all the bluebells coming out, aren't they so pretty?" Was she the Lake District's politest and most charming mountain biker? Quite possibly, once again.

Shortly afterward, the path bent downhill through a deep green forest to the left and I arrived at Coniston, where I ate another reasonable sandwich – this time at the Crown Inn, on a corner in the centre of the attractive village (population: 928). The sandwich was mid-table so far as the sandwich rankings went, the Fox and Hounds in Ennerdale Bridge still solidly in first place, the King George IV by Eskdale Green in second and the Wasdale Head Inn in third. I dropped my backpack off at my hotel, The Sun – a formidable abode partly covered by vines on a hill overlooking the village – and went to the Ruskin Museum.

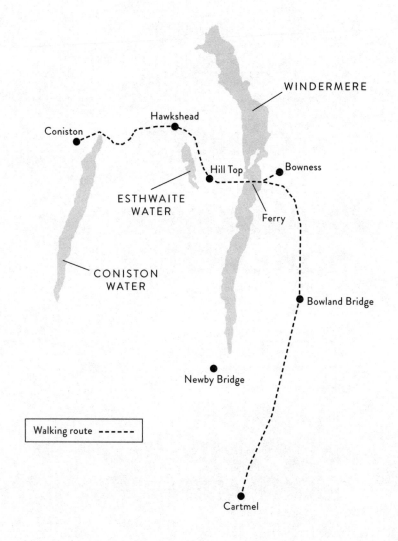

WINDERMERE

Hawkshead

Coniston

Hill Top

Bowness

ESTHWAITE
WATER

Ferry

CONISTON
WATER

Bowland Bridge

Newby Bridge

Walking route ------

Cartmel

CHAPTER EIGHT

CONISTON TO CARTMEL, VIA HAWKSHEAD AND BOWLAND BRIDGE

"REJECTING NOTHING, SELECTING NOTHING [AND] BELIEVING ALL THINGS TO BE RIGHT AND GOOD"

On a long walk around the Lake District, it is almost impossible not to *learn* things. Information about the many and varied goings-on of the Romantic poets of the late eighteenth and early nineteenth centuries, for example, was beginning to seep in (hard not to really when Wordsworth and Coleridge and the others had been up to so much). I was accumulating an understanding of the early days of mountaineering. I had heard of the scandal of the Maid of Buttermere. I had delved into the fascinating aspects of the conservation of freshwater mussels. I had been made aware, courtesy of Kristin back in Ennerdale, of the headbutting perils presented by sheep. I had found out, the hard way, that it was not a very good idea to go up Blencathra when it was windy and cloudy. I knew that sixteenth-century German miners were responsible for Cumberland sausages, or at least so it was said. I also knew a bit about old slate and lead mines as well as the workings of fell farms, the state of the local job market (not nearly enough staff) and the draining effect of second-home ownership and holiday homes on communities. Sure, I had heard of John Ruskin before coming and vaguely understood he was a nineteenth-century writer/thinker who was both an art critic and a social reformer, but I knew little beyond that.

I was, however, on the cusp of learning quite a lot more.

The Ruskin Museum was down a side alley in the centre of Coniston, although it was not just about Ruskin, a little oddly. It was also about Coniston and the local area in general. So, upon entry, you discovered that the name "Coniston" came from the Old Norse *konigs-tun* (king's settlement), referring to a Viking king called Thorstein. After this, a display in a corner went into some detail about how The Sun hotel, where I was staying, was once the headquarters of The Fell & Rock Climbing Club (founded in 1907). Coniston had been chosen in preference to Wasdale Head for the location of its meetings. This had been because it was served by a railway, the Coniston Railway, originally constructed to transport copper ore and slate in 1857, with passenger carriages brought in soon afterward on the 8½-mile line from Broughton-in-Furness. This mountaineering section of the museum also featured the same picture of Owen Glynne Jones, the pioneer climber, as was found at Wasdale Head Inn. A description praised his achievements but also mentioned that he was "famously short-sighted, abrasive and boastful". Jones appeared to have been a controversial character one way or another, with fellow climbers sneering at his method of sometimes using a "top rope" to dangle from a cliff face so that he could inspect a section of tricky rock before making a first ascent, which they believed was cheating.

At the very back of the Ruskin Museum was a wing devoted entirely to Donald Campbell, the daredevil speedboat driver who had died on a boat named *Bluebird K7* after attempting to break the world water speed record on 4 January 1967 at Coniston Water. In pride of place were the remains of the *Bluebird*, which had crashed at around 300 miles an hour. The boat was in the middle of being conserved and brought back to working order by volunteers, although judging by its still destroyed state, this looked as though it might take a while yet. Newspaper photographs from 5 January 1967 captured the boat as it flipped over. "SO DIED A BRAVE MAN: MOMENT OF HORROR IN BLUEBIRD'S DEATH DIVE", ran the headline in the *Barrow News*. Campbell's body had sunk to the depths, only to be recovered in 2001.

So not much of Ruskin at all in the Ruskin Museum, to start with.

Farther along, a display on Herdwick sheep explained they were an endangered species at the end of the nineteenth century and had to be re-established, and that Herdwick mutton was once considered such a delicacy it was served at Queen Elizabeth II's coronation banquet in 1953. Beside this display, a few dusty old cabinets teemed with clay pipes, collections of lace and ancient spearheads. But then, round a corner, there was a great deal indeed on the writer John Ruskin, seeming all-round genius and apparent oddball.

Ruskin was born in 1819 in London and died in 1900 at Brantwood, a mansion on the other side of Coniston Water that he had bought in middle age (this was also open to the public, effectively a second local Ruskin museum). His father had been a prosperous wine merchant and Ruskin had received private tuition before attending the University of Oxford. His private life had been tangled: he had married a distant cousin, Effie Gray, but for unknown reasons had never consummated the marriage. Gray had left him, and he had subsequently fallen in love with a young Irish girl, Rose La Touche. The pair never married, although Ruskin had proposed, and it is a grey area at what age precisely his love for her began. Some believe it was when she was 17. He had met her when he was aged 39 and she was 9. The historian Ian Thompson, in his first-rate book *The English Lakes: A History*, wrote matter-of-factly: "Rather like another well-known Victorian, Charles Dodgson [author, as Lewis Carroll, of *Alice's Adventures in Wonderland*], he related better to pre-pubescent girls than he did to mature women." La Touche had died young – in 1875, aged 27 – and her death had pushed Ruskin into bouts of deep depression. He took refuge in the Lakes, which he had remembered fondly from childhood visits, hence his decision to move from London and buy Brantwood.

Ruskin's working life, however, had burned brightly. He had taught at the Working Men's College in London and then also at Oxford, his lectures popular due to his lively delivery and eccentric style. His breakthrough as an art critic had come early, when he was 24, on the publication of a much-heralded celebration of the art of J. M. W. Turner. In this, he had highlighted the honesty of Turner's work, which he admired as he believed Turner painted as he saw things, not as he was supposed to see things (which was why Turner was not appreciated in some quarters at the time). Ruskin was a great advocate of close observation: "The greatest thing a human soul ever does in this world is to see something and tell what it saw in a plain way. Hundreds of people can talk for one who can think, but thousands can think for one who can see. To see clearly is poetry, prophecy and religion, all in one."

Judging by Ruskin's many words of wisdom scattered about the museum, covering a wide range of subjects, he was clearly extremely quotable. A video section in a corner provided a loop of readings by an actor.

On art:

> Fine art is that in which the hand, the head, and the heart of man go together.

On wealth and life:

> There is no wealth but life. Life including all its powers of love, of joy, and of admiration. That country is the richest which nourishes the greatest numbers of noble and happy human beings; that man is richest, who, having perfected the functions of his own life to the utmost, has also the widest helpful influence, both personal, and by other means of his possessions, over the lives of others.

On industrialization:

> We have much studied, and much perfected, of late, the great civilized invention of the division of labour; only we give it a false name. It is not, truly speaking, the labour that is divided; but the men: divided into segments of men – broken into small fragments and crumbs of life; so that all the piece of intelligence that is left is not enough to make a pin, or a nail, but exhausts itself in making the point or the head of a nail.

On nature:

> Go to nature in all singleness of heart, and walk with
> her laboriously and trustingly, having no other thoughts
> but how best to penetrate her meaning, and remember
> her instruction; rejecting nothing, selecting nothing;
> believing all things to be right and good, and rejoicing
> always in the truth.

Ruskin had campaigned for free education for all, free museums (he
had founded the Ruskin Museum in Coniston after fundraising for a
building, which was in fact why it was named after him), free libraries,
the welfare state, environmental conservation, the formation of the
National Trust, fair rents, clean city air and social reform in general.
His influence went far and wide, not just in Britain. Mahatma Gandhi
said that Ruskin's work *Unto This Last* had changed his life: "It was
impossible to set aside, once I had begun. It gripped me." Leo Tolstoy
was a fan. So were D. H. Lawrence, Marcel Proust, Édouard Manet and
William Morris. Of the first Labour members of parliament elected in
1906, the author said to have most influenced them was Ruskin.

* * *

"He was a critic of capitalism! He was ahead of his time!" said Erik,
yet another Ruskin admirer – a passionate one.

Erik was a Dutch tourist visiting the Lakes on a walking trip with
his French partner, Brigitte. When I entered the Ruskin room, they
were standing in a gloomy corner discussing Ruskin (loudly) with
David, a tourist from Surrey.

They were clearly having a great time.

I joined them for a while.

Erik was especially animated: "Ruskin believed capitalists,
particularly J. S. Mill, were wrong! Wrong! Ruskin was painting and

writing in a form of poetry about nature and he was combining the two in his watercolours." Erik was pointing at these; some were displayed alongside sketches. "It is clear when you see them that nature is more important to him than capitalism! Nature, not capitalism!"

Erik paused to see whether David and I were getting this; Brigitte seemed to have heard the gist of it before. We indicated we did, and Erik continued: "If man is only interested in making the most money and working less hard, if this conception of economy is the basis of humanity, well Ruskin believed that in this model man does not exist at all. That is what Ruskin believed! He believed that humanity should value the beauty of nature and protect other people. Nature! Humanity! He said it is not the economy that is important: life is important!"

Brigitte seemed to have caught something of Erik's fever. "What we see in the world now," she said. "What do we see? Climate change! The haves! The have-nots! It is incredible how he was so advanced!"

David was getting into it too. The trio was positively fizzing with enthusiasm for Ruskin, speaking with exclamation marks (apologies for so many). "For me, it's about nature and being closer to nature: nature, nature, nature!" David said. "I love William Wordsworth and William Morris, but I adore Ruskin! I like returning to Coniston and going to see Brantwood, I find the Lakes a very spiritual place. Ruskin is part of that. I come every year. It feels as though there is a connection here with people who have passed, like Ruskin. The fells, they're always the same – the same as when I last left them. I adore it here!"

The conversation continued in this vein for some time in the gloomy corner of the Ruskin Museum, which was otherwise empty of visitors. Then we all went out to see Ruskin's ornate Celtic cross-style gravestone in St Andrew's churchyard, just around the corner, as though we had joined a tour together. Erik, Brigitte and David gazed on in silence, for the first time, by the graveside.

Quite an unusual museum visit.

Perhaps that was appropriate, though: after all, Ruskin had evidently been quite an unusual man.

Snakes, slates and estates
The Old Man of Coniston and Brantwood

Coniston was more touristy than Cockermouth, but less so than Keswick. As well as many of the usual outdoor-clothing shops, it was home to a clutch of drinking holes including the Crown, the Yewdale, the Black Bull, The Coniston Inn and the bar at The Sun hotel; it also had an Indian restaurant, the museum, a tourist information office, Brantwood (across the water and which I wanted to visit) and a gift shop selling fudge, Lake District-edition Monopoly boards and gimmicky fake £100 notes with pictures of the Beatles instead of the Queen. The village was half a mile from the gravelly beach of the lake, where a watersports centre, café and jetty for boat rides were also located.

One of the highlights of Coniston was the Old Man of Coniston (803 metres), a fell looming to the north-west in bulbous crags as though the mountain was bubbling up from below. I had a good view from my room at The Sun and my plan was to make an ascent in the morning. It would be another Wainwright bagged, my third after Haystacks and Scafell Pike. The name of the fell had a pleasant ring that had raised my curiosity.

The Sun was not serving meals. "There's no food," said the man who handed over the key. "We don't have a chef. After Covid, people decided they preferred to work in cafés during the day, not in the evenings at bars. A friend of mine who runs a hotel in Blackpool has given up and closed down it's so bad."

So I went to the cosy, low-beamed Black Bull, where Coleridge had stayed on his semi-suicidal expedition, for a pint of smooth, creamy Bluebird Bitter, brewed by the Coniston Brewing Company (I could hardly believe how many breweries there were in the Lakes), and a decent Cumberland sausage and mash. In 1802, the poet had "dined on Oatcake & Cheese, with a pint of Ale, & 2 glasses of rum and water sweetened with preserved Gooseberries". As the waitress collected my empty plate, she stopped to say that a colleague, who had been leaving the pub looking glum, had just discovered she had been given a parking fine. New tourist-season parking rules had begun after a winter lifting of restrictions and her colleague had forgotten. "It's hard for her," the waitress said. "Now she's working for two days for nothing, like." All her wages would go to covering the ticket.

The waitress returned to the long, well-varnished bar, which had dried hops dangling above it, and a tourist in front of my table accosted a waiter, who was in the middle of serving dishes to another table, demanding "mint chocolate chip and vanilla ice cream on one plate… that's mint chocolate chip: you've got that? And vanilla: you've got that? On one plate. Do you have any milk for my coffee?" The waiter looked befuddled: *who was this man in the first place?* It did not seem that he was on a table he had been serving, but he nodded. The man glared at him.

Working in tourism in the Lakes clearly had its moments.

I returned to the dimly lit bar of The Sun, where I met Alan Piper, the owner and landlord, who joined me for a drink in the hotel's front lounge, which had smart leather sofas and armchairs and a view of the village. He preferred to talk there as it was quieter than the bar, where a group of mainly locals had gathered after the day's work, some on nearby farms, and were busy exchanging tales.

Alan wore a brown jumper and jeans and might have passed for an off-duty farmer himself. He had a broad smile and, like the regulars, was in a talkative mood. He was "nearly seventy", had been running The Sun hotel for 22 years and was originally from Merseyside but had lived in Essex for a long period when he was in IT and project management: "I did twenty years in the City. I made some decent money and bought a divorce and a pub." He was referring to The Sun, which he had spotted for sale in an advert in *The Westmorland Gazette*.

Parts of the hotel by the bar went back "at least" 400 years, to when The Sun was an inn on a key packhorse trail to the western Lakes, although it was extended to its current shape around the 1920s.

"We have eight rooms and eight real ales," said Alan, who had a no-nonsense, keep-things-simple approach.

He pointed at wood panelling in the lounge. "I did those," he said. "I also knocked seven bells out of the bar [making improvements when he bought The Sun]."

"Coniston is not like anywhere else in the Lakes. It's quite isolated as the valley opens to the south," Alan said, sipping his pint. "It's old-fashioned England. Nothing like Windermere and Bowness, they're like Blackpool. Keswick's a nice town, though."

He began talking about Donald Campbell. "He spent his last night here," Alan said. "He was a bit of a serial shagger, allegedly." A film about Campbell's tragic water-record attempt, covering his complicated love life, had been partially filmed at the hotel: *Across the Lake* starring Anthony Hopkins (1988). Framed newspaper cuttings from 1967 and old pictures of the accident were in the bar.

Alan told me that staff shortages were such a problem he was trying to arrange a work visa for a chef named Brenda he knew who lived in South Africa. But that was clearly the tip of the iceberg. After a sip or two and a pause, he said: "Actually, I'm thinking of selling this place soon. I don't think there will be lack of interest. It's lovely now." He was referring to his renovations. "It's a lovely place to be." Then he paused again and asked: "You don't know anyone who's interested, do you?"

* * *

Having resisted the temptation to buy a lovely historic Lake District hiking hostelry the night before, despite my growing fondness of lovely historic Lake District hiking hostelries, I climbed the Old Man of Coniston in the morning.

The trail began directly behind The Sun and the landscape was a patchwork quilt of colours beneath a splendid mackerel sky: tan and bleached yellow grassland, mustardy gorse, slivers of slate gorges, indigo crags above cinnamon scree. All about, inky shadows of clouds shifted across the scenery as though on urgent assignments, so the fells never seemed to stay quite still. Climbers with ropes ascended the trail heading for tricky cliffs that the main hiking paths avoided – the first proper mountain climbers I had seen. A quarry lay to one side as the path curled up to the motionless surface of Levers Water, a tucked-away tarn above Boulder Valley. The sky there was so perfectly mirrored on the water that the horizon and small lake seemed indistinguishable in places.

A narrow, twisting path led steeply onward to a ridge. I took another path there with the curious hump-shaped contours of Dow Crag rising to the right. It began to snow lightly at the summit, where I had my picture taken by a fellow hiker. It had taken about 2 hours to reach the top and a dozen or so people were milling about. The landscape beyond the long strip of Coniston Water tapered to an estuary and the Irish Sea. A good morning's work; no problem after the long slog over Hardknott and Wrynose the day before. I liked the Old Man of Coniston.

Snaps taken, I descended a path with a more direct route back to the village. It was the busiest yet, scores of people coming up. "Come on then!" a father said to his children, jockeying them on despite looking exhausted himself. Shortly afterward, I almost stepped on a little green-and-yellow snake with a zigzag pattern, an adder maybe, that was around 2 feet long. It slipped away as my right boot seemed to sense danger and halt mid-movement. I asked a fellow walker if she had seen it. She had not but was unsurprised. "You should go to the Malvern Hills," she said. "There are loads of them there. If they bite you, you won't feel great, they are poisonous, but you won't die."

This excitement aside, the return to the village was unremarkable.

Apart from meeting Brendan, that is.

Brendan Donnelly ran Coniston Stonecraft, a slate-processing company making signs for houses, panels for kitchens, clocks and wine-racks among much else, all out of slate. The business was based in buildings that were once part of the railway when it came to collect copper ore and slate from mines. The railway had closed during the British railway cuts of the 1960s. There were three seams of slate around Coniston, mined to order these days rather than the whole time. Brendan had six employees and two apprentices. He was Cumbrian and looked the part in worn old boots, a gilet and a squashed-down cap. He had a ruddy complexion, broad shoulders and strong opinions about second homes and holiday homes.

"They kill the area," he said. "I don't blame people for selling or buying, but you can't have everyone aged fifty-plus if you want a thriving community with cricket and rugby clubs and all those types of things. When I was younger there might be twenty-five mountain rescues a year. Now the average age of mountain rescue volunteers is something like over sixty, but there are five hundred call-outs. In twenty years' time will there be mountain rescue? If you take away the community, everything eventually collapses. All the lads who work here come in from Barrow [21 miles to the south]. Twenty years ago, they'd have lived locally. I read recently that Glenridding Cricket Club couldn't get the numbers. Well, what happens with something like that? The danger is it just folds."

Brendan believed that the Lake District National Park was being too protective of the local landscape, blocking new housing and business zones: "They don't want anything new, anything to happen to their precious park. Some of the things they do are very good: build out of local stone and don't go above a certain height. But I can't afford to live here. I live in Stafford. It takes three hours to drive here, I stay one night a week and go home. There's a six-bedroom lovely big house near here. It was bought by a lovely lady from London. But she's not here all the time."

The community was in dire trouble, Brendan said, before going on to explain the subtle variations in colour between Elterwater slate ("light and dark, and a wonderful sea green"), Kirkby slate ("blue-grey and darker with fine lines") and Coniston slate ("more of a silver-grey"). Brendan said that Chinese and Brazilian slate is much cheaper, but people should "take into consideration that it's travelled halfway round the world, spewing out diesel, instead of thinking it magically appeared here. This country has enough of its own slate to last forever. Importing kills our indigenous slate industry and it's not as good either."

We ended up talking a long time, and then Brendan looked at his watch: "Oh no, I'd better go back." And off he went to the old, converted railway shed, where a sound of whirring and the slicing of slate began soon after.

* * *

Brantwood was on a slope on a stretch of land known simply as "east of Coniston". It took about an hour to walk round the edge of the lake to Ruskin's old house. On the way, I passed the Swallows and Amazons Café and a notice that said that the Old Man of Coniston was known as "Kanchenjunga" in Arthur Ransome's evocative children's book *Swallows and Amazons*, while the local Bank Ground Farm was "Holly Farm" in his story.

A bulky pale-pink-and-cream building rose to the left up a drive: Brantwood. I was soon inside, inspecting the writer's Venetian-style dining room, a study with mineral collections and an octagonal desk, a drawing room with a strange harp-like instrument, a side room with a cabinet containing a (more than slightly weird) lock of Rose La Touche's hair, and his bedroom, which had an odd, turret-like corner chamber where Ruskin liked to gaze out in privacy across the lake to the Old Man of Coniston. Gilt-framed portraits and landscapes lined the walls, many extremely valuable.

Out in the garden, banks of azaleas and rhododendrons bloomed close to a secret spot where a peculiar stone chair known as Ruskin's Seat was placed by a tree, facing inland rather than to Coniston Water. This was positioned so Ruskin could examine the woodland above, said the gift-shop assistant. "His chair faced the moss and bracken and a stream. It was because he liked to concentrate on details," she said. "He visited here as a child and he always remembered it. After his first mental breakdown, he came here to feel better." According to biographers, from 1889 onward, he was so unstable he gave up writing altogether and was cared for by a cousin.

Brantwood seemed somehow to capture its illustrious and mysterious former resident in one: highly imaginative with lofty thoughts and a practical nature (he had more or less rebuilt Brantwood to create his dream retreat), yet with an unmistakably discordant, melancholic streak. As David had said back at the museum, there was a definite feeling of a connection with the unusual genius at his hideaway by the lake.

I returned along the lake and called Kasia from The Sun hotel.

News was still not good with the Ukrainians in Siedlce.

"They've been crying and stressed out and they don't understand why the visa for Anna is taking so long. I tried to calm them down and reassure them. I don't know why they'd refuse one and not the other." Kasia was talking about the British authorities. "If they both had letters with visa approval, they could have flown back with me." Kasia was about to return to London. "Now they have to sit and wait. I feel for them. I just said they can stay as long as they want at the apartment. Go and find a school for Anna in Siedlce, if needed. We prepared some more food for them: a jar of pickled cucumbers, some eggs, fresh bread, a stick of sausage and jam. Lena became very talkative and told me her whole life story. They're so worried. I sat down with them and had a cup of tea. They have been to Warsaw twice and even went to the zoo. They liked it a lot. At least they were doing something, so they don't sit and worry all the time. Though they do a lot of that as well."

To add to their personal troubles over seeking asylum, back in Ukraine, Russia had just launched a major offensive in the Donbas region in the country's east, while yet more missiles had struck Lviv in the west. There I was tramping round the Lake District enjoying the views, seeing tourist sights and having a great time meeting all sorts of people and staying at old historic English hiking inns as events in south-eastern Europe seemed to worsen by the day.

Ruskin probably would have had something to say about that (he did seem to have had views on most things).

Pottering on
Coniston to Bowland Bridge, via Hawkshead and Near Sawrey

To reach my next overnight stay in the village of Bowland Bridge, about a dozen miles south-east, involved passing the shores of two more of the Big 16 lakes: Esthwaite Water, a tiddler in the rankings at 1½ miles long, and then Windermere, the largest of the lot at 10½ miles. This trek meant skirting Esthwaite, crossing Windermere by ferry, shunning Bowness to the north (although I would be back) and turning south to tramp through remote countryside marked by a winding dotted green line on the trusty Ordnance Survey map.

The way ahead covered Beatrix Potter-land. First, the village of Hawkshead, where a gallery of watercolour illustrations from the author/illustrator's books for children – many inspired by local scenery – was to be found in the former offices of her husband, William Heelis, a solicitor. Next, a few miles on, came another, smaller village called Near Sawrey, where Potter's home at Hill Top farm was located. I was about to dip into prime tourist territory before disappearing into the fells on the other side of Windermere.

Having made the acquaintance of a sweet pair of septuagenarian sisters in the breakfast room of The Sun – one of whom, Linda, was about to take the other, Andrea, to visit a cairn she had erected on the fells to remember her Lakes-loving husband, Michael, who had died during the pandemic – I crossed the head of Coniston Water and ascended a hill. The path there led to the grounds of a country house hotel, Monk Coniston, where someone sitting on a bench asked: "Seen any snakes today?" It was the adder expert I had met descending the Old Man.

Very small world, sometimes, the Lake District.

Giant redwoods, Monterey pines, Japanese red cedars, Scotch pines and monkey puzzle trees loomed in a shaded wood beyond, leading to Tarn Hows – a man-made tarn considered a "beauty spot", with car parks, a refreshment kiosk and plenty of tourists strolling about with guidebooks. Yes, all very nice in its own way, the tarn glistening enticingly in its hollow in the hills all surrounded by trees. Not a touch on the desolate splendour of Levers Water, though, way up on the mountain.

Over a field and down a lane, I arrived at Hawkshead, which was without doubt the most charmingly quaint, daintily pretty, picture-perfectly picturesque, beguilingly bijou chocolate box of a place I had visited yet (insert further flowery adjectives as appropriate). A tourist-information sign went as far as to declare it "the prettiest village in the Lake District".

Vehicles were banned except for delivery vans. Rows of whitewashed cottages on narrow cobbled lanes twisted every which way leading to tiny squares with old-fashioned hostelries (including the popular Red Lion and the Queens Head), well-attended tea rooms, arts-and-crafts shops, Peter Rabbit shops, outdoor-clothing shops, general gift shops, jewellery shops and crystal shops. In short, a lot of shops. Hanging baskets overflowed with pink and yellow pansies. Inviting little whitewashed B & Bs posted "no vacancy" signs, mainly. One of these, Ann Tysons House, was where Wordsworth had boarded while at Hawkshead Grammar School, though there was no one about when I went by.

Everything was unashamedly "olde worlde" and pitched at tourists, of which there were many, even more than at Tarn Hows. The adjectives were running free and the tills were ringing, not to everyone's approval, naturally. Capturing the concerns of many to this day, the eminent author and climber Alan Hankinson, in his 1991 book *Coleridge Walks the Fells: A Lakeland Journey Retraced*, wrote of Hawkshead: "The whole place, it seems, has abandoned itself to the need to separate tourists from their money."

So this was nothing new, the village had already sold out to the tourist pound and, supposedly, "abandoned itself" no less than 30 years ago. Yet, if anything, tourism had become even more buoyant in the Lakes since then, well established as the "main source of income" of the economy: 19–20 million annual visitors spending a staggering £1.48 billion and bringing "great benefits" and being "vital" to the region, according to the Lake District National Park. The people in charge more than approved, even if so many voices all along the way on my hike, so far at least, had their doubts; Brendan from the slate works just the day before, for example. It had all been foreseen by Wordsworth, of course, who had expressed so many worries about trains and mass tourism in his *Guide to the Lakes*, which was first published *210 years ago*:

> Is then no nook of English ground secure
> From rash assault?

Being in Hawkshead brought it all into sharper focus.

No more "wander[ing] lonely as a cloud", at least not for a while.

Quite a few tourists were at the Beatrix Potter Gallery. I joined them, examining the many exquisite watercolours. Potter, who was born in West Brompton in London in 1866 and died in the Lake District in 1943, had bought Hill Top farm in nearby Near Sawrey in 1905 to be a countryside retreat. She had used a small inheritance and the proceeds of *The Tale of Peter Rabbit*, published three years earlier, *The Tale of Squirrel Nutkin* and *The Tailor of Gloucester*. She moved to live there full-time in 1913 after marrying Heelis, who had been handling her local Lakes affairs as she steadily acquired more and more of the surrounding countryside and farms, many of which had been under threat from development, possibly as mansions with estates for wealthy outsiders.

Potter's approach worked wonders. Under her watch, Herdwick sheep (soon to win prizes) were bred in vastly greater numbers and many struggling farms were saved. Her acquisitions on the back of the success of her stories about the likes of Jemima Puddle-Duck, Mr Jeremy Fisher and Mrs Tiggy-Winkle continued, and all her land was left to the National Trust in her will. She had known Canon Rawnsley since happy childhood visits to the Lakes when her parents had been acquaintances of the Trust's co-founder. Rawnsley had become a close friend, encouraging Potter to complete *The Tale of Peter Rabbit*, her breakthrough book, and helping find a publisher, which had been extremely tricky. In turn, Potter's generous bequest was key to kick-starting the National Trust in its early days. She had got the ball rolling and, at the time of writing, more than 20 per cent of the Lake District National Park's 912 square miles of land was overseen by the Trust, while 70 per cent of the world's Herdwick sheep roamed on the Trust's 90 farms run by tenant farmers.

"To me this is where it all started," said Nate, who was working on the ticket desk and was so tall he could hardly fit in the cramped building's front room. "Potter employed Heelis and she ended up with fifteen farms covering four thousand acres. That's a lot of places."

He was not wrong. Potter, Rawnsley and the other co-founders of the National Trust, whose instincts aligned with Wordsworth's warnings, had performed great deeds.

Like a dutiful tourist, I moved on to the next tourist site.

This was a distinguished building with narrow leaded windows and a sundial on a slope that made the whole structure look a bit tipsy. A sign by the door said Hawkshead Grammar School dated from 1585 and was attended by William Wordsworth from 1779 to 1787. Sadly, the school was closed, only opening Thursday to Monday and it was then Wednesday. So, I could not see where the young poetic rascal had carved his name on a desk (I was not having much Wordsworth-tourism luck). Instead, I went to the twelfth-century stone church, St Michael & All Angels, just behind his old school and where the Poet Laureate-to-be and Lakeland defender used to go for Sunday services. This was a fine old church with odd, imperfectly round columns matched by odd, imperfectly semicircular arches on each side of the nave that were much admired in architectural circles.

I picked up a free parish pamphlet and went to a daintily quaint tea room to read about the pressing matters of the day. A spring garden competition was calling for entries. Platinum Jubilee celebrations were being planned for the Queen. A drystone wall rebuilding party was seeking volunteers. New road signposts were planned to deter drivers from following satnav directions down unsuitable lanes (and having to be rescued by tractors).

The editorial, however, was on a completely different subject: "We are in a state of shock because something we thought impossible has happened: for the first time in 83 years, one European country has invaded another." Readers were called upon to donate items to be transported on a freight lorry to the Ukrainian border. Yet again, the Russian invasion looming large.

Close by – everything was *close by* in Hawkshead – I dropped into the post office, which was hung with the Nepalese flags of the Nepalese owner, Mohit, who had met his English wife, Carolyn, in Kathmandu 30 years ago, he told me as I posted home several newly acquired Lake District books from the portable library. Feeling fleet of foot, I proceeded down a lane past a large car park toward Esthwaite Water, which shimmered in the sunshine. It was dead quiet along a bluebell-lined path that followed the water's edge for a short distance.

Esthwaite was far enough away from Hawkshead's olde-worlde centre – about a quarter of a mile – not to draw the masses and also lacked a complete, convenient circular path. A solitary swan occupied the often-overlooked lake, which was otherwise empty aside from three fishermen in waders from Manchester seeking trout, bream, pike ("there's a forty-pounder out there"), roach, perch and eels. They had caught "nothing today" and had set off at 8 a.m. from the city to the lake.

"It's for sport," said Ian. "We catch 'em and put 'em back."

At Near Sawrey, back in the thick of tourist things, a chaos of cars was honking, blocking the street and attempting to manoeuvre in and out of the main car park for Hill Top. Potter's farmhouse was a little further on, beyond cottage terraces with colourful tulips in their front gardens. The winding lane was busy, as was Potter's garden and farmhouse. Inside, a bald National Trust employee with heavy-framed glasses explained that Hill Top had been Potter's favourite farmhouse.

"She bought it in her late thirties and she was from a privileged background," he said. "This was her first independent purchase. She would come on writing retreats, and while she was here, she bought more properties. Because of social convention she couldn't live here alone full-time. She moved to a cream house [Castle Cottage] across the way once she was married, you can see it from the front gate. But she didn't want to spoil it here. Hill Top really was very personal to her. It is pretty much as she left it in 1943."

Hill Top opened to the public in 1946. On first inspection, it seemed terribly twee: pale-pink rooms with porcelain and shell collections, polished horse brasses, mounted butterflies and doll's houses. But then you went upstairs to what felt like the beating heart of the cottage: the study. This was entirely different. Wood-panelled walls had been hung with giant landscape oil paintings. A model of a ship rested on a side table. A comfortable-looking dark-green sofa was positioned against a wall. In the corner by the only window, a solid writing bureau was bathed in pale afternoon light. There was no clutter. It was calm and restful, the landscape paintings seeming to bring the countryside into the room. The bedroom, next to the study, was simple in style too with a sturdy four-poster, fireplace and not much else. And when you went back downstairs, you realized that the jamboree of possessions on display was there for the tourists really, not exactly as it was in her day. At Hill Top, which looked from the outside like a plain pebble-dashed nineteenth-century farmhouse, Potter had created a delicious writer/artist's den in (what was then) a peaceful village in the middle of the Lakes.

No wonder she loved it so much.

* * *

From Near Sawrey the green dotted line cut across to a church on a hill with a Ukrainian flag fluttering on a pole in the graveyard. A first glimpse of Windermere's vast inland sea revealed a lake on a totally different scale to the others, perhaps Ullswater excepted. The ferry, which left every 20 minutes, was waiting and the vessel glided serenely across England's largest natural lake, with the marina at Bowness a forest of masts rising ahead and sunlight falling on the fells above Ambleside way to the north. About a dozen vehicles were on board, drivers staying in cars for the 5-minute journey, with as many foot passengers.

On the other side, I trudged up a hill past a series of plush-looking places to stay: Lindeth Fell country house hotel, Aphrodites Boutique Suites, the Windermere Boutique Spa Suites, the LA23 Lakes Apartments ("luxury boutique self-catering with hot tubs") and then, plushest of all, Linthwaite House, statues of lions pawing the sky by the entrance.

YHA Ennerdale, Denton House hostel or the Wasdale Head Inn, as much as I loved them, these were not.

Behind Linthwaite House, a footpath led to a field with a track along drystone walls that proceeded to a woodland trail that followed on to a tarn by a farmhouse with a yelping dog. This wound on to yet more fields and drystone walls. A purple haze hung across the valley ahead and there were *no other tourists at all*. The green dotted line continued to weave onward, and I arrived at a farmhouse where an elderly man had just returned from shopping. His name was Eric –

his wife was Ellen – and their farm had 87 acres. Eric had bought it 47 years ago "without looking" for £7,000.

He asked me: "Would you like a Bluebird Bitter?"

I said I would, and I stood talking to Eric as the late afternoon lilac light slowly faded.

Eric was the son of a famous speedway racer, Bill Kitchen, once captain of the England and Wembley motorcycle speedway teams. He was aged 89, from near Lancaster and looked a little like the actor Robert De Niro, with an easy-going manner and time to reminisce. "I've let it go wild now and it's great," he said, referring to the farm; there were no cattle or sheep any more. Prices of properties in the area had ballooned recently. "A few years ago, I was offered a million for that barn," he said, pointing across to a simple stone structure nearby. "But we didn't want neighbours."

His father, Bill, had travelled around the globe for competitions, often going to Australia on six-week journeys by ship. Eric also had an interest in motorbikes and had become involved with the International Motorcycling Federation, often as a photographer at events: "I've been to Japan twice, America – east coast and west – Finland, Sweden."

He owned a company that supplied spare parts for cars which he had begun as "one man with a van in 1963"; now he had 83 employees and 50 vans covering Lancaster, Barrow, Blackpool, Kendal and Penrith. Eric let this information drop into the conversation in a by-the-by manner. Then, his eyes gazing upward, he asked: "See that white cottage?"

I could see a cottage up the side of a hill in an extremely out-of-the-way position.

"From 1925 to 1935 Arthur Ransome lived there. Low Ludderburn cottage, it's called." This was where Ransome had written *Swallows and Amazons* and lived with his Russian-born wife Evgenia. They had met while he was reporting for British newspapers on the Russian Revolution in 1917, when he had also got to know well both

Vladimir Lenin (with whom he had played chess) and Leo Tolstoy; Evgenia had been Tolstoy's secretary. "Yes, they were up there," Eric said, quite casually.

He looked at the patchwork of fields in the valley below, dreamy eyed for a moment. "Used to be hounds and horses running across there during fox hunts," he said.

"That must have been quite a sight from up there," I replied.

"Oh no, I'd be down there, I used to join 'em back in those days," he said.

Ellen opened the farmhouse door and, in a manner that suggested she was quite used to him nattering away to strangers, asked: "Are you coming in?"

"Aye," he said, and he gave me directions across a stile and a field to The Hare & Hounds Inn, known well to Eric, in the village of Bowland Bridge.

I traversed the field, hopped over another stile on a drystone wall, joined a narrow country lane and soon arrived at my digs for the night.

Style, substance and a good pie
Bowland Bridge to Cartmel

"Oh, you all look so Miami!" a short, slim, energetic man behind the bar was saying to three women wearing high heels and bright satin shirts who had arrived just before me at The Hare & Hounds Inn. They were ordering gin-and-tonics and did indeed look as though they might be about to embark on a night on the tiles on South Beach. Latest pop music played – the type that gets shortlisted for the cool Mercury Prize, rather than the more mass-market BRIT Awards – as well as old hits by David Bowie and the Rolling Stones. The little bar, with its stripy sofa, exposed stone walls and little circular tables, was packed and buzzing with a crowd of mainly twenty- and thirty-something hipster clientele, although some extremely hip older hipsters were knocking about too. It was traditional – The Hare & Hounds dates from the seventeenth century – but somehow vibrantly modern all at once, and you got that as soon as you walked through the door.

The Miami trio collected their drinks. I asked the short, slim, energetic man if I could check in. "Absolutely, welcome, welcome!" he said. His name was Simon Rayner-Langmead, formerly a PR executive in fashion and hospitality, and his co-owner, Andrew Black, was the ex-publisher of the ultra-trendy, cool, hip, happening, zeitgeisty *Wallpaper** design, fashion, arts and architecture magazine. Both hipsters too, naturally, having met in hipster circles in London.

Simon took me to my room, named "Pip", an elegant chamber with pistachio-coloured walls and an oatmeal carpet. A wicker-framed bed (extremely comfortable with good linen) was in the middle with a bedside table bearing a copy of *Adventures in Wonderland: A Decade of Club Culture* by Sheryl Garratt, while opposite was an oval mirror in an ornate wooden frame carved with delicate roses set on a Louis XVI table with a green marble top. A huge bathroom with pomegranate-scented toiletries and both a claw-foot bathtub and a large walk-in shower was on one side. Best room yet, in a hipster way.

I went straight down and was given a table in the bar close to the sofa with the Miami trio – none was available in the restaurant as all were booked on this midweek night – and tucked into wild garlic and pearl barley (delicious, with chunky barley, a subtle garlic flavour and a decent portion) followed by a beef and ale pie with a rich gravy, lots of tender beef, mash mixed with spring onions, snap peas and a punchy horseradish. The miso cod and the Moroccan spiced lamb tagine had already sold out or I would have tried a more adventurous main. No regrets, however. What a beef and ale pie it was, more than a cut above the average. Best meal of the hike so far.

A curious little Tracey Emin original drawing depicting a skinny woman wearing high heels entitled *Dog Brains* hung on a wall (a self-portrait). Candles flickered. Hipsters chattered. Sipping a glass of

South African Merlot (first wine of the trip), I listened to the hipsters for a while, occasionally flicking through the pages of *Catcher in the Rye* by J. D. Salinger, which I had borrowed from a shelf in the hall as reading material. Books like this were scattered about in a library-like nook by the stairs.

One of the hipsters, wearing a black jumper and Converse trainers, was saying how each morning he checked Reuters, Associated Press and the BBC "first thing when I get up" so he would be ready for his work, something to do with financial investment. Another, an architect with multicoloured socks and an Elvis Presley quiff, was doing up a house: "We think the kitchen should have the lake view. I'm trying to convince the owner." One of the Miami trio was discussing research for a television production: "You can get lost down so many rabbit holes online – and it's so, so slow." She was referring to the broadband in the valley. A local campaign was under way to raise funds required for a "hyperfast community fibre broadband". The group discussed this for a bit. A large sum had been collected already, but £60,000 more was needed. Private investors, I gathered, were promised a return of 5 per cent per year. All this was a whole new intriguing world away from the old boozers I had visited so far. A metropolitan gathering of sorts was in full flow, deep in the countryside: FTSE, not sheep prices; fibre optics, not flooding; interior design, not drystone walls.

Simon and Andrew, a larger man with floppy grey hair, a grey hipster beard and a lumberjack shirt, joined me. Simon had been brought up in Cumbria and Andrew was from New York City. On a visit to the area, Simon had spotted that the then owners of The Hare & Hounds – which had recently "changed hands several times and never really hit the mark" and had long ago been run by the Preston and Liverpool footballer Peter Thompson – were looking to sell. Having talked about running a pub for years "mostly when drinking in Soho House [the private members' club in London]" and with Simon "tired of the fandango involved with representing luxury brands", they went for it, taking over the year prior to my visit: "People were asking us: '*Are you insane*? There's still a pandemic.'" said Simon, but the pair wanted to do something for themselves rather than bosses for once, said Andrew, whose first taste of the hospitality industry had been as a dishwasher, then as a waiter at a New York restaurant: "Everything I learned about business, I learned as a waiter: thinking on your feet, listening, negotiating and persuading."

They were almost immediately hit by a lockdown that closed the pub. However, this did not hold them back as they began a pizza van, which was parked in the car park and therefore legal for trade. The pizzas proved a hit and since the lockdowns had ended they had been doing so well at the inn – which I learned of from a glowing review in *The Times* – they were even considering branching out with another. "We have been blown away by the incredible support from locals," Simon said. He explained what he believed made a good pub: "At so many pubs-with-restaurants you can only go when you're eating, but this is a pub where you can have a drink too – a proper pub that's not so fancy that you can't come in with wellies and a dog." It was, he said, 70 per cent locals the evening I was visiting, and there were indeed a couple of fine hounds with their owners in a corner by the fireplace. "Above all else, we believe service is most important. You can't have a pub that is all style over substance."

Certainly not the case at The Hare & Hounds. Pubs, as I had been increasingly finding, were so often the beating heart of Lakeland villages and Simon and Andrew had laudably brought another one to life.

* * *

Well fed, I set off southward on a beautiful sunny morning, hoping to be even better fed in the much larger, culinarily famed village of Cartmel, about 9 miles south. Down a quiet lane flanked by bluebells I went, promptly becoming extremely lost in a wood after failing to follow the little green dotted line of a footpath, scrambling about and recovering, getting extremely lost in another wood, scrambling about and recovering, tramping for a very long way up a hill, passing a reservoir with a couple of fishermen (the only people, aside from farmers, I had laid eyes on all morning), taking a tunnel beneath an awful dual carriageway (the A590, the worst road yet), passing through the village of Ayside (where a Ukrainian flag fluttered by a cottage), walking down a very long lane and arriving – a great deal of gently rolling countryside behind me – at the extremely pretty village of Cartmel, where I had a table at an extremely fancy restaurant booked for lunch.

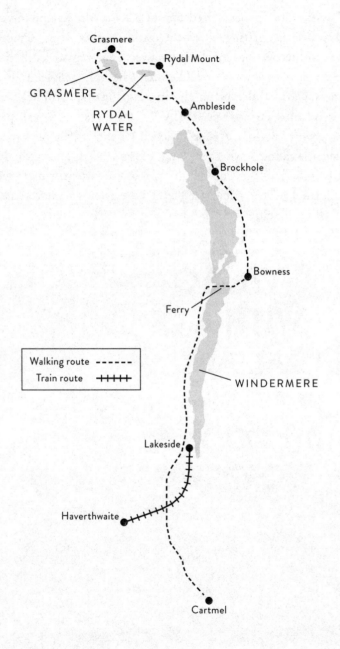

Grasmere

Rydal Mount

GRASMERE

RYDAL
WATER

Ambleside

Brockhole

Bowness

Ferry

WINDERMERE

Walking route – – – – –
Train route ++++++

Lakeside

Haverthwaite

Cartmel

CHAPTER NINE

CARTMEL TO AMBLESIDE, VIA BOWNESS, WITH A LOOP TO RYDAL AND GRASMERE

FOODIES AND WORDSWORTHIANS

Cumbria was in the midst of a culinary celebration – high fives all round – having just achieved more Michelin stars, the highest restaurant accolades, than any county outside London. That was the breaking news before I came on this Lake District walking tour.

The announcement by Michelin had been on the front page of a copy of *The Westmorland Gazette* I had picked up at the little café/shop on the platform at Oxenholme Lake District Station on the west-coast mainline. From here you catch the connection to "Windermere" along the tracks that Wordsworth hated so much when it opened in 1847, arriving, back then, at the tiny hamlet of Birthwaite that was to become known as "Windermere" (about a mile from the lake). Cumbria had been awarded a total of ten Michelin stars, with the brightest shining stars of the lot belonging to L'Enclume in Cartmel, which had moved from two to three stars, the top score possible, and was the only restaurant in Britain outside London to have achieved this pinnacle of eating. In the history of the awards, just 11 restaurants in the United Kingdom had reached such dizzy foodie heights. The result was that the county now had one Michelin star for every 48,000 people, compared to one in every 98,000 in London.

L'Enclume was run by Simon Rogan, in his mid-fifties and originally from Southampton, who had opened his fine-dining sensation with his partner, Penny Tapsell, two decades earlier in an old blacksmith's workshop. He had a farm-to-fork sustainable cooking "philosophy" and ran a 12-acre farm on the edge of Cartmel called Our Farm, which I had walked by on the way into the village and which supplied his two Cartmel restaurants, the other being Rogan & Co, with one Michelin star.

Rogan described his reaction on first hearing he had joined the Big Three club to *Cumbria Life* magazine: "I was a quivering wreck, my mouth went dry, I couldn't speak, I was absolutely gobsmacked." It had been the culmination of a lifetime's work: "It's something you dream of as a chef and anyone who says they don't is a liar." The other Michelin-star winners in Cumbria had been The Dog & Gun Inn near Skelton, The Old Stamp House in Ambleside, Allium at Askham Hall in Askham, The Cottage in the Wood in Braithwaite, HRiSHi at Gilpin Hotel & Lake House in Windermere, the Forest Side in Grasmere and Rogan & Co. Each had been awarded one Michelin star.

On a day trip to the county two months before my hike, I had arranged to meet Gill Haigh, managing director of Cumbria Tourism, at its slate-clad head office on the edge of the village of Staveley, not far from Windermere Station.

"As a local person living here there's a pride, I think," Haigh had said. "Those restaurants [the star winners] are all over the county. There's been this renaissance in food, but I think that goes hand in hand with the community, the culture of the county, the way things are farmed and also with tourism." Cumbria had become one of the best destinations in the UK for a "gourmet escape", she said, and this was unlikely to change any time soon whatever happened at future Michelin awards.

This breakthrough culinary moment, however, had not been without controversy. The writer and broadcaster Stuart Maconie, whose local was The Dog & Gun, had reacted with frustrated resignation at the way *The Times* had announced L'Enclume's third Michelin star. This was what the paper had written: "To northern cuisine such as bread and dripping and chips and curry sauce can now be added raw venison in coal oil and seaweed custard." To which Maconie had dryly responded: "Of course, we should be used to it by now. But it's still breath-taking to see such naked bigotry and snobbery passing as wit." Typical of the "snooty old Thunderer", the paper's nickname, to be so condescending to food in the North, which he said was "probably into its third decade of its food renaissance". Hadn't the snooty old Thunderer noticed? Next time a journalist "bother[ed] to visit us up here in the frozen, uncivilized north" maybe they would be in for a surprise. Touché!

Fine-dining hiker
Cartmel

Having paced past the grey stone bulk of the church of Cartmel Priory, running late, I arrived at the grey stone building of the one-Michelin star Rogan & Co where various diners' knives, forks and spoons paused in mid-air upon my entry to the elegant restaurant. This was where I was having lunch. L'Enclume, unsurprisingly, had been fully booked.

Spotlights attached to old beams shone down on well-spaced slate-and-wood tables at which smartly dressed folk were chattering and laughing. I sensed a momentary disruption in all activity on tables closest by, like in a western when the outsider swings open the saloon doors. I could not blame them for staring. I was, frankly, in a poor state. My Craghoppers jacket and North Face walking trousers had collected various sprigs of bramble and pieces of bark, accompanied by mud streaks, from the various scrambles through the trees near Rankthorns Plantation and High Loft Wood. I was sweating profusely and red-faced having had to speed up for the last few miles or else miss my precious dining slot. My backpack still bulged with books despite efforts to post various tomes back. *Had I come to the wrong place*, a few of the glances I was receiving suggested.

I was not, to be fair, your average fine diner.

"That looks heavy, sir, how far have you come, sir?" asked a tall Jeeves-like maître d' in a tweed jacket. He had perfectly groomed blonde hair clipped short at the sides, a pristine, well-shaven complexion and a ramrod-straight posture. He had clearly assessed his new fine diner (me), got the measure of him and was unfazed.

I said I thought I had come about nine miles.

"Well, you've made it now, sir," he said, brightly and somehow reservedly all at once, gesturing toward a slate-grey table in the corner by a front window.

Given I was 15 minutes late and appeared as though I might have just come from an SAS training course, he was being more than understanding. I had also made a mistake and taken The Hare & Hounds Inn key with me, rather than handing it in when I left. I had called The Hare & Hounds while scrambling toward Cartmel to say I would post it back asap, but the person who took the call said that a member of staff who lived close to Cartmel could pick it up from the restaurant if I left it there. When I explained all this to the maître d' at Rogan & Co, an eyebrow quivered ever so slightly and the pupils in his pale blue eyes seemed to dilate a fraction, but he, again, took it all in his stride.

"Very good, sir," he said. He took the key.

I sat on a retro blue-velvet chair from the 1960s, ordered an Anvil pale ale and perused the menu. I already knew that the restaurant offered a three-course set lunch with options for each course and that it was £79 (this was three and a half times the cost of a night at Denton House hostel in Keswick). "Dumplings with onion dashi and lemon thyme" along with "smoked eel with ramson" (another word for "wild garlic", as I understood it) featured among the starters, while mains included "ox cheek with glazed mushrooms and whey onions" (I had never knowingly consumed a "whey onion") as well as "roasted king oyster mushroom, grain ragout, egg yolk and truffle". For pudding, the fine diner could indulge in "buttermilk custard with rhubarb and sorrel" or "chocolate fondant with mandarin and sea salt". Even The Hare & Hounds, which had pushed my Lakeland hike's culinary experiences to new Himalayan levels, could not match this. Step aside Cumberland sausage and mash and fish and chips (as much as I loved them both), the taste buds were in for a *flavour explosion*, as I believe the presenters put it on the cooking contest programmes.

Old hits played softly: The Smiths, the Eagles, Tears for Fears. Pretty cherry blossom poked out of vases. Yellow-backed Simon Rogan books for sale were stacked neatly by the door. Little succulent plants in pots were placed here and there. Through the window I had a view of a cottage covered in wisteria and a neatly cut hedge. It was all very pleasant.

The fine dining soon began. Before the starter even arrived a plate of pop-in-the-mouth "snacks" was delivered: beef dumpling with bone marrow, cod's roe tartlet and a creamy parmesan sable. Pop, pop, pop. Explosion, explosion, explosion. The plate was whisked away. An immaculately dressed and groomed waitress with a ramrod-straight posture, again, and tattoos of stars behind one ear, Mrs Jeeves to the earlier Mr Jeeves (but more hipster by far with the tattoos), appeared holding a piece of slate with a toasted English muffin and some apple jam on it, plus a separate plate with a terrine of Gloucester Old Spot pork. Eating this was like enjoying another (extremely well-made) snack with yet more explosions: this time of the apple and salty pork. "Get stuck in, use your hands, don't worry," advised Mrs Jeeves, noticing I was hesitant. I did as I was told. It was marvellous. The slate and the plate were whisked away. Another plate arrived, with guinea fowl served in a white chocolate-and-parsnip purée (if I have that correct) and four tiny parsnips that poked out from the plate like up-turned golf tees amid the bone-marrow gravy. I ate the dish using a dainty knife and fork with pointy handles that reminded me of chopsticks. Another winner: rich but not too rich, the guinea-fowl breast stuffed with delicious herbs of some sort and the parsnips offering little earthy-vegetable side explosions (though the whole dish could have done with some French beans or something green, in this culinary hiker's humble opinion). I polished off a chocolate fondant with a little river of chocolate flooding out, tinged with the flavour of mandarin. Marvellous, too.

Mr Jeeves came over and I learned that his real name was Patrick from Slovakia. I asked him if Mr Rogan was around for a quick chat and he replied: "I don't think it's as easy as that. It must be pre-booked. He may not be in the village." He said this in an earnest yet sympathetic manner. Then he told me that a sous-chef named Tom Reeves had been in charge of Rogan & Co that day, not Mr Rogan himself.

Patrick disappeared. He returned shortly afterward and said: "He's not available I'm afraid. He's a busy man with a business to run and

I'm afraid I don't know where he is right now." Which was fair enough, I had not made an appointment and the Rogan empire was vast, extending to restaurants as far away as Singapore with possible spin-offs to come in America and the Middle East, such was the renown of his excellent cooking. This was big business, even bigger with the three Michelin stars. I thanked Patrick for trying and asked him what Slovakians thought of the war in Ukraine – after all, the country borders Ukraine. He said, after expressing concerns for Ukrainians: "I don't think there is anything for us to worry about. We are just waiting for it to be over."

Patrick left and Mrs Jeeves came over once again and I learned that her real name was Amy, originally from Essex but now living in Grange-over-Sands, just to the south of Cartmel. She said everyone had been delighted by the award of three stars at L'Enclume and that she often enjoyed helping out on Our Farm. Mr Rogan, she said, was "really down to earth and lovely" and she was proud of the Cartmel restaurants' sustainability. We talked for a while. Then she packed the delicious sourdough bread that I had not finished in a takeaway box, a single eyebrow only slightly quivering when I made this request (the bread would be good for a snack later and I did not want to waste it), and I thanked her and made my way into the old square in the centre of the unofficial culinary capital of Cumbria.

Yes, the bill for this extravagant lunch had been high but, overall, I agreed with the verdict of *Cumbria Life* magazine: that Rogan "managed to navigate a path that is neither pretentious nor elitist, albeit at prices that not everyone can afford". Anyway, I could make up for the splurge in a few nights' time when I was due to stay in a remote (free) bothy.

It had been quite a meal.

Long walk to Tourism HQ
Cartmel to Bowness

So began an unexpectedly long walk.

When planning this Lakeland hike, I had added the foodie diversion to Bowland Bridge and down to Cartmel to get a feel for this more than up-and-coming side of the region. Looking at the map back then, seeing the distance from Cartmel up to Windermere to catch the same short ferry as yesterday to Bowness, I had thought: *no problem, I can do that after lunch.* I had a room reserved at a place called Puddle Duck Lodge in the booming Lakeland tourist centre of Bowness. How could I possibly resist the *Puddle Duck Lodge?* Just stroll up the lake to the Puddle Duck for a late afternoon nose around Lakeland's holidaymaker HQ. No problem. That, at least, was the theory.

After inspecting the fine medieval interior of the church at Cartmel Priory and Mr Rogan's shop selling tea towels, hampers and more yellow-backed books, I nonchalantly set off, a fine-dining lunch inside me and a one-Michelin star spring in my step. It was past 3 p.m. I exited Cartmel's tangle of lanes feeling slightly observed for no good reason – there was a *Midsomer Murders* mystery feel to the village that I could not quite put my finger on – crossed a deserted racecourse and, shortly afterward, entered thick woodland with a velvety carpet of bluebells.

This led to a series of fell farms. Up and down the footpath I went beneath a cornflower-blue sky marked only by the vapour trail of a solitary plane. This was joyful territory with resiny pine forest opening to hazy views of the Irish Sea. I passed an empty tarn with tall feathery reeds, Bigland Tarn, and a field of distinguished white horses. I fancied I heard a train whistle as I moved from High Brow Edge to Low Brow Edge, considering what this might mean in terms of the telling of a tale. Across the way, I could see the Old Man of Coniston, the knobbly silhouette of its peak rising to the west. The path traversed a cattle field where no cattle took chase. I came to the dreaded A590, crossed it and passed the Newby Bridge and Swan hotels, having taken a bridge over the river Leven, and arrived at the southern tip of England's largest natural lake. I soon realized that what looked like a fairly short ramble up the shore to Ambleside was not that at all: a further *7 miles* were required.

My energy levels seemed to collapse at the very thought of what lay ahead; I had already gone a very long way. In this suddenly exhausted state and having discovered the ferry from Lakeside, at the southern end of Windermere, to Bowness had finished for the day, I trudged mutteringly onward along the lane (my mutterings mainly themed on *why had I not looked at the ******* map properly*, or words to that effect). This was a definite low point. I followed a long road, trying to find a better path by the lake, but failing. Darkness was beginning to descend. I was tempted to call a cab. My portable library seemed heavier than ever. In a state of half-madness, I dragged myself on, arriving at the other shorter ferry, the one I had taken yesterday and which operated till late, crossing Windermere and locating Puddle Duck Lodge, where a tall man answered the door. I could barely speak. The tall man led me upstairs, showed me my "dedicated bathroom" down a hall and took me to a tiny, pristine, very comfortable white bedroom, asking me as he did: "Would you like brown toast with your breakfast, would you like milk with your coffee, would you like a yoghurt, would you like butter on your toast, would you like orange or apple juice?" He repeated back my answers as though giving evidence in the High Court. When he left, I promptly collapsed on the tiny single bed. My tiny pristine white room, I noted, was decorated with Union Jack and Ukrainian flags as well as Beatrix Potter-style paraphernalia. I stared at these decorations with no thoughts going through my mind other than: *why, why, why didn't I read the map right?*

Feet aching badly but in need of sustenance, I shuffled to the nearby Westmorland Inn, ordered a pint and a packet of dry-roasted peanuts and sat in an armchair in a corner with a cushion that (annoyingly) slipped down the chair the whole time. I was too tired to move to a better place to sit. I was too tired to do any more than "be", in the Westmorland pub in an armchair with an annoyingly slipping cushion while sipping my pint and eating my dry-roasted peanuts. I even took off my boots and rested my feet, which seemed to have started pulsing weirdly, on top of them.

I was sitting near an elderly couple, who were arguing quietly a couple of tables away.

The woman, quite fierce and leading the disagreement, favoured Boris Johnson, the then prime minister, and his approach to Brexit.

"At least he got it done," she said.

The man murmured something.

"Bollocks!" she replied. "You're just a Remoaner."

The man murmured something else.

"Don't tell me what I can or cannot do," she replied. "I'm not going to stick at home twenty-three hours a day."

The man sighed and said: "Anyway, would you like another drink?"

"Go on then," she said.

I shuffled back to the Puddle Duck Lodge, my feet seeming almost to have seized up, and looked at my phone walking tracker: I had covered 24 miles and taken 52,969 steps that day. Two miles off a marathon. What on earth had I been thinking?

* * *

When in the heart of tourist-land, be a tourist.

Breakfast was delivered on a tray to your pristine, comfortable white bedroom at the Puddle Duck. This was the policy. The Puddle Duck had a lot of such policies and a sizeable laminated booklet outlining them: "No visitors in rooms without prior arrangement", "no muddy footwear", "no washing clothes in rooms or erecting washing lines in the room or garden", "no hot food other than breakfast in rooms", "no cooking of any kind", "no hanging of clothes or towels (wet or dry) on the hand rails or curtain pole etc. as most of the furniture is hand painted so please respect this", "no celebration banners/balloons to be attached to the furniture or walls without prior permission". A lot of "no"s and that was just a few of them. The laminated booklet continued: "Anyone found breaking these rules may be asked to leave and will still be charged." Jenny and David, the owners, clearly ran a tight ship. Having read this on arrival, I had naturally been ultra-careful, watching my every move in the almost certainty that I would surely, at some point, make some terrible mistake. *Do not, whatever you do*, I kept saying to myself, *attach any celebration banners to anything*. I had kept a keen eye on myself. I had only just pulled through.

In the hall before leaving, I asked Jenny and David, the tall man from last night, about the ferry to Lakeside. After yesterday's exertions, I wanted to go out on the water of England's largest lake to be a regular tourist, Bowness-style, enjoying the gently passing scenery on a purring pleasure boat before checking out the old Lakeside & Haverthwaite Railway (the source of yesterday's train whistle).

Jenny and David told me how to go about it: tickets for both could be bought down by the pier, they said. Then they told me they had been involved in a church fundraiser for Ukraine and had considered taking in a refugee. "The problem is, we're fully booked in the summer," said David.

I complimented them on the pristine cleanliness of Puddle Duck Lodge and Jenny said: "When we bought this place in 2018, we took seven months cleaning it. I don't like going anywhere dirty." I could tell. I could not recall staying in a place quite so spotless, nor so super-efficiently organized. Ever.

Down the hill I went past a Polish shop, a Bargain Booze off-licence, a parade of specialist hiking shops, art galleries, pubs, ice-cream parlours, jewellery shops, a Tesco Express, fish-and-chip shops, a Chinese, a Thai and an Italian restaurant. Bowness was already buzzing with tourists, even early on a weekday in April. I purchased a ticket from Windermere Lake Cruises and joined quite a few fellow holidaymakers on the *Swan* ferry.

We were soon gliding past Belle Isle. A commentary on the speakers explained this was the only inhabited island on Windermere. We also learned that the short ferry I had taken across the lake yesterday was in the location of a service that could be traced back to 1438. We wove between red marker buoys indicating shallow sections and were told that the *Swan* dated from 1938, was made in Barrow-in-Furness and had a capacity of 533 passengers. We passed millionaires' lakeside mansions that Wordsworth (more of whom later) would have had more than a few thoughts about, youth hostels, yurts and forests, fells rising beyond. At the Lakeside ferry mooring, we passengers disembarked, crossed from the mooring to a platform – a matter of a few yards – and boarded a burgundy-coloured steam train. This soon chugged away down the line for 3 miles, steam sliding past the carriages in a thick silver fog. As we followed the winding river Leven, we were told, in yet another commentary, that the line dated from 1869 and had been closed to passengers in 1965 before being reopened by enthusiasts in 1973. We arrived at Haverthwaite, disembarking and strolling along the platform for a while to stretch our legs – Haverthwaite seemed to consist of this station, a large car park next to it and not a whole lot else – before re-embarking and returning on the steam train to the ferry, and sailing back to Bowness.

A peaceful morning… and easy on the feet.

Nosing along the A591
Bowness to Ambleside

Tourism completed for the day – or so I thought – I ambled toward Ambleside, yet another Lakeland honeypot, 5 miles to the north, at the top of Windermere. The plan was to use Ambleside (population: 2,596, to Bowness' metropolis-like 3,814) as a base to visit the

Wordsworth houses at Rydal and Grasmere, staying two nights at YHA Ambleside to keep down costs, which had begun to spiral thanks to hipster nights out and stuffed guinea fowls with white-chocolate purées and fancy miniature parsnips shaped like up-turned golf tees. From Ambleside, the trail would lead on to the peaceful delights of Langdale Valley, the "tourist zone" of Hawkshead, Bowness, Ambleside and Grasmere in the central-southern Lakes complete.

Bowness had felt like a traditional British seaside resort that just happened to be on an inland sea rather than a salty one, surrounded by mountains and full of quite a few hikers, although most tourists seemed happy enough in the restaurants and pubs and taking boat trips (nothing wrong with that).

Leaving the town centre of Bowness behind around 2 p.m., I soon arrived at a building by the water that looked like an avant-garde modern-art gallery in California or perhaps northern Spain, all angular roofs on a series of connected barn-like buildings with high windows and decked terraces. This was the quite new (2019) £20-million Windermere Jetty Museum, right on the northern edge of town. Feeling it would be churlish to ignore a quite new £20-million museum that happened to be on the route, and wondering what it was all about, I went inside.

By chance, as I did, the marketing manager for the Windermere Jetty Museum, Sorcha Hunter, was in the lobby. Seeing me nosing around, she came over and cheerfully offered to give me an impromptu tour, which was very nice of her. Sorcha had ginger hair and lavender-coloured painted fingernails and was both extremely enthusiastic and clued up about the Windermere Jetty Museum, as well she might given her job, I suppose. But it all seemed genuine, and I quickly understood why.

Sorcha showed me *Dolly*, "the oldest mechanically powered boat in the world, which is actually in the *Guinness World Records*". *Dolly*, built in 1850, had been raised from the depths of Windermere in 1962 and was mounted in a side room next to a collection of old life jackets. She showed me Beatrix Potter's rowing boat, in which

Potter had spent many hours rowing around on Moss Eccles Tarn. She showed me a steam launch named *Branksome* dating from 1896, on which Prince Philip had travelled during a visit to Windermere in 1966, the lovely original walnut panelling and velvet upholstery still in place.

Sorcha showed me old speedboats. She showed me newer speedboats, some that had taken part in speed-record-attempt races on Windermere, although a speed limit on the lake had been set at 10 miles an hour since 2005, partly due to concerns for safety with so many people on Jet-Skis. Then she told me about the pioneering days of seaplanes on Windermere. She told me about the importance of boats to tourism in the Lake District, especially after the Kendal–Windermere railway had been completed in 1847, "bringing working people from nearby cities"; this was when Bowness had become Tourism HQ and was partly why it remained so today although roads had also improved somewhat since the mid-nineteenth century. In 1869, Windermere Iron Steamboat Company had run cruises on the *Lady of the Lake* from Lakeside in the south, when the railway to there had opened. The railways had been key to opening up the lake.

This heyday of tourism on the water lasted until around the 1960s, when people began jetting abroad to the sunny climes of the south of Europe. "People would go out on their boats and show off," Sorcha said. "It was a real social scene on the water, and it was incredibly important to demonstrate your wealth and the fashions of the time – the innovations of boat building. We are a county of lakes and boat builders. That's why going on the lake is still so popular. It's a beautiful lake and people enjoy being on the water." The Jetty Museum, which had received cash from the National Lottery Heritage Fund and Arts Council England to cover the £20-million makeover, was home to 11 vessels that were registered with National Historic Ships UK.

Sorcha took me to see the peaceful waterside café. Then she took me to an area with elaborate outside heated seating pods designed by the artist Charlie Whinney. She showed me the museum's working heritage steam launch, *Osprey* (1902), which was varnished and polished and ready to take a tour later in the day. She showed me a pond for model boats, and a spot at the front of the museum with an "augmented reality experience" in which you could see a boat's propeller with bubbles rising off it mysteriously appearing out of thin air in 3-D, if you pointed your smartphone in the right direction.

In half an hour, without my having had an appointment, I had enjoyed a very good look about the Windermere Jetty Museum.

Thank you, Sorcha Hunter.

I walked on.

I was following pavements along the A591. There was no other way. People did not seem to say hello when they passed, unlike just about everywhere else I had been. It felt almost as though I had entered the "urban Lakes", even though no such thing existed; how could there be anything remotely *urban* about a region with a population of 42,000 people and dramatic fells rising all about amid sheep farms and dreamy waters? I dropped by at a place called Brockhole, a visitor centre run by the Lake District National Park, with adventure activities, a large car park and a small museum (free entry) in the former second home of an eighteenth-century wool merchant. The museum was full of stuffed creatures including herons, otters, black-headed gulls, pike, trout, kestrels, golden eagles, red squirrels – all sorts, with plentiful panels on the wildlife and history of the Lakes. An intriguing little pit stop.

Not long after, I reached YHA Ambleside, which had a great lakeside location on the southern edge of Ambleside, about a quarter of a mile outside the town centre. It was, said the receptionist, taken over mainly by "two parties of rugby lads with their dads". The receptionist seemed to be warning me about this. These lads, pre-teenage and teenage, and their dads were running rampant all over the place, I already saw; the lads leaping into the lake in boxer shorts, the fathers loping about drinking pints and wearing Hawaiian outfits – including grass skirts (some of them) – as a Hawaiian evening was planned in the restaurant/bar a bit later. YHA Ambleside could take 250 guests and was the largest hostel yet on my journey; again, I had a private room (thankfully).

I dropped off the backpack and ate a pizza on the terrace, watching the sun set, reading Wordsworth's *Guide* and listening to the twang of hula-hula music.

Wordsworth seemed to spend a great deal of his *Guide* discussing what "the man of genuine taste" might and should appreciate, i.e. what he, Wordsworth, the Poet Laureate-to-be, considered to be of "genuine taste", I was beginning to notice. His views were wide and varied.

For one thing, he believed that there should be better organized trees on the islands of Derwentwater: "If the wood upon them were managed with more taste, they might become interesting features in the landscape." For another, he believed that old-fashioned cottages and dwellings, as opposed to flashy mansions of the Brockhole type, were "models of elegance" that gave "high gratification to the man of genuine taste".

He disliked tourists in general: "The lakes had now become celebrated; visitors flocked hither from all parts of England; the fancies of some were smitten so deeply that they became settlers; and the islands of Derwentwater and Winandermere [the name Wordsworth gave to Windermere], as they offered the strongest temptation, were the first places settled upon, and were instantly defaced by the intrusion."

He disliked larch plantations, which altered the "original appearance of the rocky steps", preferring "native hollies and ash trees". He disliked houses that were painted white – a pet hate; he preferred "something between a cream and a dust colour commonly called stone colour". He was not a fan of the European Alps, he said in an aside, considering the lakes of the Lake District "much more interesting".

He approved of the opinions of Thomas Gray, formed during Gray's visit in 1769, a year before Wordsworth's birth. He even quoted Gray describing Grasmere: "No flaring gentleman's house or garden-wall, breaks upon the repose of this little unsuspected paradise; but all is peace, rusticity, and happy poverty, in its neatest and most becoming attire."

A generation on, however, Wordsworth said he was offended "at almost every turn, by an introduction of discordant objects, disturbing that peaceful harmony of form and colour, which had been through a long lapse of ages most happily preserved."

In his *Guide*, Wordsworth was *going off on one*, in a most delightful Poet Laureate-to-be way. I especially enjoyed the part in which he praised the little chapel at Buttermere, now with Wainwright's memorial, of course: "A man must be very insensible who would not be touched with pleasure at the sight of the chapel of Buttermere, so strikingly expressing, by its diminutive size, how small must be the congregation there assembled, as it were, like one family." I had been touched there too (so seemed to have passed the Wordsworth sensibility/*taste* test).

Wordsworth saved his harshest criticism for outsiders building big new abodes:

> It is probable, that in a few years the country on the margin of the Lakes will fall almost entirely into the possession of gentry, either strangers or natives. It is then much to be wished, that a better taste should prevail among these new proprietors; and, as they cannot be expected to leave things to themselves, that skill and knowledge should prevent unnecessary deviations from the path of simplicity and beauty along which, without design and unconsciously, their humble predecessors have moved. In this wish the author will be joined by persons of pure taste throughout the whole island, who, by their visits (often repeated) to the Lakes in the North of England, testify that they deem the district a sort of

> national property, in which every man has a right and
> interest who has an eye to perceive and a heart to enjoy.

"Pure taste", "genuine taste", an "eye to perceive" and a "heart to enjoy"; Wordsworth clearly believed the average Joe needed to work on these things.

With his use of "a sort of national property", however, Wordsworth had been in effect calling for what was to come: the National Trust. He was way ahead of his time, a trailblazer for commonly owned and protected green spaces before the modern national-park system had even begun; Yellowstone National Park in Wyoming, Montana and Idaho, considered the first national park anywhere, was only formed in 1872. It took until 1951 for that to happen with the creation of the Lake District National Park, although the National Trust, begun in 1895, had been quietly and cannily snapping up so much land before then.

What Wordsworth would have thought of the "pure taste" of pizzas and lagers and men in straw dresses and twangy Hawaiian music was another matter; though YHA Ambleside was not (seemingly) for the time being in the "possession of the gentry", at least. So the old Lakeland Bard ought to have been happy about that.

The sun dropped beyond the fells as a last blaze of golden light slowly faded across the jade-sheen of Windermere and the sky bloomed above in crimson and pink. What a very fine setting for a hostel.

I read a text from Kasia that said that both Lena and Anna had had their visa applications accepted: "It's great news today. More later." Not just great, *fantastic* news. Kasia had to call her parents in Poland to discuss the details of getting the pair to Warsaw airport; we would talk the next day.

I continued boning up on Wordsworth, drinking beer and watching the shifting colours in the electric sky, jolly hula-hula music drifting on to the terrace, fathers in straw skirts occasionally skipping by.

All quite normal at YHA Ambleside, it would seem.

The big Wordsworth day lay ahead: Ambleside proper followed by Rydal and Grasmere awaited.

Hikers, bikers and a cult
Ambleside to Rydal and Grasmere and back

Ambleside was home to a great many shops selling walking stuff. To get there, I had passed a Roman fort with fewer remains than the one at Hardknott, the giant beer garden of Waterside Inn, Ambleside Manor (a "vegetarian country guest house") and a pretty park with a croquet lawn, tennis courts and crazy golf. The spire of St Mary's Church, designed by George Gilbert Scott, Victorian architect of London's St Pancras Station, shot up behind the park and I went to see the stained-glass windows in honour of William and Dorothy Wordsworth in the Wordsworth Chapel to the left. Then I walked up a street with both a Co-op and a Spar supermarket, arriving at Market Cross and what seemed like "base camp" for Lakeland hikers and climbers.

Serious-climber shops offered ropes and crampons, while an assortment of less technical shops sold hiker basics, the most prominent of these being Gaynor Sports, which claimed on a sign to be "BRITAIN'S LARGEST OUTDOOR SUPERSTORE". Inside, a dizzying array of waterproof clothing, fleeces and boots was to be found, a veritable cathedral to casual rambling gear. I walked around in a daze – overhearing one shop assistant saying to another that "there's going to be a hell of a lot of mountain rescue today", as the wind was up to 65 miles an hour on Helvellyn – and being tempted by all sorts of new, latest-design waterproof clothing, even though what I had was fine and no way could I buy anything as the backpack was jam-packed. There was a definite moreish quality to walking stuff and I seemed to have fallen for it hook, line and sinker: a proper newborn Mountain Warehouse man.

Outside, I came to Stock Ghyll, a stream that once powered cloth mills and which led up to Stock Ghyll Force, a waterfall. This stream was notable for a little stone house, Bridge House, that spanned the water and dated from the seventeenth century; an icon of Ambleside, having survived so long and said once to have been home to a family of eight. The Armitt Museum was a little further on with an excellent second-hand bookshop in which I had to control myself (I had also seemed to have fallen hook, line and sinker for old books on the Lakes), an exhibition on Beatrix Potter's farms and an upstairs library. Here I talked to a woman who was busy at a computer digitalizing the correspondence of the local sociologist and writer Harriet Martineau (1802–1876), who had written her very own *Complete Guide to the English Lakes* in 1855. As a volunteer, she had also digitalized the letters of the Armitt sisters, who had been behind the museum, which opened in 1912. "You have to go through all the boring stuff," she said. "But then you get an interesting occurrence. It's social history actually, keeps me out of mischief."

Beyond a police station and a fire station outside the Armitt Museum was The Knoll, a grey stone building where Martineau had lived, now a private house. From there I walked down a lane and across a field, listening to the "tap tap tap" of woodpeckers and arriving at the sixteenth-century Rydal Hall, an imposing building run as a retreat by the Diocese of Carlisle and where I met the Christian Motorcyclists Association UK. A gathering of men and women in black leather with white crosses on their backs had assembled by the entrance to Rydal Hall, outside which several dozen shiny bikes had been parked. The association was about to hold its annual general meeting.

"There are seventy-two of us for the AGM and we will worship and praise together," said Paul, secretary of the Lake District and Lancashire branch, who was grey bearded and wore badges stitched into his leather jacket that said: "JESUS, LORD AND SAVIOUR, CHRIST", and "I'M NOT PERFECT, JUST FORGIVEN". I complimented him on his gleaming motorbike. He replied: "My ride is irrelevant, it's just a bike. The relevance is we are Christian and we take the good words of Jesus Christ on the road – to bikers, motorists and anyone else who needs our help, support or prayer."

He asked about me and I explained *Lost in the Lakes*.

"We aren't lost, brother," he said.

Mike Fitton, national chairman of the Christian Motorcyclists Association UK, motto "Taking the Gospel to Bikers", sauntered up, also wearing a leather jacket with a white cross, also grey bearded, but his was less bushy than Paul's. He handed me the *Biker Bible*, which included a "contemporary English version" of the Bible as well as articles with headlines such as "With God nothing is wasted", and "Saved at the gate of hell!"

"With compliments," he said as I took the book. He said that 120,000 copies of the *Biker Bible* had been distributed by the Christian Motorcyclists Association during the past ten years. "We're not a club, we're a Christian mission to the motorcycle world. To every aspect of the motorcycle world we are sharing the Gospel message. It's a bikers' community with regular rallies, we meet at bikers' cafes and go touring. We are motorcyclists but foremost we are Christians and we've been doing it thirty-five years. Christians who are bikers, not bikers who are Christians."

Brief sermon from the national chairman over, Paul of the local branch added: "We only plant the seeds, and God waters them. We're going to room three [at Rydal Hall] for lunch. Goodbye! God bless you!"

As I have said previously, you never quite knew whom you might meet on a walk in the Lakes: all sorts of hikers, even Christian bikers.

I continued down a path to Rydal Mount, Wordsworth's old house, where he lived from 1813 to 1850 and where he died.

During Wordsworth's years at Rydal Mount, tourists would come just to gape at him. He was an early nineteenth-century literary star (before Charles Dickens swept the floor in that regard), having made his name with his poem "Lyrical Ballads", co-authored with Samuel

Taylor Coleridge. Yet he was deemed the genius of the two, which Coleridge had himself conceded, perhaps explaining the latter's opium habits and predilection for risk-taking climbs: *what was the point with such a brilliant fellow poet making him look average?*

The two had joined forces and travelled together to the West Country when younger, with Dorothy always in tow. Earlier, before meeting Coleridge, Wordsworth had travelled to France on a walking tour – 20 miles a day quite normal – reaching as far as the Swiss Alps and Italy and enjoying the excitement of the Revolution. During this jaunt he had even fathered a daughter, Caroline, with a woman named Annette Vallon, but war between France and England got in the way of keeping in touch, although he honoured a financial commitment. Perhaps if war had not happened Wordsworth might have moved across the Channel and the history of the Lakes and Wordsworth would be quite different, as Hunter Davies has suggested.

The poet had just enough cash to keep going when he returned, partly thanks, initially, to a bequest of £900 by an artist friend, plus sponsorship by the Wedgwood family and money from a debt due to his late father finally being paid. This settlement allowed him to marry his childhood sweetheart, Mary Hutchinson of Penrith, with whom he was to father five children (though three died before their parents did). Wordsworth became Poet Laureate in 1843 on the death of Robert Southey of Keswick, and his reputation was completed with the posthumous publication of "The Prelude", a poem about his early life.

It was strange to see Rydal Mount and imagine tourists in the days Wordsworth lived there, gathering nervously at the end of the lane for a glimpse of the great Poet Laureate – and you could understand why he chose Rydal, with its commanding position and views of Rydal Water to the west and the verdant valley leading to Ambleside to the east. Neatly tucked away, yet not quite in the sticks.

A guide named Clara showed me round, a private tour as no other tourists had booked this time slot. We took in the drawing room with its old chairs, tables, cigar boxes, top hats, inkstands and so on, plus original portraits of the poet and his sister that define public understanding of their appearance. Wordsworth: aquiline nose, sharp chin, inquisitive eyes, high forehead. Sometimes looking a bit smug. Dorothy: head slightly bowed, demure and pensive yet knowing-looking, and, later in life, quite determined and tough.

The house was owned by the Kean family, Clara said, who "only come here for holidays".

Clara was Hong Kong Chinese. "I've been here since 1991. I've been working here eleven years and still have a lot to read." She was referring to Wordsworth's life – she was currently enjoying learning of the poor behaviour of Coleridge when the trio took a tour of Scotland.

"I heard that he died in the attic study," Clara said, when we went upstairs to a room with glorious views, old letters and a portable writing bureau, which felt like the beating heart of Rydal Mount, even though Wordsworth's had come to a stop there.

After investigating the well-looked after garden, I walked from Rydal Mount to Dove Cottage in Grasmere along a 2-mile track with a fine view of Rydal Water to the left – this track is known macabrely as the "Coffin Route" because it was the way corpses were taken in medieval times to the church of St Oswald's in Grasmere. I was bang on time for my meeting with Michael McGregor, director of the Wordsworth Trust, on the terrace of the café next to the whitewashed facade of Dove Cottage.

* * *

I had been talking to a couple on a neighbouring table when Michael arrived: Anne and Mick. Anne was reading a quote from inside the brim of her coffee cup. It was from Wordsworth, and it said: "My heart leaps up when I behold a rainbow in the sky". Anne said: "I think that's beautiful. My daughter died five years ago and we have adopted rainbows as a way of remembering her. So this is very special. She lived her life to the full, but yeah, little signs like these: we look for them and we see them everywhere."

It was a fitting moment: Wordsworth's poetry still touching people's lives, with the person responsible for ensuring the word still got out pulling up a chair.

Michael ordered a coffee and asked if I would like another. He was a genial, softly spoken man, aged 56, and had been working at Dove Cottage on and off since he was 22. He wore a grey jacket and a blue spotted shirt and had amused gimlet eyes. He was from Blythe, north of Newcastle, and had applied for a position at Dove Cottage after studying English at Leeds University. A friend had pointed out the advert for a Wordsworth job in Grasmere and he had gone for it, despite not being a Wordsworth obsessive. Michael had first worked in the gift shop, then conducted tours, acted as assistant to the director, then taken over as director himself.

"I love poetry," he said, explaining his career path and quickly getting down to basics: "We have about forty-five thousand visitors a year, back in the early 1990s we were getting eighty-five thousand visitors."

What had happened?

"The successive Iraq wars and foot-and-mouth, then there was SARS," he said. Severe acute respiratory syndrome. "These were natural shocks to the system really."

The result had been a big drop-off in visitors from Japan and the United States, meanwhile competition from other attractions in the Lakes, such as the adventure centre at Brockhole, had also affected domestic tourists. Other factors were the rise in self-catering accommodation – "on a wet day people might come to us or they might watch Sky TV" – as well as the simple fact that "people may think: *well I've been there, I've done that, I don't want to go again*".

To counter this, the Wordsworth Trust had recently redeveloped the museum and improved the gardens so those who had been before might be tempted back.

The subject soon turned to Wordsworth himself, naturally. Why was there still such a fascination with the poet more than a century and a half on?

Michael, unsurprisingly, was ready for this. "A lot of what Wordsworth articulates about his relationship with the natural world, particularly the natural world of the Lake District, is very much echoed in what people come here for today: that sense of solace, that sense of rejuvenation, that sense of slowing down from the hurly-burly of their daily lives, you know," he said. "This was Wordsworth, two hundred years before mindfulness was trendy. This was what Wordsworth was talking about. *Why don't you slow down? Why don't you spend half an hour watching a butterfly?*"

He paused and said: "There was a time after Wordsworth's death in 1850 when the Lake District was really known as Wordsworth-shire." Such was the cult following of his poetry. "It's moved away from that, partly because the Victorian veneration of Wordsworth as the great philosophical poet has waned, and one of the challenges we've had is keeping interest in Wordsworth going on the curriculum at schools. So a lot of our work now is finding various routes into the curriculum. We work directly with schools."

I asked Michael whether Wordsworth's popularity had ironically led to the tourist invasion that he hoped to avoid.

He was, unsurprisingly, ready for this too. "It's a very interesting point actually. We all know that Wordsworth campaigned against the railway coming, which is why the railway stops at Windermere now. What Wordsworth wanted, and he wasn't against tourism per se, what he was reacting against was that sense of mass tourism. Because for Wordsworth, it's all about the individual connection and I suppose his concern was that he wanted people to have the right views, the right perspective, the right attitude in terms of how they approach the Lakes. And it is a connection that is very much about individual connection rather than mass connection."

Did the director of the Wordsworth Trust think Wordsworth, so concerned about what was the *right attitude* and *taste*, was a bit of a snob?

Michael paused, chuckled and chose his words carefully: "We know Wordsworth started off as a radical poet. He wrote a letter to the Bishop of Llandaff, which if he'd actually sent it, would probably would have got him tried for treason. He was a staunch republican in his youth. And 'Lyrical Ballads' is very much about his challenge and Coleridge's challenge to the world of poetry. Poetry can be about a whole range of different people, so it can be about the dispossessed, it can be about the homeless, it can be about people with mental illness. So Wordsworth had that inclusivity in his poetry. So I don't think he was trying to keep the hoi polloi out. I think he worried that industrialization had dulled minds, and everything was becoming mechanized and everything was about mass production and so Wordsworth feared that actually mass tourism becomes an extension of that with trainloads of people coming up from the great conurbations."

Michael paused again, seeking the right way forward: "It's all about connections with Wordsworth and connections were being broken. He writes a lot about the connection between the farmer and his land, you know, and how that connection is broken by government policy and by industrialization, with people losing their land. Wordsworth, throughout his life, had a strong sense of the importance of education and he wanted his poetry to live and do good. It wasn't just passive, you know. But as with everything with Wordsworth, it's complicated. Wordsworth moved from a republican view to a Tory view to a High Church view in his later life. Younger poets felt he'd betrayed them, betrayed the cause."

I asked Michael about Wordsworth's effect on railways in the Lakes.

"Well, the plan was to run it right through up to Keswick [from Windermere]," he said. "It would have transformed the Lake District completely. You'd have been able to stop in Grasmere. In a sense what we've got in terms of all the traffic congestion on the main road through the Lake District comes from that. Of course, in Wordsworth's time the main road through the Lake District was this road here, the one that passes right in front of Dove Cottage. It's very difficult to know how it would have panned out."

Wordsworth's intervention, however, had been crucial: "He was, in the 1840s, a very well-known figure, he was Poet Laureate, and finally, after years of critical ridicule and public neglect, he *finally* had become the recognized poet of his generation. When you look at the trajectory of Wordsworth's poetry, we like to claim that Wordsworth's golden decade was the period from 1798 to 1808 – that broadly coincides with the Dove Cottage years. But when he was writing what many consider now to be his greatest poetry, that was the time at which he was, critically speaking, getting savaged by the press. People didn't understand him. Coleridge says of Wordsworth that he was striding so far ahead he was almost disappearing in the distance. And what it needed was, as it were, for public taste and appreciation to catch up. It's always that thing when anyone is doing something that is absolutely radical and new, it takes time for it to become the norm. So, the critics absolutely savaged his focus on the poor and the dispossessed – on what they called not fit subjects for poetry. And for Wordsworth really, when it was getting into the 1830s and the 1840s, that's when people started to recognize *actually he is one of our greatest poets*. If he'd spoken out against the railway at an earlier period, he wouldn't have had the same profile really."

I asked Michael about Wordsworth's regular use of the word "sublime" and "sublimity" in his descriptions of the Lakes in his *Guide* (you can't help but notice this).

"The *sublime* was fashionable parlance at the time," Michael replied. "It goes back to the mid-eighteenth century really, that sense of the sublime and the picturesque. It's about a combination of beauty, horror and immensity, that was kind of how it was defined. So, it's that sense of something that is awe-inspiring and just a little bit scary as well. A bit dangerous. So, it has a kind of different meaning to its present-day meaning really. So that's why Wordsworth would have used it, though after Wordsworth embraces the picturesque, he ends up rejecting the picturesque because it's such a limiting view of the landscape and a very formulaic view of landscape."

Michael said that in the early eighteenth century "there was no such thing as the Lake District. Cumbria was a place you got through as quickly as you possibly could. Because it was a scary place. It was wild, sparsely populated, and so there was a sense of: there's nothing there. Nothing to look at." How Daniel Defoe had found it on his *Tour Through the Whole Island of Great Britain*. "It was only really from the 1750s onward when artists actually started to come here, particularly from the 1790s and the start of the Napoleonic wars when people couldn't go to Europe any more. That was when people started to consider that what was considered threatening was actually also something attractive." People then would come seeking the "picturesque", a term popularized by an eighteenth-century cleric named William Gilpin, who had even written a book on the "rules" of understanding what was picturesque, suggesting where to stand to view scenes to their best advantage. Some visitors, such as Thomas Gray, would carry a Claude glass, which was used to witness such points to their greatest advantage, to make the very most of the picturesque.

Michael continued: "Wordsworth has this phrase which he writes in his greatest poem "The Prelude" about being 'fostered alike by beauty and by fear'. For Wordsworth, everything is not some kind of bucolic idyll, the Lake District is a tough place, you know. It's a place to live, it's a place to farm, it's also a place where the landscape can be threatening."

That, said Michael, was *sublimity*.

I asked him about Wordsworth's dislike of mansions built by wealthy industrialists from Manchester and Liverpool. "Wordsworth said that if you are going to create a human structure within the landscape, you should work with the 'invisible hand of art'." This was why he did not like whitewashed buildings. "Yes, well Dove Cottage *was* white actually because it was a pub. For Wordsworth, the idea of creating these big statement properties that glared down at everybody and drew the eye, well that was anathema to him."

I asked Michael about mass tourism now and people coming to Dove Cottage: "I think Wordsworth would be quite pleased. Wordsworth had a very sure sense of his own destiny, absolutely. But he would have worried about the loss of the individual connection with the landscape."

I thanked Michael for his insights – Wordsworth did somehow seem to hold the key to understanding the Lake District – and took a picture of him outside Dove Cottage. Then I went round the old house, admiring the rusticity of it all: the flagstone floors, open fireplaces, low ceilings, beams, creaky staircases, thick stone walls. Then I went to the brilliant museum outlining Wordsworth's life and Dorothy's, explaining how, when they lived at Dove Cottage, they would walk for mile upon mile in the fells (Dorothy would make the 8-mile round trip to Ambleside to collect the post several times a week). Displays included a pair of William's old socks (remarkably well preserved) as well as his walking stick, old sandwich box and postbag. Then I walked into the centre of Grasmere, about half a mile on, to see William and Dorothy's graves in the graveyard of St Oswald's Church. Then I looked through the windows of the various outdoor-clothing stores, stopped for a sausage roll and a pint in the garden of Tweedies Bar and returned to Ambleside along a green dotted path to the south of Grasmere and Rydal Water. The wind had picked up and was funnelling through the valley, turning the surface of the lakes into a series of swirls like the strokes on a Van Gogh painting. Banks of bluebells swept to the shores in a purple haze. Wild swimmers were splashing about. I headed for St Mary's steeple and returned to the youth hostel. I was about to visit my favourite valley yet.

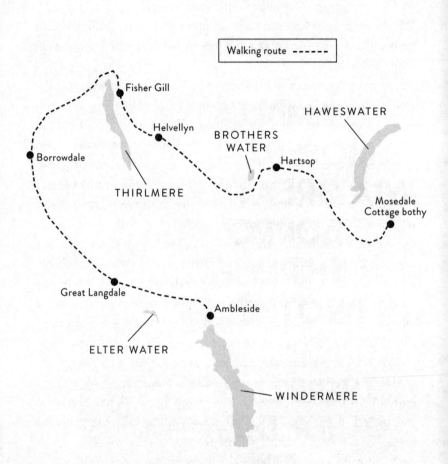

Walking route -------

Fisher Gill

Helvellyn

BROTHERS
WATER

HAWESWATER

Borrowdale

Hartsop

THIRLMERE

Mosedale
Cottage bothy

Great Langdale

Ambleside

ELTER WATER

WINDERMERE

AMBLESIDE TO MOSEDALE VALLEY, VIA GREAT LANGDALE, BORROWDALE, THIRLMERE AND BROTHERS WATER

"THERE'LL BE NOTHING OTHER THAN TOURISM ONE DAY"

There can be few greater pleasures than setting forth early as the sun rises in the Lake District – as I may have stated previously – heading up into the fells (Loughrigg) with no one else about and moving onward via remote lakes (Elter Water), passing joyous waterfalls (Skelwith Force), finding yourself following the rush of a river (Great Langdale Beck) through a cool, deserted woodland leading to a mighty valley.

This valley was officially split into two: Little Langdale and Great Langdale. I made my way through Elterwater village, where a troop of artists with easels was meeting by a circular bench outside the Britannia Inn, about to set off on a day's painting. The water of Great Langdale Beck was crystal clear ("pellucid" was Wordsworth's favoured description of such becks) as I took a path marked the "Cumbrian Way", stopping to fill my water bottle at a tap provided for hikers outside Wainwrights' Inn in the village of Chapel Stile, where disused slate quarries rose on the north side of the beck.

Beyond Chapel Stile, Great Langdale valley opened out, a sweep of mighty fells rising on all sides, and I plodded onward to a National Trust café at the foot of a path that led steeply upward to Stickle Tarn. Shunning this, I continued along a trail by a drystone wall and soon dipped down to my destination: the Old Dungeon Ghyll inn, where I sat at a picnic table by a magnolia tree in the sunshine outside the old stone building – like Wasdale Head Inn, but much smaller, a famous climbers' lodgings – and met a woman saying her name was Su Sea.

Valleys, waterfalls, a Mersey derby and Extinction Rebellion
Great Langdale and up Stickle Tarn

There can be few greater pleasures, after a delightful sunny morning hike in the Lake District, than relaxing at the picnic tables outside the

Old Dungeon Ghyll on a sunny afternoon. This, I can confirm, was an excellent way to while away a couple of hours.

I was too early to check in and the pub had yet to open; a member of staff at the check-in desk kiosk inside had said: "We're opening for food at noon, but though I say that, it may be 12.15. Getting staff is a nightmare. I'm not sure when exactly he is coming in." By "he" the check-in person was referring to the barman.

So, I sat outside at a picnic table, the fells soaring above and blazing orange in the sunlight, talking to Su Sea. "Don't give it too much of a glowing write-up," said Su Sea, who had dyed orange hair, rosy cheeks and was in her sixties, incredibly laid-back, well spoken and accompanied by an ageing lurcher named Tilly. She was talking about the Old Dungeon Ghyll, which I could already tell was a great place, surrounded as it was by so many towering fells in its isolated spot. A message that read "REBEL FOR LIFE" was attached to Su Sea's handbag and she told me she had a house in Oxfordshire that she rented out, using the proceeds to travel about the country living in a Volkswagen van, which she had owned for ten years, usually staying at campsites. "There are too many people around already really. They set up tents, scatter beer bottles and sometimes even leave tents." This, she said, could happen when younger visitors had bought tents for a party in the countryside and simply could not be bothered to clear up; they would rather just abandon everything and return home.

Su Sea had walked up to Blea Tarn that morning and had discovered some campers who had pitched tents illegally on National Trust land. "I kind of lost my cool a bit," she said. "I told them to wake up and move on." She had thought they were the type who would scatter bottles and perhaps ditch their tent. "But then I discovered they had children, so I softened and talked to them."

I said I liked the message on her bag. "That's an Extinction Rebellion thing," Su Sea replied. I asked her how she had become involved with the radical anti-climate change group – had she ever superglued herself to a motorway? "Oh no," she said. "But only because of the dog. When she's gone, I'm going to get much more involved."

Tilly was getting on a bit: "She's fourteen years old and quite deaf; about ninety-eight in human years, you know." Tilly looked at me as though sensing she was being discussed. She had a large shaved patch with a stitched-up scar on one side and did not look in the best of ways. "That was where she got attacked by a Jack Russell."

Su Sea said she had been involved with some Extinction Rebellion activities: "April 2019, I think it was. We took Marble Arch. I had a tiny tent. Ten nights they let us stay there, then they kicked us off."

I asked Su Sea, who said she was born in South Africa, if that was her real name. "Oh, I go by many names," she replied. "I just liked the sound of this one." She talked a bit more about Extinction Rebellion: "The only way is to go more extreme. A letter came round recently from the group. It said that Extinction Rebellion is really just messing about right now. Unless you are prepared to go to prison, nobody's going to take any notice." Would you do that, I asked. "Possibly," Su Sea replied. "But I want to see my dog out first. If I could take her to prison with me, I'd do it."

What did she like most about the Lake District? She was a regular visitor to Great Langdale, knowing many of the locals. "For me, it's the wildness," she said. Then she looked up and smiled. "Ah, here's the gaffer."

Neil Walmsley was the gaffer/landlord of the Old Dungeon Ghyll inn and had been since 1983, along with his wife, Jane. He came over to say hello to Su Sea, telling her he had just returned from a cruise around the Azores and the Canaries.

Neil, aged 75, had been a keen fell runner when younger and was also a talented musician; each Wednesday jams with fiddles and guitars were held in the Hikers' Bar, an old cowshed where the stalls had been converted into drinking booths. The inn attracted many hikers and climbers coming to explore famous close-by fells, including Crinkle Crags, the Pike of Blisco and the Langdale Pikes. Many famous mountaineers had visited over the years. John Hunt, who led the first successful ascent of Mount Everest in 1953, plus Chris Bonington and Ian Clough, the first Britons to ascend the north face of the Eiger in the Swiss Alps, had all dropped by. There was also a rich history of hospitality, having been known as Middlefell Inn back in 1885, when charabancs (horse-drawn vehicles) would come from Little Langdale and a horn would be blown to indicate how many guests were coming and meals required. In the early twentieth century, it was bought by the distinguished historian G. M. Trevelyan, who gifted the property to the National Trust.

"I know all this area like the back of my hand," said Neil, "I know every rock."

These days for physical activity Neil would go wild swimming each morning, sometimes at Chapel Stile, other times at Mickleden Tarn. He said: "You've got to reset. Instead of gardening, I go swimming in the river." He recommended a 16-mile "Langdale Horseshoe" walk. Then he told me that during the Covid lockdowns, he was too sad simply to throw away his barrels of ale that could not be sold, so he had turned his favourite (Old Peculier) into vinegar, which had helped pass the time with no guests about.

Neil and Su Sea got talking.

I went into the old cowshed bar.

On the walls were old mountaineering pictures, while pewter tankards hung behind the counter and simple wooden furniture was dotted about on a red lino floor. Flames flickered in a metal fireplace to the left as you entered. It was gloomy, with just the dancing light of the fire – and also brilliant. The ghosts of a thousand stories or more told of an evening seemed to hover in the air, almost whispering. Flapjack and currant slices and sandwiches were for sale. A central partition marked the old cow stalls, all of which were empty (but they would not be later). A roughly constructed painting of a hellish scene hung in a corner: a climber, it would seem, was holding aloft a tankard in one hand and what would appear to be an ice axe poking cheekily into an angel's rear-end in the other, while all around the edges of the composition, devils and angels cavorted amid mountain crags and madness. The barman, who had turned up at noon, despite the doubts of the check-in person, said deadpan: "This place is an old cowshed. Sometimes the cows were better behaved than the locals are now."

He passed over a pint of Old Peculier. A man entered, a local, and said to another drinker: "I lost eight thousand pounds gambling when drunk…" I did not catch the rest of the conversation though sensibly, it would seem, he had given up alcohol and was on soft drinks.

I went back into the sunshine outside. There, a hiker on the picnic table next to mine said to me: "Oh my knees. I can't go far these days. She had hip replacements when she was forty-five, she's absolutely fine." He was indicating his wife. "I do like it through the valley," he said. "It's fine in the valley." This was where they had been walking that morning as the hills were too much for him. He paused and looked at the fell-tops. "But I'd rather be up there."

The couple was from south Gloucestershire. "We're on our first day, we're also going to the Yorkshire Dales, a week here, a week there. Just testing out the knees today. We only did two miles. I fell in love with the Lakes when I was seventeen. Back then, Larry, a mate of mine, had said: 'We're going to go to the Mendip Hills, I've got my father's car.' So we drove off and I said, as we seemed to be going in a strange direction: 'Which bit of the Mendip Hills are we going to?' And he said: 'The Lake District.' I just fell in love with it straight away on that trip."

He had taken his wife to the Lakes for their honeymoon. She said: "I had to go. It was rocky and wet, that much I remember."

Their names were Roy and Jill Benny. "For forty years we have been coming to the Lakes: Keswick, Ullswater, Langdale, all over. The last time, we took the caravan," said Roy. This time they were staying in a self-catering place. When Roy was aged 21, he had gone up Scafell Pike with some friends: "We got absolutely lost. At 7 p.m. a mist came down. We were on the verge of panic. Then an experienced fell walker came by, gave us some food and a compass and we got back at 11 p.m.

and the pub had just shut!" This seemed to have been a more frightful scenario than getting lost in the dark on England's highest mountain.

I went to check in, ringing a bell at the reception kiosk.

A man in his twenties appeared, glaring at me. I said I would like to check in.

"Two secs," he said and disappeared.

I never saw him again.

As I waited, a waiter materialized from a door next to the reception kiosk. He seemed agitated. "I don't know where I'm going, so I'm not going to bother," he muttered to himself, swivelled around and returned to the kitchen with two plates of food. Shortly afterward, a woman with an exasperated expression appeared with these plates and took them to the outside tables.

The waiter, having seen me, entered the reception kiosk and asked me what I wanted.

I said I wished to check in.

"I don't know how to do it, but I can try to figure it out," he said. He bashed away on a keyboard for a bit.

"What the fuckin' 'ell," he then said. "'Scuse my French. Me and IT are no bloody good."

As he did so, the exasperated woman from earlier arrived in the reception kiosk, shooed the waiter away, checked me in, gave me the key and wished me a good stay (in about 30 seconds flat).

* * *

With the afternoon free, I went up to Stickle Tarn (473 metres).

A steep path with plenty of boulders to scamper over led to the little lake, an inky black pool surrounded by a half-crater of cliffs with a dam on the side facing the valley. It was Zen-like, so quiet and still as though the mountains had been waiting for you (the hiker) and were silently considering their new arrival. A fisherman was trying his luck near the path. I asked what he was hoping to catch, and he said:

"I'm trying for trout, Arctic char and pike. Haven't had a bite." This seemed to be the way fishing often went in the Lake District.

It had been quite a way up to Stickle Tarn, more than anticipated – about 40 minutes. On the way down I stopped at a pretty waterfall tumbling between boulders in an especially picturesque manner (of which Reverend William Gilpin would no doubt have approved). Then the track curled onward to the New Dungeon Ghyll inn, rival to the Old Dungeon Ghyll and about a mile down the road back toward Ambleside, where a barman from Liverpool had just turned the television channel to Liverpool versus Everton in the Premier League.

I asked him which team he supported.

"Neither mate," he replied. "Formula One: Red Bull, that's me."

The bar was called the Walker's Bar and, as if by some sort of mysterious magnetic attraction, suddenly the whole room filled with a great number of Liverpudlian walkers, both Liverpool- and Everton-following Liverpudlian walkers, but mainly Liverpool fans. They proceeded solemnly to pick up the lyrics of "You'll Never Walk Alone" by Gerry and the Pacemakers as the Liverpool Football Club anthem was sung at the ground. This was quite moving and rousing, and the smaller group of Everton supporters did not seem to take offence at their neighbours' soulful crooning.

The television had awful, shaky satellite reception, so that you might be watching it live, or it might pause for 2 seconds and then everything would speed up.

A middle-aged woman across the bar yelled: "Come on, Mané!"

She was referring to the Senegalese Liverpool striker, Sadio Mané, who had just squandered a decent chance.

"I want us to win but I don't want Everton to go down," said a man sitting next to me, quite out of the blue. He could tell I was neutral as far as the game went. By "down" he meant relegated to the football division below.

Conversation, as it seemed it always did in the Lakes, began to flow. The man was with his wife, and they had just been up the Crinkle

Crags fell. Their names were Nick and Carrie. They asked about my ascents in the Lakes, assuming reasonably enough that this was why I had come on a walking trip: to bag Wainwrights.

I mentioned the Blencathra debacle.

Carrie said: "You can't see the path in the mist up there. Blencathra has to be done in the dry. We've only managed it once."

"We were the same when we started," Nick said. "Nervous about getting up. Then, slowly, we gained confidence. In 2021 we completed the Wainwrights. It had taken us six years. It had all started when we suddenly realized we'd done fifty of them. We decided to go for the rest of them."

Carrie said: "When you've done it, gone to the tops, good weather and bad, it won't worry you any more."

Nick said: "I was never interested in the Lakes. Never thought it was something I wanted to do." The couple lived in Carlisle. Carrie was a haematology nurse; Nick worked at Nestlé, which had a plant by Carlisle where dry cappuccino mixes were produced, among other products.

Carrie said: "As a nurse I'm in quite a stressful job. It's a clear-your-head moment to be free and get away from it all here."

Nick said: "I just like getting up at 3 a.m. and heading off, it's good for the soul." This was what the couple did, making a day trip of it from Carlisle. "You don't think about the stresses of everyday life."

Their next hike was planned for Austria, tramping between Vienna and Salzburg, they said.

As Liverpool won, to great cheers – "Yeaasss get in there!" yelled the middle-aged woman of earlier, who had steadily increased her vocal contributions as the match unwound – the pair gave me a plan for tomorrow's walk, pointing out the route on my map. Which was very nice of them, each bit carefully explained.

Walking camaraderie in the Lakes, which you soon find just about everywhere, could be just as strong as the lure of the scenery.

"So you're nooot owoot all day"
Pike of Blisco, Great Knott and Crinkle Crags in Great Langdale

With a morning free, I planned to go up the Pike of Blisco (705 metres), Great Knott (696 metres) and Crinkle Crags (859 metres).

Three Wainwrights in one day… I was beginning to lose count. Anyway, Nick and Carrie thought I could manage it and the peaks were neatly located next to each other, connected by ridges on a fairly straightforward circular route.

A handful of clouds dotted the sky looking like little explosions of chalk as I scampered up a stone path, hounds barking in the valley below and sublime Wordsworthian views unfolding with every step. *Sublimity* was just about everywhere that April morning, *picturesque sublimity*, even: great fells and cliffs and crags all over the place positively oozing the sublime.

You could see down to the "ODG" (the Old Dungeon Ghyll, my lodgings): a dot amid trees and sheep paddocks. It was, as ever, inspiring to look back and admire just how far you had gone, the mountains shooting up, forming a giant U-shape around the valley: the work of shifting Ice Age glaciers of 13,000 years earlier, which had cut through the volcanic landscape of 400 million years before. Way back then you would not have wanted to go for a gentle hike around the Lakes as: 1) There were none; the lakes only formed after the glaciers passed through, dragging boulders that formed barriers to create the pools of water – the lakes – when the ice eventually melted, and 2) The lava flows and eruptions might make it decidedly tricky to follow all the little green Ordnance Survey dotted lines.

Looking back was, of course, one of the great thrills of hiking: giving yourself a little mental pat on the back every now and then. Facing north-east you could see a sharp ravine up to Stickle Tarn, a sleek vertical slice in the terrain beyond the National Trust tea room. I looked at it and thought: *did I really nip up and down that before watching the Liverpool–Everton match at the New Dungeon Ghyll Inn over several pints with Nick and Carrie?* It seemed quite a climb.

After clambering over lichen-covered boulders, however, I soon reached the top of the Pike of Blisco, where a slender elderly man with a stick pointed the way to the summits of Great Knott and Crinkle Crags. He was the only other person up there and, very helpfully and patiently, went into some detail regarding boulders and tracks through the crags that needed to be negotiated.

I thanked him and then he said, somewhat fiercely, taking me aback: "But don't blame me if *ya* get lost."

Then he tipped his cap and went on his way.

After dawdling on the summit, I followed a trail down, catching up with the elderly man a few minutes later. He was off on a similar route. We fell into step for a while. He was aged 78 and embarking on a long hike to distant fells. When I explained I aimed to return to the ODG for lunch he looked at me with frank disappointment and commented: "So you're *nooot owoot* all day."

Then he offered some advice.

"I've been active all my life and I intend to keep it that way," he said. "The secret to the fells is to pace yourself."

I thanked him yet again and moved on ahead, hoping that when I was aged 78 I would have the wherewithal to climb the Pike of Blisco as a "starter" for a day-long ramble across England's highest fells.

Cliffs shaped like church organ pipes rose to the right as the trail turned from step-like stones to scree. Dark-coated Herdwick sheep munched on vegetation on vertiginous slopes. A little water pool, a tiny tarn, reflected the sky almost perfectly.

At the top of Great Knott, I looked across that patchwork landscape of Great Langdale valley. More chalk-explosion clouds shifted imperceptibly above, casting shadows on the bright pastures of farmland and scree below. Becks whispered in the depths of the valley. The Irish Sea gleamed still and solid on the horizon.

Coming to the rough ridges of Crinkle Crags, I heard voices. These belonged to Ross and Jan, retired teachers from West Lakes Academy, which was a secondary school in Egremont, a market town to the west, near St Bees. Both were lean and rosy cheeked with matching black plastic gaters over their boots, walking sticks and woolly hats. They went hiking twice a week, usually, and lived in the village of Lamplugh, close to Loweswater. Ross proceeded to tell me about a legendary Lakeland hiker who was not Alfred Wainwright. This legendary Lakeland hiker was named Bill Birkett, who had recorded 550 peaks over 1,000 feet in the Lakes. This put Wainwright's 214 somewhat in the shade, though Wainwright's were more cherry-picked and mainly higher, and Ross pointed out that Wainwright had also written a follow-up book to his *Pictorial Guide* called *The Outlying Fells of Lakeland* focusing on ones on the edge of the Lake District. These amounted to 116 more, which Ross had also "done", of course.

Ross said that he had completed the Wainwrights a dozen times, although he had once met a man on a trail by Grasmere who claimed to have done them an incredible *57 times*. This was nothing compared to the Lake District fell legend Joss Naylor, who had ticked them all off in a *single week* once back in 1986, he said.

Ross was in the middle of doing the Birketts because "I enjoy it and it's good for your health".

Jan added: "Especially your psychological health." But as she was about to continue, Ross said "excuse me" and began striding at speed up a side path to a mini hillock/peak to the right. This was one of the Birketts. Within a minute or so he was up, where he posed for a moment at the summit as though having conquered Everest and proceeded to spring down again. "Look at him," said Jan. "He's as fit as a butcher's dog. He's got an official book at home where he marks everywhere he's been."

Ross rejoined the path ahead of us and said: "Come on Jan!" She and I had paused to chat.

We caught up and we all continued together to the mysterious rocky peak of Crinkle Crags, where Ross began talking about the second homes in the Lakes: "Yes, it's a big problem: not enough young blood coming in. Where we live it's just ordinary folk, though you do get a few Airbnbs."

With that, he sprang off once again to surmount another Birkett to the left, and Jan told me that during the pandemic lockdowns "people came in tents and quite a few times there were what I would call festival gatherings, throw-away tents and chairs".

We discussed this for a bit, stopping to look back at Great Langdale valley. Then a voice said: "Come on Jan!" It was Ross, a bit further along again.

We hurried up, reached Ross and they parted, heading north-west. More Birketts beckoned, as did lunch at the ODG.

* * *

The ODG was probably my favourite Lakeland stopover and was named after a waterfall I never got round to seeing somewhere near Stickle Tarn. The hotel's charms were many and varied: its isolation, the quiet of the valley, the smart refurbished rooms, the atmospheric lounge with squashy sofas, old maps and a striking painting of three climbers from the early days of fell walking entitled *The Solitary, The Wanderer and The Poet*. Then, last but far from least, there were the people. Not just fellow hikers, locals too, who were to be found most evenings in the Hikers' Bar. After an afternoon reading M. A. Comley's harrowing page-turner *To Make Them Pay*, I met many of them.

There was Phil, a retired engineer, and Linda, a retired support worker, from Liverpool, sitting in my cow stall as I ate a giant chilli con carne. Phil said: "People go to Ambleside and Windermere and they say they've been to the Lakes, but they've not been to the Lakes until they've come to Langdale." The pair had been coming on holiday to the ODG for 20 years. They told me how their son was a pilot and had once invited the former prime minister Tony Blair into his cockpit and how Phil had been brought up in the house on Forthlin Road next to the musician Paul McCartney: "I remember him and his brother. My mother said not to play with them because they were a really really rough family. Their ball always used to come in the garden. She didn't want us to have anything to do with them."

Then there were Gail and Mike, who ran neighbouring Middle Fell farm.

This duo had a great deal to say on a variety of subjects and they operated in a tag-team style. After being introduced by Phil and Linda, I joined them for a while.

Mike, who was in his seventies, said that the policies of the National Trust and the Lake District National Park were "geared toward tourism. People come and dump their cars and don't care where they've parked. Tourists. There's no one to call up about it. No one gives a shit. All they want is more tourists."

Gail said: "We feel, as a farming community, completely overrun. The south of England beauty spots are better looked after. Here we have potholes in the roads. Our county is full of second homes and it's very easy for them [second homeowners] not to pay council tax. They don't bring any money in."

Mike: "Eighty-seven per cent of the houses of Little and Great Langdale are second homes or holiday homes. The local community is dying. There are very few well-paid jobs, just hospitality, farming or quarrying. The price of property is prohibitive: four hundred and eighty thousand pounds for a two-bed flat in London and you can afford a house here."

Gail: "It's four hundred and fifty thousand pounds for a two-bed terrace here. If you're a local person on thirty thousand pounds a year, you're never going to afford that. There's a darkness, an undercurrent to the Lakes that no one ever shows. 'It's great,' people say. But it isn't. What we're saying is that tourism has taken over to the detriment of the real Lake District. But the approach of the authorities here is: *more, more, more.*"

Mike: "There'll be nothing other than tourism one day."

Gail: "We're not bitter and twisted people. We're not saying there should be no tourism. Just less tourism. I get upset because the Lake District as I know it has become shabby and neglected. You can't expect farmers to do the job of the local council. We can't fill potholes and pick up litter. It's turning into a theme park."

Mike: "Maintenance of gates is left to the farmer. I have a lot of fears for farming in the area."

Gail: "People say they've never seen a poor farmer. If you live in a high rise in Birmingham, you may think farmers are rich because they drive around in Range Rovers." She paused: "I don't want to bombard you with moaning. We do love living here."

Mike: "It's better than a proper job."

They both worried about the future, when Brexit would kick in and the European Union's CAP, supporting farming production, was due to end.

Mike: "In the next five years there's going to be trouble for farmers. *Farmers* are not subsidized. *Food production* is subsidized. CAP has been a hundred per cent successful. It has provided a consistent supply of quality food at a good price. Only one and a half per cent of the population are farmers. But if food gets too expensive, whichever party is in charge will not be re-elected. CAP wasn't done so farmers could have Range Rovers. People think food is expensive now but with the way things are going with cheaper imports, we face a disaster. A disaster for British farmers. And I think the way British government policy is going, it will end up that way."

An acoustic guitarist in a corner began strumming "Lust for Life" by Iggy Pop as a man named Leo cut in. Leo was curly-haired and in his mid-thirties, a footpath builder and renowned local rock climber who had been listening to us. He was caressing a pint glass and had his legs stretched out casually toward the fire. He had a deep, rich voice, a whimsical yet theatrical manner and referred to himself playfully as "Leo, the lion of Langdale".

Leo: "On a lighter note, you see that cannonball there." I did, something that looked like a cannonball at least, protruding from the bar wall. "That cannonball there comes from when the Cavaliers and the Roundheads were here. There was a big battle. That cannonball pitched up on top of Side Pike, reportedly, where that window is, that was the front door. It bounced twice, reportedly, and sunk in that bar there."

I looked at the "cannonball" and said something along the lines of "that's quite a story".

Leo paused, sipped his pint and then added: "On a lighter note, that cannonball is not a cannonball, it's called a bullock in local terms." This was a rounded piece of slate. He had been pulling my leg.

Leo told me a bit about the local area: "In Langdale, Vikings had influence. That's *lang dale* (long valley). We also have the Ullswater *hipe*. It's a short sharp inhalation." He made such a sound. "It's a pulmonic ingression. Only two lots of others do this: Scandinavian reindeer herders and Zimbabwean cow herders. Well, it was the Vikings that brought this to Ullswater."

Leo told me about his job as a footpath builder, which he had been doing for a group called Fix the Fells for 16 years: "It's a good job. It's hard, but it's good. I'll quote a bit of Wordsworth: 'Work, where you can, in the spirit of nature, with an invisible hand of art...' that's landscaping. If I've put one stone out of place, I'll go back and fix it, even if it takes all day. I'll redo it. I want it to feel as though you're springing up the fell."

The guitarist strummed. A couple in a corner stared into their smartphones. A barman told me he had an idea for an international fast-food chain to rival McDonald's that he would call "Chip Butty World". Another barman looked at my map and said "that's about right" when I showed him where I was going tomorrow. Three men with foxhounds arrived to many hellos from the other drinkers.

I left for my room, the sound of stories, gossip and laughter seeping through the floorboards. What a great place... even if some of the tales told by the fire did not perhaps bode all that well for the Lakes. But, as I have said, my aim was to tell the story of this hike how it was – and that was how it was at the ODG.

"Getting ready for the Ruskies"
Great Langdale to Thirlmere

From Great Langdale valley you crossed into Borrowdale Valley, on my route. This was a long, testing hike, with the backpack once again as RAF Eurofighter Typhoon jets looking like evil black birds occasionally soared by, so low you could almost make out the pilots. After a split second, the boom and tear of the jets would hit you. Then they were gone and echoey, thundery sounds would emanate from valleys beyond. A bald Geordie hiker passing by, with a tattoo on his leg of the actor Jack Nicholson as he appeared screaming through a doorway in the film *The Shining*, looked up and wryly commented: "Getting ready for the Ruskies, oh aye."

Over a footbridge at the end of the valley, a path wound up to Stake Pass (at about 450 metres) and then zigzagged down extravagantly to Borrowdale, following Stake Beck through rolling grassland. I stopped for lunch at The Langstrath Country Inn in the quiet village of Stonethwaite (good smoked salmon sandwich, slightly pricey lime-and-soda), and kept going to the bigger village of Rosthwaite. There, I poked my nose into Scafell Hotel to see the honours board of the Borrowdale Fell Race – more than 17 miles long and including Scafell Pike and Great Gable. A man with the surname "Lightfoot" had appropriately won this famous contest many times.

A path went sharply up from Rosthwaite to a tucked-away spot called Watendlath, where a Ukrainian flag hung by a café facing a tranquil tarn. There, I received a call from the owner of the Fisher Gill

Camping Barn by Thirlmere: "The door is open. Two others said they would come but I haven't heard from them, so you'll probably have it to yourself. I've left wood for the fire. Can you leave the kitchen clean and tidy please?" The owner would not be around for my stay, so I could let myself in and out the next day.

Watendlath led to High Tove (515 metres), a boggy fell that descended through woodland to Thirlmere, where a landslip seemed to have blocked the way to the south. Luckily, I was heading north, soon arriving at the long stone curve of a dam built in 1891 to form a reservoir supplying water to Manchester, in the process wiping out the hamlet of Armboth (much to the outrage of John Ruskin). Then, after getting lost in woodland and crossing the ever-awful A591, I found my camping barn (a hundred metres or so from the ever-awful A591).

It was 6 p.m. No one else was there and I suddenly realized I was very tired indeed; it had been a 17-mile day. I walked along the A591 for a quarter of a mile and ate Cumberland sausage and mash (the best yet) from an almost-empty pub, the King's Head, where a sign said: "SERVING STRICTLY RESIDENTS ONLY, NO WALK-INS", but the kindly barman took pity on me. That said, when I asked if I could also come by in the morning for breakfast (as I had no food with me), he gave me a look that suggested I was pushing my luck and added solemnly: "I'm sorry, but that would be beyond the pale."

Back at the camping barn, I lit the fire and heard the latest about Lena and Anna from Kasia: "Their host is waiting for them at the airport. Their flight was delayed an hour, but they are on their way. Anna had learned a poem in Polish to say thank you to my parents. They really liked the apartment while they were there, and they were so careful not to make anything dirty. Really nice people." Their host's line manager at the company she worked for had generously donated a laptop for Anna to use to do her school lessons.

Afterward, I settled by the fire and picked up an old *Metro* newspaper left by a former resident of the barn. The front-page headline read:

"BORIS COMMONS APOLOGY! I'M TRULY SORRY", with a subhead "PM: IT DID NOT OCCUR TO ME THAT I BROKE MY OWN COVID LAWS AT DOWNING ST BASH". A picture showed the then ruler of the United Kingdom looking dishevelled and slightly manic.

Troubles in Europe, yes, and at home too. I fell asleep to the gentle crackle of the fire. What a peaceful and good-value (i.e. cheap) place. I can highly recommend the Fisher Gill Camping Barn.

Euphoria, exhaustion and recovery
Thirlmere to Brothers Water

Helvellyn (950 metres) awaited, another big one.

Past windows of contented-looking breakfast eaters tucking into bacon and eggs at the King's Head, I plodded up a very long steep path that meandered to Brown Cragg, White Side, Lower Man and, finally, the summit of Helvellyn, going steadily and pacing myself as my wise acquaintance from the Pike of Blisco had suggested. Three weeks ago, I would not have dreamed of taking on this hike with the backpack. I had, it would have seemed, *progressed* – hiking-wise.

This ascent, however, was the mere start of the day with various further lofty Wainwright fells to come: Nethermost Pike (891 metres), High Crag (884 metres), Dollywaggon Pike (858 metres), Fairfield (873 metres) and Hart Crag (822 metres). These linked spikes in the landscape would lead to my next lake: Brothers Water, a small one in a delightful hidden valley.

Six Wainwrights in a day, doubling the total to a dozen so far, by my calculations. To be honest, though, I was not really sure how many I might have bagged, maybe there had been a few I had simply not noticed. That was quite possible, not that this bothered me in the slightest. The main thing was moving on in this big, peculiar, wobbly circle around the Lakes, seeing Britain's favourite national park from another route/perspective and *not stressing at all* about peaks or marking them down as "bagged" or "done". I was on a long gentle amble, letting whatever might happen do just that, though the hike was beginning, as the circle was nearing its return to Penrith, to be a *slightly hillier, less gentle* amble than before.

It was a windless day and I had a spring in my step despite having had no breakfast (and despite no lunch to come either, aside from the odd hotel biscuit: I had really messed up on the eating front with the camping barn being so isolated and no shop about). The sun slowly leaked through high milky-grey clouds as a path wound up an exposed mountainside. In an hour or so I was up. Standing at the top of Helvellyn and gazing down on the pair of ridges suited to much more experienced walkers – Swirral Edge and, even more terrifying in appearance, Striding Edge (the one Merv back in Penrith had warned me about) – I was overcome by a great sense of achievement, bordering on euphoria, faced by this classic Lakeland vista. A German hiker was by the spot marking the top, the only other person. He seemed quite satisfied too, staring out at Ullswater on the horizon. "I came crawling up there this morning," he was pointing to Swirral Edge. "I do not have a head for heights. On the right was a sheer drop. I was terrified." He shuddered at the memory of it. "I camped down there by that tarn last night." He pointed to a distant inky-coloured tarn in a crater below. "I shouldn't have. It's illegal. The national park people do not like it. But I cleaned up and left no mess." He had tried to traverse Striding Edge yesterday but had backtracked. "I gave up and went down again. It was just too much."

The German made his way down the path I had ascended.

Two other hikers arrived and one asked: "All right, mate, how do you spell Helvellyn?" I told him and he put this into his GPS device and said: "Ahhh." It appeared he had only just then realized he was at the summit. I do not think Tim, the Wasdale Mountain Rescue veteran, would have been much impressed.

Three others passed as I walked on along a wide ridge toward Dollywaggon Pike, and one of them, an American, enquired: "How's it going on Striding Edge?"

Striding Edge, which curved thinly downward like the tail of a lizard, was clearly the big attraction up on Helvellyn; perhaps it was the danger the ridge represented, the scene of so many an accident and fatality over the years. I told them I had not been across it, and they appeared momentarily disappointed I had not just risked life and limb that morning. Were they about to attempt the infamous ridge? The American replied: "Yeah, today's the day. I'd only ever do it in perfect conditions like this, man."

I wished them luck. The American gave me a fist pump as though I had scored a touchdown or hit a home run. "See I told you, it's universal, man," he said to his friend. "A universal greeting." He turned to me. "Have a good day, man." And they went on their way.

The summit of Helvellyn was a particularly *sublime* spot and this *sublimity* continued on the trail down to the glittering, lavender-blue curves of Grisedale Tarn. Sunshine had broken through and the landscape had transformed into a world of mysterious long shadows and dazzling patches of light on the boggy, boulder-strewn, tumbling slopes.

"Bonnie day!" said a man in a flat cap coming up from Grisedale, getting it in one.

By the tarn, I crossed some stepping stones and continued slowly and laboriously up a scree-strewn path to the top of Fairfield, trudging onward to Hart Crag via places called Flinty Grave and Scrubby Crag, where I asked a man with his daughter for directions to Brothers Water. I was, I realized as I did so, exhausted, extremely hungry, thirsty, waterless and lost.

"Nice to see someone using one of those," the father said in jolly tones, looking at my map, not quite assessing my state; I had tried not to seem as desperate as I felt. Using their GPS device, he established that I should have turned left about a quarter of a mile back. Retracing my steps, I located a tricky-to-discern track and crossed a boggy field, arriving at a curious, thin ravine. The path at that point turned into an almost stepladder-steep series of rocks, requiring a great deal of concentration, before dropping to the valley floor between crags and a place called Priest's Hole Cave, a mouth-shaped hollow in a cliff somewhere above that was popular with wild campers. At the bottom of the long descent, I reached the swirling eddies of Kirkstone Beck and followed the stream for a while, arriving, beyond a campsite, at Brotherswater Inn. This was where I had booked a room for the night.

It had been an 8-hour, 13-mile, 362-floor hiking day. More "floors" (ascent) than on any day so far.

* * *

In rapid succession, I went to my neat little en-suite room, with its tartan curtains and pictures of hunting scenes; I dropped off my backpack; and I went to the restaurant, where I found that Mark, the genial duty manager, who had been at check-in, had placed a pint of iced water beside a menu at a corner table with the best views toward Hart Crag. He had also arranged three mini tasting glasses of the inn's local ales. After downing the pint of iced water, I sampled these ales and opted for Brotherswater IPA, yet another local brew, this one produced by Tirril: The Lakeland Brewery. At the risk of repeating myself on the subject: flabbergasting how many of these there were round about in the Lakes; it was almost as though anyone not involved in tourism or farming must be toiling in some local craft brewery or other.

Mark, originally from Solihull, seemed to have a sixth sense regarding his guests. Or perhaps he just had eyes: breakfastless and with limited water and just a few "room biscuits" during the day (purloined from previous lodgings), I had almost staggered into the inn around 4 p.m.

Mark brought the ale; I took a good long sip of this ale and I asked him if I could have safely filled my water bottle earlier from the stream below Priest's Hole Cave. "Oh, I wouldn't touch that," he said. "There's lead from the old silver mine in that. It's not as polluted as it used to be, but it's still there."

He took my food order: steak and ale pie, which was soon to arrive with a veritable mountain of chips, snap peas, carrots and courgettes. I wolfed down the lot while taking in my surroundings: little clusters of circular tables and chairs beneath varnished beams, a well-swept terracotta tiled floor, framed prints of local scenery – including one of Brotherswater Inn by the talented local artist Judy Boyes – old black-and-white pictures of the Windermere ferry, shiny rows of pewter mugs, a fireplace prepared and ready for lighting later. It was all spic and span and in good order. Beatles and Jimi Hendrix hits played quietly on a stereo: not too loud, nor too quiet either, just the right volume.

Mark swiftly retrieved my empty plate and returned soon after, on this occasion to pass the time of day. As I had arrived between usual lunch and dinner, there was a lull in proceedings at the Brotherswater Inn.

He was interested in my next day's hike up three more Wainwrights: The Knott (739 metres), High Street (828 metres) and Mardale Ill Bell (760 metres), taking the Nan Bield Pass and staying at Mosedale Cottage bothy – a free night in an unsupervised old building – before passing a place called Sleddale Hall and arriving at the eastern market town of Shap, where I would be meeting Kasia, who was back from Poland. Mark was a more-than-proficient climber, having travelled to Corsica and Sardinia for three years to devote himself to the "fantastic climbing" on those islands, such was his passion for the pursuit. He had done so after his children had grown up, having sold his house to pay for the adventure; he already had grandchildren, though he looked in his early fifties.

Mark's ears had pricked up at the mention of Sleddale Hall. This was where much of the cult, tragicomic 1986 film *Withnail and I*, starring Richard E. Grant (Withnail) and Paul McGann (Marwood, the "I"), had been filmed. *Withnail and I* covered the story of two out-of-work actors in the late 1960s attempting to soothe their woes in the Lake District after borrowing a dented old Jaguar Mark 2 from Withnail's eccentric uncle, Monty (played by the late Richard Griffiths). On the spur of the moment, the odd couple drive up the M6 to a deserted cottage owned by Monty, declaring to nonplussed passers-by in the fells: "We've gone on holiday by mistake," and generally fooling around. I had been to the hall before – when it was derelict, many years after the film had been shot – having driven up to the Lakes in a Jaguar Mark 2 myself, with a pair of friends who were *Withnail* fanatics. This had been for a newspaper article celebrating various locations connected to the film, not just in the Lake District. I was curious to see the spot again as it happened to be on the way to Shap.

"Oh, I'm a big fan," said Mark, his eyes lighting up. "It's always on resume-watching."

He began quoting lines from the film: "We want the finest wines available to humanity. And we want them here and we want them now!" This was Withnail's theatrical, comic, bombastic (drunken) demand made during one scene to a prim, outraged tea room owner, while on an excursion from their cottage to Penrith.

"I often watch it when it's miserable to cheer me up," Mark said.

He told me about his career, first as a pharmaceutical supplier, commuting from Keswick to Lancashire, and later in an outdoors shop in the Lakes after he realized he "could not bear the commute any more", before he bought a motorhome and went travelling to Europe to go climbing, and returned to the Lakes to find other work. He advised me which specialist outdoor shop chains had the best knowledge/service. Then he gave me some fell-hiking advice for the next day, as he knew I would probably be stiff and the way ahead was demanding.

"Slowly, slowly, cross your arms like this," he said, shuffling very slowly indeed with his arms crossed on his chest. It was almost as though he was moving in slow motion. "You won't get there any quicker rushing as you'll just be going stop-start, catching your breath." He watched my attempt to emulate his shuffle. "Maintain your height!" He showed what he meant: keeping your back straight, no hunching. That was the way to do it.

The Brotherswater Inn was yet another great pit stop, and Mark was yet another friendly fellow fell walker. Being a long-distance fell walker, I was learning, opened doors: people seemed curious about your (half-mad) route.

To the bothy
Brothers Water to Mosedale Valley

The name of Brothers Water may derive from two brothers who are said to have drowned in 1785 while ice skating on the small lake (½ mile long and ¼ mile wide). The veracity of this is uncertain, but the lake had at one time been known as Broad Water, strangely so given its size. Some believe the appellation comes from the Old Norse word *brothir* (also meaning "brother"), though the tragic story of the drowned brothers, true or not, seemed to stick in your mind while beside its tranquil shore.

Strolling along the gravelly edge, I paused for a while near a fine old maple tree as a pair of RAF Eurofighter Typhoon jets roared by shattering the peace – reflecting that Wordsworth would probably have quite a bit to say about them, if he was troubled over the disturbances caused by steam trains – before giving directions to a solitary (quite lost) Geordie hiker and admiring the magnolias, rhododendrons and daffodils in the gardens of cottages in the quaint village of Hartsop, once a lead-mining hub.

Ahead lay a rapid rise to the heap of rock called Knott (reached via Mark's excellent shuffling technique), below which a secret valley with a lonely lake known as Hayeswater lay between plunging cliffs of pewter-coloured scree, looking as though not many people went down there. The landscape had an elemental ruthlessness with humpbacked fells rising beyond like mysterious mountain kingdoms in the clouds. Two

Herdwick sheep stood on the edge of a steep incline, way up at 800 metres, facing one another as though having a gossip. Ravens swooped by the cliffs above Hayeswater, croaks reverberating across the valley.

The long grassy plateau-like passage of High Street led onward. This had been a Roman road and you could still see the ancient tracks. The trail swooped to the craggy summit of Mardale Ill Bell, with the neat circle of Blea Water below, followed by a pretty little tarn and then the lead-grey, S-shaped expanse of Haweswater. There was not a single building down below that I could see. This corner of the Lakes felt forgotten, overlooked in favour of the bright lights of Bowness and scrambles of Scafell Pike.

While admiring the scenery and eating a sausage roll by a cairn, however, three male hikers appeared from below – Stevie G., Stevie W. and Graham – accompanied by a golden retriever named Charlie. They were on a practice hike ahead of an ascent of Ben Nevis as well as somewhere called the Devil's Ridge in Scotland later in the year; they were hale and hearty, middle-aged, dressed in an assortment of expensive-looking walking gear. Jolly good fellows one and all, "from Blackpool way". They helped with directions to Mosedale Cottage bothy, Charlie ate the last of my sausage roll and we parted on our separate ways, whereupon I soon met a tall bald man, wearing what looked like black eyeliner, who was holding a stake-like walking stick. He said he was doing Wainwright's "outlying fells", that the boggy paths ahead were tricky to follow in Mosedale and that he had passed the bothy and taken a look inside: "It's a bit spooky in there. You're the only resident."

This tall bald man was to be the last human being I would lay eyes on for around 20 hours.

Crossing bogs in the afternoon sunshine, I located Mosedale Cottage bothy.

It was indeed spooky and empty – and quite wonderful too.

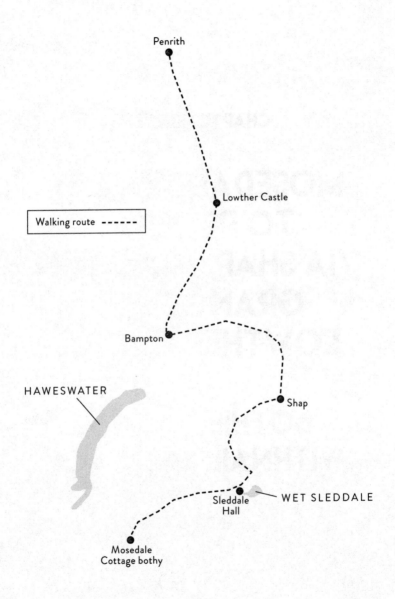

Penrith

Lowther Castle

Walking route ------

Bampton

HAWESWATER

Shap

Sleddale
Hall

WET SLEDDALE

Mosedale
Cottage bothy

CHAPTER ELEVEN

MOSEDALE VALLEY TO PENRITH, VIA SHAP, BAMPTON GRANGE AND LOWTHER CASTLE

BOTHIES, BOGS, WITHNAIL AND BACK

Many people say the Lake District is desperately overrun by tourists. This cannot be claimed of Mosedale. I had a small valley of rolling grassland with a few Herdwicks, plus the Mosedale Cottage bothy, entirely to myself.

Not really having understood bothies, I had nevertheless always been intrigued by the idea of them. I had come across this one simply by looking at Google Maps and working out what seemed the halfway point between Brothers Water and Shap. Mosedale fit the bill and the only place to stay appeared to be the bothy. On realizing this, I had looked up what you are supposed to do at a bothy in terms of booking ahead. You did not need to. You were just meant to turn up. So, I had bought a sleeping bag that claimed to offer protection against temperatures down to –15°C, which I had been carrying the entire trip, the bulky object taking up a fair bit of space in the backpack.

Online pictures had shown that Mosedale Cottage bothy had comfy-looking leather sofas by a burning fireplace, as though it was the inviting lounge of a cosy country inn. Following the boggy path to the secluded cottage, tucked behind trees by a stream next to a disused quarry, I came to a little house on a prairie with a yard that had a burned circle in the middle from old fires, a grim toilet outhouse, whitewashed walls and a shiny green door with a notice: "THIS BOTHY IS MAINTAINED BY THE MOUNTAIN BOTHIES ASSOCIATION. PLEASE KEEP THE PLACE TIDY." All around was boggy rolling grassland, as far as the eye could see.

Inside, I could recognize the lounge from the photo, minus the leather sofas and the fire in the fireplace, which was empty and without fuel. Beaten-up old chairs were placed on the dusty flagstones, lined against the walls as though you had entered a dental surgery. A dented gas lamp was on a windowsill. The walls were filthy, cobwebs in the corners. Someone had written an unprintably disparaging remark about Prince Andrew on a door to the sleeping chambers, which consisted of wide wooden "beds". I selected one of these and put my backpack in what seemed to be the best spot.

Back in the lounge was a "bothy book" next to a lovely old copy of *Lakeland through the Lens* by W. A. Poucher, a *World Atlas of Wine*, *A Vision of Britain* by the then Prince Charles (Andrew's less-disgraced older brother, soon to be king) and a publication about exploring the Lakes during full moons, the bothy no doubt being a good location for that. This bothy book was full of juicy tales of former occupants. A recent visitor named Bertie had discovered that a can of Guinness had exploded in his sleeping bag on transit to the bothy and a companion had written of this accident: "He completely lost his [****]. Love this bothy. Ten out of ten for laughing at other people's misery!" Nathan, who had stayed a few days earlier, had needed to be pulled out of a bog courtesy of one of his mates. Susan had only just found the bothy as fog had descended on the final stretch: "Not sure what would have happened if we hadn't." Meanwhile, another recent group said: "We came for a little mish from Newcastle." What *mish* meant I was not quite sure. "We're the Geordies. We are mental. We're off our [****]-ing heads! Belter night." Which gave a better understanding, perhaps, of what *mish* might mean.

Aside all this and much more, there were plenty of grumbles about other guests, mainly previous ones who had left litter: "Yeah, you lazy [****]s who left your litter behind, stay in the city nobheads!" Another former resident named Stuart was upset about a group of fellow guests from Poland who had politely written in the bothy book thanking the Mountain Bothies Association for its hospitality and signing off as "Team Poland". "Kept up by loud music and even louder conversation until 1 a.m.", Stuart wrote beneath their entry. "Be less 'Team Poland' and have more respect for fellow bothy users." People having fun: *tut tut tut.* Generally though – aside from hamming-it-up "do not stay, evil entity present" type remarks – all was positive: "great hideaway", "a sanctuary", "such respite", "perfect", "loved our rabbit stew/lamb hotpot/fresh fish with asparagus and new potatoes", all cooked on the stove that had no fuel.

The answer to this wood and coal dilemma seemed to be to bring your own. "Biked up with beers and firewood", said one entry. "Enjoyed a grand night in luxury!" So far as food was concerned, I had a can of beans, a can of tuna and two bread rolls bought from the shop at the campsite at Brothers Water. Drinking water could be had from the stream, according to the tall bald man who looked as though he was wearing eyeliner. I had only brought a couple of cans of Coke Zero. I was not, you might say, the best-organized bothy dweller.

Mosedale Cottage bothy turned out to be both the best and worst of nights.

On the positive side, there was the silence (save for the odd sheep) and the seclusion in the hidden grassy hills. There was also a blazing sunset, followed by the fading light on the fell-tops, a sequence of periwinkle blue, cornflower, lilac, deeper lilac, purple, deeper purple and jet black. There was the canopy of stars. There was the candlelight (I had brought tea lights and matches). There was the reading of a book by candlelight in your very own private bothy in your very own private Lakeland valley.

But it was cold, very cold and it got colder, −3°C at its chilliest. In a scarf, woolly hat and gloves, fully dressed in my sleeping bag suitable for temperatures as low as −15°C, I shiveringly dwelled in my "bed" room reading the final harrowing pages of *To Make Them Pay* – murders galore in Workington – waiting for the magic sleeping bag to work. This did not happen. As the temperature dipped, so did mine. Meanwhile, the wooden "bed" was hard, especially, I noticed, on the hips.

The reason for these discomforts was simple: *I had not bought a camping mat.* You needed a camping for the sleeping bag to function properly and not to feel the hard wood below. Of course you needed a camping mat.

I tried to sleep. I did so for maybe half an hour. I awoke shivering. I could not get back to sleep. I put on another fleece. I located the flimsy orange "emergency shelter" and put that over me as a canopy of sorts, hoping this might somehow work. It did, up to a point. The temperature in this canopy went up as though I was in a small, not-very-hot hothouse that seemed to have been created by my breathing. Condensation began to drip from the emergency shelter, which was irritating, but I was reasonably warm even if my hips hurt when I turned from one side to another, and it was damp. I was still fully clothed and wearing my woolly hat and scarf. In this condition, I slept at Mosedale Cottage bothy, waking at the crack of dawn, feeling strangely refreshed, to eat the remains of the beans and tuna and a bread roll for breakfast. I rolled up my sleeping bag, signed the bothy book – "I came on holiday by mistake" – collected my rubbish and stepped forth across the bog toward Shap.

Withnail and a familiar face
Mosedale Valley to Shap

From a distance, Mosedale Cottage bothy looked idyllic, so inviting and perfect with its little ring of trees way back across the bog. Frost gave the grass a crunch where it had not already melted in the early light. This meant that sometimes you would step on solid-looking frosty terrain, thinking it must be firm ground, only for your foot to disappear in the treacly mire below.

Squeaking skylarks and trickling water provided an accompaniment to the *squelch, squelch, squelch* of boots. The sky was cloudless. The green dotted line of the Ordnance Survey map snaked between the damp hills of Wainwright "outlying fells".

After a while the route wound down a sharp slope arriving at Sleddale Hall, the cottage known in the film as Crow Crag, where so much of the half-crazed action took place in *Withnail and I*. It was there the unemployed acting duo comically attempted to pluck and cook a chicken in the cottage's wood-burning stove using an old boot to prop the bird up. It was on the field close by that they had run-ins with the local poacher (played by Michael Elphick), who mistrusts the Londoners and waves an eel at them in a pub as a warning in another scene, to which Withnail replies: "Don't threaten me with a dead fish!" The unexpected arrival of Uncle Monty at Crow Crag late one night scares the life out of them both: could it be the enraged poacher coming to get them? This paranoid ineptitude in the "real" countryside of the Lakes – quite different to the experiences of tourists staying at guest houses or hotels in "unreal" Ambleside or Bowness – was all part of the film's comedy and enduring appeal. Even the local tourist board promoted *Withnail* breaks.

Since my last visit, Sleddale Hall had become a private home. From a distance as I crossed the slope above, I could see a figure unloading groceries from a vehicle and I pondered asking if I could look around inside. Two considerations, however, stopped me in my tracks. The first: having seen the old cottage just about as it had been originally in the film, I did not want to temper that memory (it had been a kind of shrine to *Withnail and I*, complete with quotes scrawled on the walls and even an "Uncle Monty's Guest Book" back then). The second: how would you like it if you lived quietly on a hillside and a dishevelled unwashed man who said he was a *Withnail and I* fan and who had hardly slept the night before turned up with a backpack full of Lakeland books and mud up to his shins.

A clink of empty bottles being dropped in a recycling bin emanated from Sleddale Hall (the ghost of Withnail?). I tramped on, happy enough to have again laid eyes on Withnail and Marwood's old stomping ground, passing Wet Sleddale Reservoir and crossing a series of fields and bogs, while trains slid along the tracks between Euston and Penrith that had brought me to the Lakes and steam wafted from funnels on the Shap limestone factory beyond the railway. Up a short lane past a particularly boggy bog, I arrived at a busy road that ran through the centre of an untouristy eastern Cumbrian village.

This was Shap.

It took perhaps 10 minutes to walk from one end of Shap to the other, popping into a post office to buy a copy of the *Cumberland and*

Westmorland Herald ("that's the bible that is," said the owner), and taking in a smart, modern swimming-pool complex, a fish-and-chip shop, a bowling club, a village hall with a Ukrainian flag flying on a pole, a charity shop where the proceeds went to community projects (what a great idea), a New Balance factory outlet shop (somewhat surprisingly) and three pubs, one of which I was staying in with Kasia that night, the Kings Arms.

Not long after I had arrived – enough time for a shower, thankfully – so did Kasia, in a minicab from Penrith Station. She was wearing a yellow hiker's jacket, a baseball cap and boots, and was carrying a (much smaller) backpack, looking ready for hiking action. We embraced outside the Kings Arms and she told me I looked tanned: even in April in the north-west of England, if you spend enough time outside, this seemed possible. Who needs summer in the Med or fake tans from a bottle? Just go rambling in the fells in the spring with snow on the mountaintops and freezing temperatures at night (though I think I may well have had a farmer's complexion, not a bronzed yachtie-Monaco look).

* * *

We investigated Shap.

This involved a series of points of call. The first being at the unexpected New Balance outlet shop, where we learned that K Shoes had closed a factory there 23 years ago and New Balance, an American multimillion-dollar trainer-making company that already had a British outpost in Flimby on the Cumbrian coast, had stepped in to rehire 25 staff. Work on making some of the country's trendiest trainers continued somewhere at the back and on floors upstairs, and discounts of 70 per cent were possible on a dizzying array of colourful footwear and running gear that would cost you a great deal more down in London. The business had been a great success story for the local economy.

"It's a nice family feel here," said an assistant, who had proudly run through the recent history of New Balance in Shap and gone on to tell us about the latest trainers that had "totally new fuel cell technology, they propel you forward at speed". At Shap, the workers helped make the "uppers", the top parts of the shoes, rather than the soles. Who would have thought it, tucked away in a little village beside the boggy fells of north-east Lakeland?

Back at the post office, where I sent home more Lakeland books as the backpack was billowing out of control again and I could do with a less burdensome hike on the final day to Penrith, the owner I had met earlier commented: "We've had people strip off in here."

He watched our reactions. We asked him what he meant.

"Strip off to post clothes back they don't need because it's got hot and they don't need them any more."

He was a chatty post-office owner.

I asked him where the centre of Shap was and he replied: "Here! This is the centre, where you're standing!"

Kasia and I went for a drink at The Greyhound, where we sat in the back garden and watched Avanti West Coast trains rattling very close by. The tracks were near the back fence and the barman told us that trainspotters sometimes came just to sit with beers and "spot" the various locomotives and carriages spinning by.

We went for dinner at the Kings Arms, eating pies near the pool table, dartboards, a "Queen: We Are The Champions" fruit machine and pictures of old Shap FC teams, while listening to coast-to-coast walkers on a nearby table talking about the benefits of merino-made hiking gear – "merino shirts, scarves, tops, hats, socks, it just feels better: everything merino!" – and how many times they had completed the coast-to-coast walk. "This is my fourth," said one unsurprisingly extremely thin man, disappointing another hiker who had just said they were on their third go. Hiker bragging happens.

Back to the beginning
Shap to Penrith, via Bampton Grange and Lowther Castle

You can usefully judge an overnight hostelry in the Lakes by its breakfast. The Kings Arms passed this test with aplomb: a strapping, steaming full English of Cumberland sausages, lashings of bacon, mounds of beans, blood pudding, tomatoes, mushrooms, slices of toast galore and all the sauces. A suitably right royal pile-up.

The waitress Yvonne was a talkative sort and told us that *Withnail and I* fans often came to Shap to visit Sleddale Hall: "Oh aye, people come from far and wide – not just this country." She loved the film: "I've watched it time and time again." Yvonne told us that each summer for the past ten years, a Withnail-themed festival-style event called "Uncle Monty's Summer Soirée" had been held at Sleddale Hall with a screening of the film and food provided. Tickets were sold and male guests encouraged to wear Savile Row tweed suits, moustaches and curly wigs to pull off an Uncle Monty look. Move over Wordsworthians, the Withnail crew has hit the fells! It must be quite an occasion.

Well-fed and informed, we left Shap, pausing to look at the jagged medieval ruins of its old abbey – "Why destroy it, couldn't they have used it for something else?" asked Kasia, referring to Henry VIII's actions in the 1540s, which was a fair point – before making off across fields and along streams with kestrels wheeling above as gently rolling hills led onward to the village of Bampton, where we had an appointment.

The Mardale Inn was another local success story. The late-eighteenth-century property, an inn since 1890, had closed in 2017 to the great disappointment of locals as it was the only pub in the area other than the Crown and Mitre, which was shut down during the Covid pandemic. Since then, however, the Mardale had been purchased by a local community fundraising group that had remarkably gathered £400,000 in less than a month. It had yet to reopen when we went, though it was due to soon. Phil and Sue Sweetland, key members of the Bampton Valley Community Pub steering committee, met us outside the pebble-dashed facade and led us into a room with simple wooden furniture and a flagstone floor. A picture signed by the actor Paul McGann showed him dressed as Marwood and Richard E. Grant as Withnail, sitting on the front steps of the inn; a nearby red phone box in Bampton had featured in the film and they had stopped by for a rest during the shoot. McGann had added a message: "My thumbs have gone numb!" This was a line from the opening scene when the pair had been experimenting with drugs. We were clearly still firmly in *Withnail and I* territory.

Phil and Sue had moved to the village from London just before the pub closed and had been "very sad" about the hostelry shutting – it had been where locals met "especially during the winter". With others on the team to save The Mardale Inn, they had attracted 500 investors. "Regulars loved the idea," said Sue. "Word spread." We sat for a while discussing the importance of pubs as village hubs in the Lake District, then we thanked Paul and Sue, wished them and The Mardale Inn the best of luck and made our way down a lane toward Lowther Castle. It was frankly amazing what crowdfunding could so swiftly achieve in a tiny village tucked away in the Lakeland fells.

More fields, streams and gently rolling hills lay ahead. It was good to have company for once. "So gorgeous," said Kasia, referring to the scenery, "I think I've said that five times." She was right, it was especially beautiful in those parts. We followed a trail lined with daffodils and dandelions into pine woodland on the Lowther Estate, not long afterward arriving at the evocative ruins of the castle itself.

The current Lowther Castle was built in 1857 by Sir James Lowther, for whom William Wordsworth's father, John, had long worked as a steward without being properly paid, seemingly out of the frugality – you might just say tightness – of Sir James. When Sir James died in 1802 (John Wordsworth had passed away in 1783), the cash due to the Wordsworth family was paid by his successor, Sir William

Lowther; William Wordsworth was to become a regular visitor of Sir William at Lowther.

Meanwhile, the castle's other big claim to fame was a certain Hugh Cecil Lowther, the fifth Earl of Lonsdale, a playboy-like character who inherited the grand pile in 1882, aged 25. He proceeded to buy prize horses for hunting and hire troops of musicians for entertaining while indulging in his passion for boxing, both trying it out himself and encouraging others – hence the prestigious Lonsdale Belt in boxing that continues to this day. Another interest was early motor cars, and he went on to be the first president of the Automobile Association. Aside from all this, he was also a renowned ladies' man who had been involved in a notorious high-society affair and was generally famed for splashing the cash, spending his inheritance like there was no tomorrow. His nicknames included "Lordy" and the "Yellow Earl", as he was fond of the colour, and he twice entertained Kaiser Wilhelm II of Germany at Lowther Castle, not to mention the kings of Portugal and Italy. Sadly, and perhaps predictably, before his death he had blown so much money he could no longer afford to live at Lowther and had had to move out.

That was the beginning of a long decline at the castle, which had fallen into disrepair with walls crumbling and contents sold off. In 2011, however, it had been opened to the public after a basic restoration (not to its original glory, despite costing £9 million) and it made a curious final "tourist sight" for this hike around the Lakes.

* * *

From Lowther, the walk up to Penrith did not take long.

Past a campsite we tramped, following the river Lowther beneath the M6 before crossing the river Eamont and heading for my starting point: the Station Hotel. Kasia was exhausted. Somehow, I had turned into a mountain whippet over the past month and thought nothing of 5 rolling miles up to the town after the 7 miles earlier from Shap. Kasia thought otherwise. A drink was more than in order for revival purposes – and, of course, to toast the trip.

As we entered the crowded bar, though, we moved to one side by the staircase to the rooms as Kasia had been sent a text by Anna that showed a picture of a stylish outdoor gas fire with a bottle of bubbly on a table with champagne flutes set beside it. She and her mother, Lena, and their host were enjoying a Saturday-night celebration for making it to the UK. It was touching to see them so comfortably and happily lodged after the difficulties of their journey and despite the troubles that rumbled on in their war-ravaged homeland.

Many people were having a good time too at the Station Hotel, which was rammed full of groups exchanging gossip, pool players celebrating good shots and folk vaguely taking in Arsenal versus West Ham on a television hung above the bar.

Among their number, at a table near ours, I was surprised to see Kathleen, the manageress who had offered tips along with Merv on my first night. I went over and said hello and she said: "You made it! Merv and I weren't sure you would." Merv was not around. He was still in the kitchen, finishing his shift.

On hearing me ask about the chef, a farmer friend of Kathleen's commented: "You're lucky to be alive, if you took advice from him."

Kathleen, who was on a night off, said to the farmer: "I told him not to go." She turned to me: "Why didn't you take your car?"

Previously, I seemed to recall, she and Merv had been recommending the bus. I explained, as I had to Peter in Nether Wasdale, that I did not have one, and I described the hike again to the farmer and Kathleen's husband, a postman, who was also there.

The farmer said: "Next time, take Merv and lose him, won't you?"

A discussion on the merits of fell walking and Merv's advice ensued. They were not walkers themselves. "None of us go hiking," said Kathleen.

Kathleen's husband said: "I wouldn't even know the way to Threlkeld." With that, though, he raised his glass, we all did.

It was Saturday night at the Station Hotel and it was time for a party. Patch, Kathleen's terrier, let out a funny high-pitched howl. Rolling Stones music played. A pool player cried: "*Yeyeees!*" Arsenal scored a goal (but no one really seemed to notice). A group of lads entered and ordered Moretti lagers.

So ended this long circular hike around the lakes of the Lake District: back where it had started… 379 happy miles on.

AFTERWORD

Sweeping conclusions, grand statements about the meaning of the Lake District and its place in modern Britain: I'll leave those to others. Instead, I have aimed in this hiking book to let the people I met along the way have their say, their voices accumulating somehow or other to form the "story", alongside the nitty-gritty of a walker following a route – I wanted to capture the reality of that too.

Voices from the fells... not just how I saw it.

I did not want to come at the Lakes with an "angle", nor did I have one, other than that I had always enjoyed the scenery. After all, I was merely an outsider passing by, shuffling along with a ridiculous backpack full of books in a big amateurish circle drawn on an Ordnance Survey map, pleased simply to make it from A to B without the need for a mountain rescue team. What did I know (aside from what I could glean from my portable library)?

Fortunately, plenty of people kindly opened up and talked to me from day one: Kathleen and Merv at the Station Hotel, Ken in the kebab shop, farmers with static holiday homes, critics from *The Durham Drinker*, bookseller/poets, campsite coordinators, café owners, tea-shop assistants, youth-hostel managers, cheerful barmen purveying Wainwright ales. And that was just in the first 24 hours.

Add ferrymen, tourist-office staff, former lead-mine engineers, National Trust membership consultants, Polish hotel managers, quarry owners, barmaids worried about the cost of living, twenty-somethings struggling to get on the property ladder, convivial mayors, folk musicians and ghyll scramblers. Sprinkle in encounters with newsagents and pipe sellers, owners of grand country estates, chicken and cattle farmers, award-winning whisky distillers, guest-house owners, pub managers, hotel owners and nuclear plant employees (met halfway up Scafell Pike) – not to mention hard-working sheep-rearing fell farmers, shepherds, champion fell runners, mountain-rescue team members, railway controllers, golf-course greenkeepers, slate processors, fishermen (rarely catching much) and the odd spare-motor-parts supplier. All had a tale to tell.

Throw in hipster inn owners, maître d's at Michelin-starred restaurants, museum marketing managers, outdoor-pursuits shop assistants, retired teachers, footpath builders, rock climbers, Extinction Rebellion rebels, New Balance employees, nurses, Nestlé factory workers, post-office owners, posties, community-pub organizers, Christian Motorcyclists Association riders and directors of the Wordsworth Trust – and you had a right mix. It all formed a heady, enlivening gathering of opinion, and I was immensely grateful to those who took time to say what was on their minds.

The people of the Lakes made the trip, not just the heady, dare I say, *sublime* scenery of the Lakes.

And those mentioned above were just the locals.

Fellow hikers brought their own perspectives and camaraderie along the long winding trails: the coast-to-coast Germans in Ennerdale, the vacuum-cleaner engineer and his pal on Haystacks, ex-prison officers, teachers, carers, well-being coaches, IT experts, whoever it might be. I wanted the random to rule in *Lost in the Lakes*. Travel writing should be like that: hit the trail and see whatever turns up. Only the journey reveals what the story will tell. Go with an open mind, eyes and ears alert. At least, that was my approach. Yes, the odd arranged meeting helped, but for the most part, let happenchance lead the way.

Which I hope has come across in these "notes" from the trail.

Many of the current difficulties facing the Lake District, of course, became clear as the miles clicked by: staff shortages caused by high local rents and other rising costs of living; the trouble of second homes and holiday homes pushing up property prices; youngsters forced out of the area; the resulting pressure on communities as schools and transport links were cut; the vicious circle this created; the concerns about *over-tourism* and traffic jams; the problems of seasonal employment; fears about climate change and the knock-on effects, especially flooding; fears among farmers over how precisely they will survive once the umbilical cord of European Union subsidies finally ends post-Brexit. These were (some of) the talking points. No use walking round the Lakes and simply admiring the mountains as though they existed in splendid isolation: "Oh, what a lovely fell", and all that.

Wordsworth (and later Ruskin) had agonized over mass tourism from Manchester and Liverpool, and the poet's prominent attack on the spread of railways had, partially at least, succeeded. Yet their dreams of protecting peaceful communities of fell farmers tucked away in the dales – lakes empty save the odd fisherman and slopes populated by shepherds quietly tending flocks – had clearly not come true.

Most of the pressing issues in the region quite obviously found their roots in one cause: holidaymakers, a great number of whom arrived in vehicles. A group called Friends of the Lake District has estimated that 83 per cent of visitors came by car. The resultant traffic congestion led to accidents, damage to stone walls and (sometimes) the requirement to reverse long distances down narrow lanes: "There is often an unbroken queue of traffic all the way through the popular settlements of Ambleside, Bowness and Keswick, causing intrusive noise and air pollution."

The Lake District has, of course, become a far cry from the romantic ideal imagined by the Lake Poets. The writer/farmer James Rebanks, author of *The Shepherd's Life: A Tale of the Lake District*, who runs a farm in Matterdale, near Keswick, has said the region is, "for better or worse, a scenic playground for the rest of Britain" as well as tourists from further afield. He added: "There are places where it doesn't feel like it's ours any more, as if the guests have taken over the guesthouse." Thoughts that more than chimed with those of Gail and Mike back at the Old Dungeon Ghyll: "There'll be nothing left but tourism one day… it's turning into a theme park."

All this said, Wordsworth's hope for a "sort of national property, in which every man has a right and interest who has an eye to perceive and a heart to enjoy" had indeed come to fruition in the form of first the National Trust – led so boldly by Canon Rawnsley and backed so importantly by Beatrix Potter – and then the Lake District National Park, created in 1951.

* * *

Rather than follow in anyone's footsteps, I ploughed my own furrow in the Lakes. Letting the main waters and meres lead the way, I wound round the peaks, avoiding them the best I could during the early days. I was not averse to trying them, I just did not trust myself particularly. What I really needed was to get from one place to another with the large backpack and *move on*.

My failure to scale Blencathra in the white-out of cloud did not help build confidence in the first week, though later on, routes that I would have ruled out at the beginning seemed fine: Helvellyn to Dollywaggon Crag to Fairfield and Hart Crag, for example, on the way to Brothers Water. All of these were classic Alfred Wainwright 800-metre summits as described in his much-loved *Pictorial Guide*, yet my aim was to get to the next place and if such monsters happened to be in the way without an obvious easier route, so be it, I would go up.

My only real climbs for the sake of climbing, on "down days", were Blencathra, Haystacks, Scafell Pike, the Old Man of Coniston, the Pike of Blisco, Great Knott and Crinkle Crags. Not a bad effort, really, but the point is that the bagging of Wainwrights, as fantastic as each may be, was not all important.

By going my own way, I felt I was giving the Lake *District*, not just the Lake *fells*, my best shot in a month, and my enjoyment of its landscapes only grew as the hike continued. It is possible to *take a trip around* the Lakes, I was finding, not just go up endless peaks – although both were eminently enjoyable in their own ways.

There is a great danger in waxing lyrical and slipping into purple prose about the Lakes, so I will put it simply: I loved it.

Each morning felt like unwrapping a present, and that gift was the looming fells and the lakes in their shades of grey and the winding paths between the heather and the bracken and the gorse and the fresh air coming in from the sea and the subtly shifting clouds and the long rays of sunshine breaking through the haze and the crags and the cliffs and the ridges and the scree and interesting people you would meet on the way. Clarity, solace and company rolled up in one; a chance for feet and mind to wander, thoughts in (better) order after plodding the fells.

* * *

I have returned to the Lakes once since April (I write this in August) to visit Kendal, which had fallen outside my walking route. I was curious to see the distinguished market town on the eastern edge of the Lakes, and also to visit the Kendal Museum to learn more about Alfred Wainwright.

The Kendal Museum was a treasure trove: old-fashioned, full of stuffed creatures in glass cabinets, racks of glittery minerals found in the fells, ancient arrowheads and Roman coins. Wainwright, who was local and worked at the town hall, was honorary curator at the museum from 1945 to 1974. His old office is in a corner now used as a herbarium, and many of the labels on displays at the museum remain in his hand. The key interest for the fell walker, though, was just to the right of the ticket desk: a cabinet in which his thread-worn tweed jacket, flat cap, crumpled rucksack, heavily darned socks, pipe, tobacco tin and scuffed boots were displayed. A signed first edition of his guide to the eastern fells was next to his old typewriter, fountain pen and the polished "BOROUGH TREASURER" sign that was once on his town-hall office door. A bronze bust of Wainwright smoking his beloved pipe stared out, showing a genial countenance captured by the sculptor Clive Bernard.

The Kendal Museum was a place of pilgrimage for lovers of fell walking, suitably unpretentious, in keeping with the "master fell walker" who spent so much time wandering the crags, often on his own with his flat cap and pens and pencils.

Later that day, I met David Claxton, secretary of the Wainwright Society, at the Rheged cultural centre on the edge of Penrith to find out more about the man who had so influenced fell walking in the Lake District.

The Wainwright Society had 2,000 members and was founded in 2002 by a group of enthusiasts. David told me that Wainwright never carried a compass, preferring to rely on his sense of direction, and that the author did not believe in hurrying around the fells: "Wainwright talks about taking time to enjoy the views and the landscapes." Those bagging the Wainwrights at great speed might miss out on much and needed to take care in their haste. Being a proficient fell walker was simple, Wainwright believed: "Fellwalking accidents only happen to those who walk clumsily. The only advice you need… is to watch where you put your feet."

The secretary of the Wainwright Society explained what he believed accounted for Wainwright's enduring appeal. "Well, a lot of people have written about the fells, but his descriptions of the routes up remain unmatched." David had not himself climbed all 214 peaks, nor did he feel an urge to do so although he regularly walked his two Labradors on Blencathra. Sometimes he did so in the company of a friend who had knocked on Wainwright's door as a boy because he wanted to see him.

"Did Wainwright say: 'Go away'?" As he might have.

"No, not at all: he was very friendly." Wainwright, who had put so much of his spare time into unpaid work at the Kendal Museum, was clearly community orientated and a much-liked local figure.

* * *

During this return trip, I also visited Derwentwater, where I went wild swimming for half an hour or so – it was more of a dip than a swim – near the main boat landing at Keswick.

The water temperature was chilly, and I wore a wetsuit as I splashed about by the jetties, overseen by Graeme Sutton of a company named Swim on the Wild Side. The water was a peculiar shade of green and I saw no fish whatsoever, while the mud by the shore felt strangely gooey and went up almost to my knees. The water was cool and refreshing, however, and my instinct was to swim out to St Herbert's Island, but Graeme wisely advised against this as it was quite a long way. This much I can report on wild swimming in the Lake District, although news stories of an explosion of blue-green algae, microbes that can destroy life in the lakes and cause rashes and vomiting in humans (and kill dogs), in the waters of Windermere were soon to make headlines. "CLIMATE CHANGE FEARS OVER WINDERMERE'S SEA OF GREEN", ran a piece in *The Times*. Abnormally warm weather had boosted the dangerous algae and I wondered what I had been seeing on my swim. The water temperature of Windermere had risen 1.7°C in 70 years and the algae were also being encouraged by phosphorous and nitrogen "nutrients" coming from sewage works during "storm overspills", farming and private septic tanks (of which there were as many as 1,900 in the Lake District that were not connected to the main sewage system).

Signs had been put up by Windermere warning: "CAUTION TOXIC ALGAE". Fingers were being pointed in all directions, but the Environment Agency, charged with protecting Britain's natural assets, said that it was working hard to enhance the lake, having invested £700,000 in the past ten years to improve the lake's water quality.

The *Daily Mail*, going for the jugular, followed up with: "WHAT HAS MADE GLORIOUS WINDERMERE LOOK LIKE A SEWER?" Meanwhile, the former Labour Party spin doctor and political commentator Alastair Campbell stated on social media: "I cannot think of any other government in Europe or any part of the developed world that would allow their equivalent of Windermere to be treated as a cesspit." Not exactly the greatest state of affairs.

* * *

Also since the hike, in quite different news, word had filtered back that Alan Dunn, the now former mayor of Keswick (mayors usually serve for a year), did not quite make it on the journey to take aid for Ukraine to Poland in the old, adapted Citroën. Sadly, he had tested positive for Covid the day before he was due to leave and a fellow Keswick councillor named Peter Terry oversaw the transport of the medical equipment.

Meanwhile, Claire Whitaker of Scalderskew Farm had texted to say that the poorly lamb that the woman hiker had brought in from the fells was "doing well" and that three sets of twins had been born in the field in front of my shepherd's hut and eight "singles" the night I stayed. Bookings for the shepherd's hut were going reasonably. The energy crisis, Claire said, was yet to affect their business as she had fixed their electricity rate for three years just before the worst of the price hikes: "I think I was pretty savvy getting that, looking back now."

Regarding second-home ownership, a policy to double charge council taxes for second homeowners across England was announced in the Queen's Speech the month after I returned, a move designed to deter ballooning houses prices in rural areas. However, Tim Farron, struck a note of realism and caution when speaking to ITV: "Let's be clear, ninety per cent of second homes are bought by people who use them as investments. They let them out for two or three months, therefore they pay no council tax and they also pay no business rates, and somebody going to the food bank in Kendal or Penrith is having to subsidize somebody with a second or third or fourth home in Ambleside or in Appleby and that's not on."

I had contacted his local office and we chatted the day after I went to the Kendal Museum. Farron had been touring his constituency that day on his "summer surgery tour" in which he had visited "forty to fifty villages" over three weeks, an impressive effort and an example of the lengths to which Liberal Democrat politicians will sometimes go to shore up support as outsiders in the British "two party" political system. We had a chat about rising energy prices and Farron referred to Boris Johnson, then the prime minister but about to step aside, as "this flipping joker who's in office but not in power meanwhile the country's going to the absolute toilet".

His tongue appeared to be nicely loosened. I asked him why the second-homes/holiday-lets issue was not being taken seriously at government level. His answer went thus: politicians do not pay attention as it affects a small proportion of the population, the Conservative Party does not worry about rural seats that it "takes for granted" and, finally, "while it has always been a problem it has become catastrophic in the last year or two". Our rulers, Farron said, were yet to get on top of the matter and the situation was spiralling out of control: "There has been a complete collapse in the private rental sector. The average income round here means you can't buy a house, but the chances are you will wait forever for a council house. We've built quite a lot recently here but it's not enough to compensate. So, the long-term private rented sector has been a kind of safety valve, which is far from perfect. But the long-term private rented sector has now turned into the short-term private rented sector with Airbnbs and the rest of the private holiday-let market." Landlords could earn "five or six times" more that way and were using "section 21 notices" to evict long-term tenants.

Did he believe second homes/holiday lets were fundamentally *wrong*? "No," he replied. "Having a second home doesn't make you a bad person. Holiday lets are an important part of the tourism economy here, but an unregulated market will mean you get too many of both and it kills the community and it robs people of opportunity. So, without being unkind to people who have holiday lets, still less to those who use them for their holidays, or indeed people who have second homes, it's a problem and we have to solve it."

His solution, he believed, would act as a "silver bullet": to reclassify accommodation as either a permanent residence, holiday let or second home used occasionally. Then local councils could set limits on numbers. At the moment, "a dwelling is a dwelling is a dwelling" and that was not subtle enough for planning requirements.

Was there simply too much tourism in the Lake District? His answer returned to the property difficulties: "I've come across people [during his summer surgery tour] who cannot find anywhere to live and, put bluntly, there's a reasonable chance that it's because [the local] holiday cottage may have been the chef's house last year. So, you replace the working-age population with holidaymakers at the risk of killing the goose that gives the golden egg – and you end up without a workforce to give them [the holidaymakers] a decent experience. So, it's not so much that there is too much tourism, but we have allowed holiday accommodation to gobble up the accommodation that was workforce accommodation and, therefore, we are not able to meet the needs of the local economy."

There was the additional problem of so many visitors putting pressure on local infrastructure and services: wear and tear on roads and busy doctor's surgeries that were not provided with sufficient resources to cope. "We are a county about twice the size of Lancashire with a population of barely a third, but add visitor numbers and we are maybe ten times bigger than Lancashire. We have absolutely no problem with any of that, but we are getting nothing for it. No funding formula adequately addresses the needs and the fact we are supporting a much bigger population. The county has roughly half a million in it but there are twenty million people in it for two months of the year, not all at the same time of course."

Tourism clearly put a huge strain on the Lakes. Meanwhile, loopholes regarding council taxes, as Gail and Mike had pointed out in the Old Dungeon Ghyll, could make a nonsense of the rules so far as many second homeowners were concerned, with young people still likely to be priced out of their own communities. As the couple in their twenties in The Crafty Baa pub in Keswick had said to Alan and me: "We can't afford the cheapest house in Keswick. Not even a terraced house in a flood-risk area." This, another aspect of tourism and the great love so many people have for the Lake District, was the burning issue across the region and, at the risk of sounding like an old colonel writing a letter to *The Times*: *something surely must be done.*

* * *

On a completely separate matter, Lena and Anna had settled into life in Worcester, where their host had agreed to them staying for a year (the initial period had been six months). Anna was attending a good local school, had passed her exams and made friends, while Lena had found work preparing flowers at a greenhouse on a farm in a village outside Worcester. Kasia and I talked to them by Zoom and Lena said that it was difficult for her mentally in the UK, and although she "thanked God" for her work, she was desperately homesick: "There are no words to express how much I want to go home." Her husband was involved with digging trenches near the Belarus border, and she was hopeful that the war would end soon: "Of course, we are worried. We did not start this. We [Ukraine] did not bother anyone, so we should not be bothered." Their apartment in Kiev had not been damaged, although Anna's doctor's home in Bucha had been destroyed and she had had to move to Poland with nothing. Anna's school friends from Ukraine, whom she kept in touch with via the internet, were scattered in France, Germany, Poland, the Netherlands and other parts of the UK.

The pair was receiving food handouts from an Orthodox church in Worcester to make ends meet – "a huge help to us" – and assisting with tidying and cleaning at the house of their host, who prepared evening meals for them. Lena was a particular fan of "chicken pie and Yorkshire pudding". She had been working weekends, getting up at 4.30 a.m. for the 6 a.m. start of her shifts. She was grateful to a local municipal pool that was allowing Ukrainian refugees, of which there were many in the city, free swims. "Our sponsors are our second family now. Our English family," said Lena, adding that British people had been welcoming. Of the future, she said: "Life is life, it is difficult to make plans. We do not know what will happen the next day, so we are trying to live day by day." Anna, who would be taking GCSEs in two years, said she liked it in Worcester and that her English was improving. "It is easier for younger people," said Lena.

* * *

The world turned while the mountains of the Lakes stayed the same as always. Wainwright's comment, "The fleeting hour of life of those who love the hills is quickly spent, but the hills are eternal", seemed as accurate today as ever.

In 1724 Daniel Defoe described the Lake District as "eminent only for being the wildest, most barren and frightful of any [land] that I have passed over in England or even in Wales". Well with all the tea rooms and cosy inns, Airbnbs, upmarket hotels and Michelin-starred restaurants these days, it's moved on a bit since then. Yet you could still find quiet spots alone in the fells, even close to the busiest tourist honeypots.

Just book a ticket to ride to Penrith or Windermere (leave the car behind).

The Lakes are waiting, down the line.

ACKNOWLEDGEMENTS

Many thanks to those met along the trails who helped bring this journey to life, I'm grateful to one and all. Thanks also to Gill Haigh of Cumbria Tourism, Michael McGregor of the Wordsworth Trust and David Claxton of the Wainwright Society, as well as, as ever, to my parents, Robert and Christine Chesshyre, and to Meg Chesshyre, Kate Chesshyre and Edward Chesshyre, Danny Kelly, Naomi Grimley, Sue Heady and Ben Clatworthy for their encouragement. I owe special gratitude to Kasia, who so caringly helped Lena and Anna make it from Kiev to Britain, who put up with me during the writing process and was there at the end in Shap. Also, special thanks to Mark Palmer, Harriet Sime and Hugo Brown of the *Daily Mail* travel section, Sarah Hartley, travel editor of *The Mail on Sunday*, Olivia Hartley and Graham Stewart of *The Critic* magazine and Steve Anglesey of *The New European*. Stanfords maps and travel bookshop in Covent Garden has offered great support (and was where I bought my trusty Ordnance Survey maps), likewise the staff of The Open Book in Richmond. Claire Plimmer, editorial director of Summersdale, has been fantastic as always, and thanks to Sophie Martin for seeing the book through production smoothly, eagle-eyed Carol Turner and Natalya Kahn for their edits, Jasmin Burkitt for her tireless publicity work and Hamish Braid for the tricky maps.

THE HIKE:
DISTANCE COVERED,
PLACES STAYED, PUBS VISITED

Day 1 – Around Penrith: 2.2 miles, 5,001 steps

Day 2 – Penrith to Patterdale: 18.9 miles, 44,737 steps

Day 3 – Patterdale to Watermillock: 14.6 miles, 35,267 steps

Day 4 – Watermillock to Threlkeld: 12.6 miles, 26,241 steps

Day 5 – Threlkeld to Keswick, via Blencathra: 15.2 miles, 39,477 steps

Day 6 – Keswick and around Derwentwater: 12.4 miles, 30,050 steps

Day 7 – Keswick to Linskeldfield: 16.3 miles, 37,336 steps

Day 8 – Linskeldfield to Cockermouth: 10.9 miles, 25,926 steps

Day 9 – Cockermouth to Buttermere: 15.7 miles, 34,925 steps

Day 10 – Buttermere to Haystacks and back: 9.9 miles, 25,207 steps

Day 11 – Buttermere to Ennerdale: 9.3 miles, 23,456 steps

Day 12 – Ennerdale to Ennerdale Bridge and back: 9 miles, 23,860 steps

Day 13 – Ennerdale, rest day: 0.6 miles, 1,476 steps

Day 14 – Ennerdale to Wasdale Head: 8.9 miles, 23,544 steps

Day 15 – Wasdale Head, up Scafell Pike and back: 7.1 miles, 18,644 steps

Day 16 – Wasdale Head to Scalderskew: 10.3 miles, 25,329 steps

Day 17 – Scalderskew to Eskdale: 18.4 miles, 33,693 steps

Day 18 – Eskdale (railway) to Ravenglass and back: 8.2 miles, 21,025 steps

Day 19 – Eskdale to Coniston: 14 miles, 31,021 steps

Day 20 – Coniston, up Old Man and to Brantwood and back: 14.8 miles, 34,603 steps

Day 21 – Coniston to Bowland Bridge: 13.2 miles, 31,983 steps

Day 22 – Bowland Bridge to Bowness, via Cartmel: 24.3 miles, 52,969 steps

Day 23 – Bowness to Ambleside: 9.4 miles, 21,816 steps

Day 24 – Ambleside to Rydal and Grasmere and back: 12.1 miles, 30,283 steps

Day 25 – Ambleside to Great Langdale, via Stickle Tarn: 12.3 miles, 31,520 steps

Day 26 – Great Langdale up to Crinkle Crags and back: 9.2 miles, 22,769 steps

Day 27 – Great Langdale to Thirlmere: 17.5 miles, 42,082 steps

Day 28 – Thirlmere to Brothers Water: 13.2 miles, 35,354 steps

Day 29 – Brothers Water to Mosedale Valley: 9.8 miles, 27,390 steps

Day 30 – Mosedale Valley to Shap: 9.3 miles, 23,375 steps

Day 31 – Shap to Penrith: 13.8 miles, 35,220 steps

Day 32 – Around Penrith: 5.7 miles, 15,986 steps

Total distance covered: 379.1 miles

Average daily distance covered: 11.85 miles

Total number of steps: 911,565 steps

Average daily step count: 28,486 steps

Note: Where walks are particularly long, it would be easy to split up journeys. I booked accommodation about two months in advance of my April trip and availability was good.

Places stayed: Station Hotel, Penrith (www.stationpenrith.co.uk); YHA Patterdale (www.yha.org.uk); Brackenrigg Inn, Watermillock (www.brackenrigginn.co.uk); Horse & Farrier, Threlkeld (www.horseandfarrier.com); Denton House, Keswick (www.dentonhouse-keswick.co.uk); Linskeldfield Farm (www.linskeldfield.co.uk);

Croft Guest House, Cockermouth (www.croft-guesthouse.co.uk); YHA Buttermere (www.yha.org.uk); YHA Ennerdale (www.yha. org.uk); Wasdale Head Inn (www.wasdale.com); Scalderskew Shepherds Hut (www.scalderskewshepherdshut.co.uk); Woolpack Inn, Eskdale (www.woolpack.co.uk); The Sun Coniston (www. thesunconiston.com); The Hare & Hounds Inn, Bowland Bridge (www.hareandhoundslakes.com); Puddle Duck Lodge, Bowness (www.puddleducklodge.co.uk); YHA Ambleside (www.yha.org.uk); Old Dungeon Ghyll, Great Langdale (www.odg.co.uk); Fisher Gill Camping Barn, Thirlmere (www.booking.com); Brotherswater Inn (www.sykeside.co.uk); Mosedale Cottage (www.crosstheuk.com); Kings Arms, Shap (www.kingsarmsshap.co.uk); The George Hotel, Penrith (www.everbrightgrouphotels.com).

Pubs visited (aside from those stayed at): Agricultural Hotel, Penrith (www.the-agricultural-hotel.co.uk); Fell Bar, Penrith (www. fellbrewery.co.uk); White Lion, Patterdale (www.thelakedistrict. org); The Royal Hotel, Dockray (www.the-royal-dockray.co.uk); The Salutation Inn, Threlkeld (www.thesalutation.co.uk); The Crafty Baa, Keswick (www.thecraftybaa.com); The Pocket Café Bar, Keswick (www.thepocketkeswick.com); The Wainwright, Keswick (www.thewainwright.pub); Fletcher Christian, Cockermouth (www. craftunionpubs.com); Kirkstile Inn, Loweswater (www.kirkstile.com); High Stile Kitchen, Buttermere (www.buttermerecourthotel.co.uk); Fox and Hounds Inn, Ennerdale Bridge (www.foxandhoundsinn.org); The Strands & Screes Inn, Nether Wasdale (www.strands-brewery. co.uk); King George IV Inn, Eskdale (www.kinggeorge-eskdale.com); Brook House Inn, Eskdale (www.brookhouseinn.co.uk); The Boot Inn, Eskdale (www.thebooteskdale.co.uk); Ratty Arms, Ravenglass (www.rattyarms.org); Crown Inn, Coniston (www.crowninnconiston. com); Black Bull, Coniston (www.blackbullconiston.co.uk); Tower Bank Arms, Sawrey (www.towerbankarms.co.uk); The Westmorland Inn, Bowness (www.thewestmorlandinn.co.uk); The

Flying Pig, Bowness (www.theflyingpigbowness.co.uk); Ambleside Tavern (www.amblesideonline.co.uk); Tweedies Bar, Grasmere (www.tweediesgrasmere.com); New Dungeon Ghyll, Great Langdale (www.dungeon-ghyll.co.uk); The Langstrath Country Inn, Stonethwaite (www.thelangstrath.co.uk); King's Head Inn, Thirlmere (www.lakedistrictinns.co.uk/kings-head); The Greyhound Inn, Shap (www.greyhoundshap.co.uk).

BIBLIOGRAPHY

Bennett, Bob *Wasdale Head and the Inn: A History* (2021, Bob Bennett)

Bradbury, Julia *Wainwright Walks* (2012, Frances Lincoln)

Brown, Jules and Longley, Norm *The Rough Guide to the Lake District* (2021, Rough Guides)

Comley, M. A. *To Make Them Pay* (2022, Jeamel Publishing Limited)

Davies, Hunter *Lakeland: A Personal Journey* (2016, Head of Zeus Ltd)

Davies, Hunter *Wainwright: The Biography* (1995, Michael Joseph)

Davies, Hunter *A Walk Around the Lakes* (1979, George Weidenfield and Nicolson Ltd)

Davies, Hunter and Holman, Tom *The Good Guide to the Lakes* (2008, Frances Lincoln)

Dearden, James *John Ruskin* (2008, Shire Publications)

Defoe, Daniel *A Tour Thro' the Whole Island of Great Britain: Divided into Circuits or Journeys* (1748, S. Birt *et al.*)

Hankinson, Alan *Coleridge Walks the Fells: A Lakeland Journey Retraced* (1991, Ellenbank Press)

Hewitt-McManus, Thomas *Withnail & I: Everything You Ever Wanted to Know But Were Too Drunk to Ask* (2006, Lulu Press Incorporated)

Hubank, Roger *Hazard's Way* (2004, The Ernest Press)

Lindop, Grevel *A Literary Guide to the Lake District* (2015, Sigma Leisure)

Martineau, Harriet *A Complete Guide to the English Lakes* (1855, Forgotten Books)

McCracken, David *Wordsworth and the Lake District* (1985, Oxford University Press)

McKay, Sinclair *Ramble On: The Story of our Love for Walking Britain* (2013, Fourth Estate)

Naylor, Joss *Lakes, Meres and Waters of the Lake District* (2021, Cicerone)

Rebanks, James *English Pastoral: An Inheritance* (2020, Allen Lane)

Rebanks, James *The Shepherd's Life: A Tale of the Lake District* (2015, Allen Lane)

Robinson, Bruce *Withnail and I: The Original Screenplay* (1989, Bloomsbury)

Ruskin, John *Selected Writings* (2004, Oxford University Press)

Schofield, Lee *Wild Fell: Fighting for Nature on a Lake District Hill Farm* (2022, Doubleday)

Symonds, Henry Herbert *Walking in the Lake District* (1962, J. and J. Gray)

Thompson, Ian *The English Lakes: A History* (2010, Bloomsbury)

Tope, Rebecca *The Ambleside Alibi* (2013, Allison & Busby)

Wainwright, Alfred *A Pictorial Guide to the Lakeland Fells* (2005, Frances Lincoln)

West, Thomas *A Guide to the Lakes* (1778, Richardson and Urquhart)

Winn, Christopher *I Never Knew That About the Lake District* (2010, Ebury Press)

Wordsworth, William *A Guide Through the District of the Lakes in the North of England* (1835, A Thousand Fields)

Have you enjoyed this book?

If so, why not write a review on your favourite website?

If you're interested in finding out more about our books,
find us on Facebook at **Summersdale Publishers**, on Twitter
at **@Summersdale** and on Instagram at **@summersdalebooks**
and get in touch. We'd love to hear from you!.

Thanks very much for buying this Summersdale book.

www.summersdale.com